A Strategy for Excellence

Reaching for New Standards in Education

by

Michael J. Bakalis

With a foreword by Lawrence N. Hansen

1974  LINNET BOOKS

Library of Congress Cataloging in Publication Data

Bakalis, Michael J.
    A strategy for excellence.

    Includes bibliographical references.
    1. School management and organization. 2. State de-
partments of education. I. Title.
LB2809.A2B34   379'.152   73-23101
ISBN 0-208-01245-1

© 1974 by THE SHOE STRING PRESS, INC.
First published 1974 as a LINNET BOOK, an imprint of
The Shoe String Press, Inc.,
Hamden, Connecticut 06514

Printed in the United States of America

For my daughters Patty and Erin

In the hope that in some small way we will
have helped to make the schools better for
their generation.

Contents

Foreword

On January 11, 1971, a thirty-two year old former public school teacher, former history professor, and former assistant dean of liberal arts and sciences stood before the Illinois General Assembly and was administered the oath of office. Dr. Michael J. Bakalis was sworn in as Illinois' last popularly elected and as the nation's youngest chief state educational officer.

In brief inaugural remarks, Bakalis called upon all who had a stake in the state's vast system of public education to reach for new standards of excellence. The new superintendent warned that a strategy of excellence would require a frank assessment of educational weaknesses, a questioning of old assumptions, and an equalization of educational opportunity. He promised a new level of participatory democracy which would make the educational system "dynamic, responsive, relevant and, most importantly, humane."

These were brave words. But despite the soaring quality of the rhetoric, no one was quite certain what his words would eventually mean in terms of the actual operation of the schools. All anyone knew for certain was that Mike Bakalis had come out of relative obscurity, engaged in a vigorous grass-roots campaign, and ridden into office with a 500,000 vote margin. With little money and with the help of a modest but spirited staff, Mike Bakalis moved throughout Illinois, meeting thousands of people and presenting his views on education. He spoke as an educator, not as a politician. His victory, though generally unexpected, was widely interpreted as a mandate for change.

Bakalis' three and one half year old superintendency has been a continuous burst of activity. With the assistance of 3000 citizens a far reaching statement of goals and priorities for Illinois education has been written and is now being implemented. Serious reform of school finance and teacher preparation programs and certification is well underway. Methods for evaluating teacher performance are being studied. Standards for the supervision and evaluation of schools have been revised so that emphasis is properly placed on educational outcomes rather than educational inputs. Local educational planning with community involvement is now being required throughout the State for the first time in history. The frauds in the State's hundreds of privately operated vocational and technical schools have been run out of business.

Rules and regulations for the prevention and elimination of racial segregation in the schools have been promulgated and are being enforced. Illinois is now funding programs for non-English speaking youngsters at a level unmatched by any other state. The Illinois Inventory of Educational Progress has been initiated to measure and to inform citizens about what students specifically know, feel and can do, and about the variables which account for differences in student performance. Experiments with the 12-month school year are being funded through the superintendent's office, as are experiments in decentralized governance of large urban school districts. The emphasis in curriculum reform is on individualization. To test various innovative approaches to individualization, career education, and equal educational opportunities, the Illinois Network for School Development has been established.

Mike Bakalis has leapt headlong into a battle that possibly could have been avoided altogether. To be sure, his behavior does not conform with the traditional role played by chief state education officers. Less than one year after Bakalis took office, *Newsweek* observed:

> Theoretically, most state superintendents are vested with some degree of authority over local school districts. But in actual practice, relatively few have dared to exercise that control, largely out of deference to the fierce independence of community school boards. Recently, however, with taxpayers in bitter rebellion against the skyrocketing costs of education—and with the schools themselves struggling to cope with a host of new social and educational problems—such a passive posture has become increasingly difficult to maintain. As a result, many state administrators have begun to exercise their power more aggressively—and few have been more aggressive than Mike Bakalis.[1]

If state departments of education are going to make a difference in the long run they must be prepared, Bakalis believes, to test the prevailing orthodoxy and to discard the myths regarding what is possible and not possible in the schools. He frequently reminds his listeners of Lincoln's observation that "the dogmas of the quiet past are inadequate to the stormy present. As our case is new, so we must think anew and act anew." To think and act anew requires first that the hard issues be raised and dealt with. It requires that educators have a global view of education and that their primary allegiance be to children, not to their own profession. This is how Mike Bakalis has approached the tasks facing him. He has a mission and a sense of urgency which often rock the educational boat and generate unaccustomed levels of consternation among some professionals and politicians. However, his tough mindedness, courage, and resolve have only served to enhance his standing among the general citizenry of the State.

Whether or not Mike Bakalis is appointed Illinois' chief state educational officer in 1975, it is unlikely that Illinois education will ever be the same again. His influence in educational affairs will be felt here for many years to come. As one commentator for *The Chicago Sun Times* noted after the third year of Bakalis' administration: "Bakalis certainly has become one of the most energetic problem-solvers this state has ever seen. Bakalis has sought to tackle problems and provide leadership, even where it has not been sought. His goal is simple: a model for the nation in the way schools ought to be run."[2]

In the essays which follow, Dr. Bakalis reveals in both philosophical and practical terms what he believes the educational enterprise must do if it is to renew itself. While developments in Illinois frequently provide a frame of reference for these essays, what Bakalis has to say is generally applicable to schools everywhere. While he does not presume to have answers to all the problems facing education, wherever possible the available options are examined. Mike Bakalis' philosophy of education, his vision, and his system of ideas are carefully set out. His objective is to show that a mood of complacency has overcome public education and that only timely and determined action can guarantee a better future.

What I find remarkable in Mike Bakalis' performance is that he not only stands for something, but for something beyond normally accepted goals. It has been said that in American political life the stand is all important. But today the stand is no less important in

public education. Allan Nevins once noted that "one of our
national faults is our tendency to pay too much attention to personalities and too little to policy and argument; we are lazy, we like
to drift, and we are willing to accept gestures for courage, and
catch words for ideas."[3] As an educator and as a politician too,
Mike Bakalis, by reaching for new standards of excellence, is
helping to change that tradition.

LAWRENCE N. HANSEN

Chicago, Illinois

Preface

Since January of 1971 I have had the honor and the challenge of serving as the chief state school officer for the State of Illinois. My tenure in office has given me a rare opportunity to be at the center of a growing and increasingly widespread movement to reform the schools of the state. Having spent the years before my election as a university professor lecturing students on institutional change, I have most recently been involved in an ongoing effort to renew, in a single state, one of the most fundamental institutions of society, the school. Needless to say, I have found that lecturing on concepts and acting on problems are two very different things.

This book is written three years after my inauguration. Had it been written one or two years ago, it would have been considerably different. Three years in office dealing with these issues on a day-to-day basis in the educational and political arenas have allowed me to approach my topic in a much more insightful and practical way. There have been successes and failures during these three years—both of which have brought forth valuable lessons. Yet while certain things have become clearer, certain aspects of my thinking more pragmatic, I have not abandoned the basic overall philosophy which led me to seek, and fortunately win, the office which I now hold. I attempted to express those thoughts in my inaugural remarks before the Illinois General Assembly on January 11, 1971. On that day I said:

> Over a century ago the Constitution of the State of Illinois had written into it a far-sighted mandate—the responsibility for public education was placed upon the state itself. It was a unique commitment and those of us here today are the beneficiaries of that charge.
>
> Today we stand on the threshold of a new Constitution and of new and more awesome responsibilities. For the world is

very different now—and if education was important in 1870, it is today the necessary ingredient for survival. Our new Constitution reaffirms the State's prime responsibility for public education and as the constitutionally defined education officer of this State, I have sworn to defend the letter and the spirit of that document.

Education in the 1970's will require more than constitutional directives—we will need a reordering of our priorities to achieve not only an equalization of educational opportunity, but also a new level of educational quality. The task that confronts us all is to forge a new and far-reaching strategy—a strategy of excellence. It must be a strategy which will have as its goal nothing less than making Illinois education the lighthouse for the nation—where all will look to find direction— where all can see what *can* be done.

I stand before you as the last man to be *elected* as Superintendent of Public Instruction for the State of Illinois. Let this signal the beginning of a time when all citizens, disregarding party but united in purpose, join together in the formation of this grand design. This must not be a Democratic strategy or a Republican one, but one that is jointly conceived by men and women who know that the future is not partisan and that our children are our future.

Today public education faces a crisis more serious than ever in the long history since its unique birth in this nation. Faculties, students and taxpayers have raised serious questions about the purpose and direction of our schools. There are those among us who foresee the ultimate end of the public schools. I am not among them. Institutions throughout our land are today old and tired—but this is not cause to doom them to extinction. Institutions, like every man and every generation, must renew themselves. Let us pledge here today to be the agents of this self-renewal—the end of which will be education which is dynamic, responsive, relevant and, most importantly, humane. Let us pledge here today a renewed commitment to the survival of public education.

All these things will not come quickly and in four years we can but begin to set the course—but begin we must. And a beginning will call for a frank assessment of our educational weaknesses and a continuation of our educational strengths. It will call for a questioning of old assumptions regarding how educational decisions are made and by whom; regarding the role of teachers, students and parents; regarding the role of this legislative body and of the office which I now enter. It will call for a participatory democracy which will truly make the educational enterprise a public one.

The challenge of this decade is a difficult one—we must broaden the base of educational opportunity even further while simultaneously reaching for new standards of excellence. Let us recognize candidly that there are those who say it cannot be done. But if one child in Illinois is denied the opportunity to reach the level of his educational potential, then all of us will be losers. If mediocrity is allowed to be our standard in education, then we must be prepared to live in a mediocre society. I did not seek this office to preside over educational mediocrity.

I am pledged to a peaceful revolution—a revolution of quality. I am pledged to an age old dream—that the truly educated society can be the truly good society, that excellence in education means not only teaching a man what he can do, but who he is and what he can become.

The eyes of the next generation are fixed upon us. It is a heavy responsibility and I ask the citizens of this State to join with me in this effort.

With God's help—it can be done.

What I hoped to do that day was to paint, in broad sweeping strokes, the general thrust of what I sought to do in the four years that lay ahead of me as the Superintendent of Public Instruction for the State of Illinois. Anyone who seeks the origins of what we have done or will seek to do need only consult once again those inaugural remarks—for the seeds of all of the programs are to be found there.

The inaugural remarks identified a number of key points which were and remain central to my thinking. The first of these was a reminder that education was historically and is today a *state* responsibility. It seemed to me an extremely important point to make because so many of the difficulties the schools faced were the direct result of the inability or unwillingness of the state to play any kind of real leadership role in public education. Local control had come to mean state neglect and state impotence. It also seemed important to stress that the task ahead was the dual one of continuing to work for an equalization of educational opportunity at the same time we made new efforts to define and achieve educational quality. Francis Keppel has dealt with this theme of moving from quantitative concerns to qualitative ones in his fine book, *The Necessary Revolution in American Education*; while John Gardner's book entitled *Excellence: Can We Be Excellent and Equal Too?* has, more eloquently than anyone, presented the challenge of equality in relation to quality.

My call for a nonpartisan design for educational excellence was, in retrospect, the rhetoric of inexperience. Political realities present at once the greatest obstacle and the greatest potential for major educational reform. Without question, the public's view of the relationship between politics and education is a naive one as well as one that is detrimental to bringing about any concrete educational change, since it demands a separation lest somehow the legendary corrupting influences of politics not taint the mythical purity of the educational enterprise.

The central point of my address dealt with the problem of institutional change. It was a call for a self-renewing process which would result in the survival of public education and its transformation into a humane institution. But it would be a survival which could only be achieved by many people questioning many old assumptions. It seemed extremely important to me that we broaden the base of educational decision-making. The citizens of a state or community are seldom asked their opinion, seldom asked to participate in determining educational policy. No one will deny such consultation is difficult. No one will deny it is a slow, tedious process. Few will ever admit that a consensus on current educational issues is probable, even if it is possible. And yet, if we do not in a real, genuine way allow people to make decisions on policy, are we not admitting the failure of the American educational system in accomplishing at least that one historic task of providing individuals with the ability and the opportunity to govern themselves? Many will argue that such involvement is not necessary. History, after all, is filled with examples of people who would not or could not participate in deciding their own affairs, and somehow they survived. Theirs were often governments of efficiency and security. There were also often governments of tyranny and despotism which eventually crushed the human spirit. "There are some,"

Thomas Jefferson observed, "who prefer the calm seas of despotism to the stormy seas of liberty." In the years ahead, in education as well as in all of our institutions, we must not choose security over freedom and convenience over democracy. And finally, I sought to return the emphasis to where it properly belongs—the child. The language of public education is child-centered; the actions and programs often fall far short from the words.

How we might deal with these necessary changes in these times of turbulence in one of the most fundamental institutions, the school, is the subject of this book. It is purposely entitled *"A Strategy for Excellence"* because it is only one man's considered opinion: it is not *the* strategy for excellence for it is doubtful that such a definitive, conclusive prescription exists.

"Excellent things are rare" Plato noted us in his *Republic*, and indeed they are. It is even rarer for us to really think seriously about the concept itself. John Gardner in his book, *Excellence*, reminds us that there are many kinds of excellence and yet in each arena of human endeavor one senses intuitively rather than empirically that an achievement of excellent proportions has been accomplished. Gardner recites some historical moments which conjure images of excellence:

> Confucius teaching the feudal lords to govern wisely . . . Leonidas defending the pass at Thermopylae . . . Saint Francis preaching to the birds at Alviano . . . Lincoln writing the second inaugural "with malice toward none" . . . Mozart composing his first oratorio at the age of eleven . . . Galileo dropping weights from the Tower of Pisa . . . Emily Dickinson jotting her "letters to the world" on scraps of paper . . . Jesus saying, "Father forgive them; for they know not what they do" . . . Florence Nightingale nursing the wounded at Balaclava . . . .

These are moments of human achievement—intellectual, moral, spiritual—which clearly rise above the standards of performance of most human behavior. Perhaps from these we can construct a working definition of excellence from which we can move to see its application in the field of public education.

Let us define excellence as that level and quality of human performance in any endeavor which cannot be surpassed by any further human effort. Excellence in any activity is the best performance possible by a human being. Such a definition is, of course, exceedingly demanding and difficult to deal with. How do we know what the best performance possible is? How can we tell that Florence Nightingale could not have done a better job at Balaclava? Or that someone else could not have been more successful at her job? The answer, of course, is that we do not know and can never know. Or when we speak of excellence being a level of human performance which cannot be surpassed by any additional human effort—are we talking abo lt the particular individual person, or humans in general? Is Florence Nightingale's performance excellent for *her* capabilities or excellent when one looks at the whole range of human potential? Such are the kinds of questions which will confront those who strive for excellence in education. They are difficult. But they must be met head on.

There are further considerations which make the pursuit of excellence particularly difficult in a society such as ours. A democratic society, no matter what its rhetoric, moves toward certain kinds of leveling tendencies. The thrust of democracy is to remove the obstacles to equality. When Jefferson talked of "self-evident truths," he spoke of all men being created equal. We all know, of course, that, aside from certain God-given rights, what he was really calling for was a society in which all would have an equal chance to prove how unequal they were. Yet even though the idea of equal opportunity is the generally accepted interpretation of equality in America, we still are uncomfortable with those individuals who are not the same as we are. The history of American reform movements is filled with examples of men and groups of men who consciously and deliberately fought to reduce or eliminate the economic and, consequently, social differences that had developed in American society. The problem is whether the entire idea of excellence is contradictory to the desire to be equal. Excellence by its very nature is special, unique, and limited. Equality by its very nature is regular, common, and widespread. "Can we be equal and excellent too?" is the way John Gardner stated the problem. The answer for our society can and must be an unqualified "yes" if we really believe that the goal of excellence is desirable.

Quality in education will not just happen. It will be achieved when educators and politicians want it to happen and are ready to exercise true educational leadership. Emerson hit upon the essence of such leadership over a century ago when he called for leaders who do not do things *for* us—but who rather restore our faith in ourselves to make a difference and control our own destinies. Today, more than ever before in public education, we need such men and women.

The road toward excellence on which we have embarked in Illinois is being traveled by thousands of people who have contributed ideas for this book. Teachers, school administrators, board members, students, and lay citizens have dedicated themselves to this effort in an unprecedented manner. For their enthusiasm, their criticism, their courage, their perseverance and their support, I am much indebted. I have also been fortunate to have been surrounded by many individuals who believe that educational excellence is an achievable goal. My prejudices make me believe that my colleagues in the Illinois State Office of Education are among the best in the nation. They continue to serve the people of Illinois with an enthusiasm and dedication that makes me proud to be a public servant. I cannot acknowledge all who make my job easier, but I would be remiss if I did not recognize one of them. Lawrence Hansen has worked with me these past three years as my special assistant. It is a title which inadequately describes the significant role he has played in my administration. Larry and I have struggled together in discussing policy and formulating ideas which I have had the occasion to articulate to the citizens of Illinois in my official capacity. Together we have discussed thoughts and words which have become the framework for dozens of speeches I have delivered. These speeches were the foundation for the present book. In many ways this book is as much Larry Hansen's as it is mine. And for his untiring efforts I can only offer my thanks.

MICHAEL J. BAKALIS

Springfield, Illinois

Chapter I

THE EMERGENCE OF STATE EDUCATIONAL LEADERSHIP

The major weakness of all state departments of education I have encountered, with perhaps one or two exceptions, is that they are too much a part of the educational establishment. That is, I found many of these agencies . . . to be little more than the "willing tools" of the interests and clientele. . . . In more than one state I heard highly placed education and political officials claim that state departments of education "follow a party line" or "reflect the public school mentality."[1]

James B. Conant

It appears that one reason state legislatures have been reluctant to make generous appropriations to the departments is that no one provides strong intellectual or political support on their behalf. The logical source of such support is the body of professional educators who often appear to have little enthusiasm with the activities of state departments of education. Most state departments are viewed in somewhat negative terms by the legislature, and these predispositions tend to reinforce each other.[2]

Roald F. Campbell and
Gerald E. Stroufe

Much of our best-selling literature in recent years has been devoted to scathing criticisms of education. On the whole, these criticisms have served a useful purpose. They have, for instance, helped to intensify public impatience with the schools. And sound recommendations, some more philosophical than practical, have emerged. Most critics, however, have one thing in common: few have ever had to run a school system involving billions of dollars, millions of students, and thousands of teachers, administrators and school board members. But it is in that vast crucible that educational policy is forged. It is infinitely easier to write a book about the failings of education than to be responsible for making the educational system succeed. Of course, I am also a critic of the schools, but unlike the Silbermans, Bruners, and Holts of the world, all of whom I deeply respect, it has been my task since 1971 to try to turn things around in one state. J. Myron Atkin, the Dean of the University of Illinois College of Education is correct when he observes:

> Regardless of the desirability of reform, schools are not able to change as rapidly as most hortatory writers wish, nor are they as pliable as critics would have the public believe.[3]

Nevertheless, improvements in education are possible, though not easy. Eventual developments will be determined to a large extent by the quality of state educational leadership.

The principal focus of this book is state leadership in education. A wide range of subjects is examined—curriculum, school finance, educational planning and others—and underlying the treatment of each is the premise that state departments of education can and will increasingly be expected to provide the essential leadership for attaining universality and excellence in education. Historically, of course, local islands of educational excellence in this nation have flourished in spite of, or at least without the assistance and inspiration of, state departments of education.

However, the role of the state in education is gradually changing, as all of public education must, if it is to survive. Hemmed in on all sides by constraints—some institutional and financial, others legal and political—state departments have played a relatively passive role in educational developments. But present demands for leadership are such that the day of the quiet regulator and statistic compiler is swiftly and inevitably passing. There is a complex of circumstances and countervailing forces which in varying ways are both helping and hindering the emergence of state educational leadership. In this opening chapter those forces are assessed very briefly and some ideas are advanced as to how they might be dealt with. Without some understanding of the environment in which educational policy is made, it is impossible to appreciate why some things happen and others do not.

The low profile of state education departments stems, in part, from an historical legacy which relegated them to important, but nevertheless mundane, functions. Traditionally, they have been expected to collect, tabulate, and publish school statistics relative to attendance, teachers, term and finances; to apportion state aid to school districts; to visit school districts and advise local school authorities; to exhort the people to found and improve their schools; and to advise the legislature as to the conditions and needs of the schools. These were the duties of state departments a century ago, and to a large extent they represent their duties today. State statutes and customs even more so have tended to straitjacket state departments, and as a result they have rarely been effective instruments for effecting educational change.

Although state departments today are large and complex organizations, there has been a curious consistency in their functions through the years, a consistency which raises serious questions about their capacity to provide desperately needed statewide educational leadership. Their effectiveness has traditionally been measured against standards which are largely mechanistic, supervisory, and regulatory in character. By virtue of legislative delegation, state departments of education are engrossed in matters relating to instruction, school law, teacher certification, pensions, statistics and reports, supervision, and transportation. These functions are not unimportant, but regrettably other crucial and clearly transcendent issues in public education have gone largely unattended. And the result is a mammoth enterprise which, despite its incredible successes, has little understanding of where it is going educationally or how it will get there. If public restiveness over education has reached the crisis stage in this country, responsibility for this loss of public confidence must be borne in large measure by the states and their departments of education.

Of course, efforts to invigorate state leadership in education, although long overdue, will not be uniformly welcomed. Some critics continuously confuse leadership with some sinister totalitarian conspiracy, while still others interpret any unaccustomed level of activism on the part of state departments as unwarranted intrusions or interference with processes and methods long considered sacred; this is particulary true of those who propose that local control of schools be absolute and irreducible. So over the years school people at all levels have grown accustomed to state departments which are relatively quiescent—state departments which occasionally manage crises, but do very little to anticipate or prevent them. The relationship of the various states to the subsystems of education has customarily been one of dignified distance, not because this arrangement was in any sense advantageous to them or to the consumers of education, but because that is the way it has always been.

This condition, of course, has had a profound impact on the actual performance of state departments. It has helped breed modest, if not meager, expectations among citizens who either oversee these agencies or who look to them for direction and leadership. The danger inherent in the resultant malaise lies in the fact that public education, like other democratic institutions, is so susceptible to leveling influences—influences which, if not steadfastly resisted, produce a deterioration of standards and the debasement of excellence at all levels. As James D. Koerner has observed, state departments of education often perform worst at their most important functions.

> In licensing teachers and administrators [state departments of education] are as rigid as they ever were; in the inspection of schools they either ignore their responsibilities entirely or impose a set of mechanical criteria of dubious validity; in research and data gathering they are simply and consistently inadequate; in operating educational establishments of their own they are without any kind of distinction in a job in which they of all agencies should excel, and in long-range planning for the state and in providing strong educa-

tional leadership they are failures—if one tries to think of a major educational reform of the last quarter of a century that has come about through a state department of education, one is faced with a formidable task.[4]

Koerner's indictment is harsh, but it is not exaggerated. The increased involvement in recent years of the federal government in public education suggests that the performances of state departments are subject to widespread dissatisfaction. Although Washington has shown little interest in supplanting the states' obligations in regard to education, the federal government's influence with regard to the formulation of state policies, priorities, and standards is clear and unmistakable. The lack of *state-initiated* policies, priorities, and standards has created a vacuum. As a result, most states have bent and swayed with the federal winds. So while the federal government has maintained a posture of non-interference with state policies, the lack of such policies has led to greater influence than the federal government ever intended. What is significant about the expanding federal role in education is the obvious suggestion that existing educational machinery, particularly at the state level, has been examined and that its concept, conduct, and performance has been found wanting. It suggests, too, that as a matter of national policy the state's role in education must be more sharply drawn and its performance greatly upgraded.

The federal government is now flexing its muscles in other ways. There is a growing movement in Congress and within the United States Office of Education to encourage improved coordination and delivery by the states of educational services. Early drafts of position papers emanating from Washington on "Special Revenue Sharing for Education" would require a state "Master Plan" for allocation of funds under three broad categories: (a) Education for the Handicapped, (b) Vocational Education, and (c) Supporting Educational Materials and Services. Two other programs (Compensatory Education for the Disadvantaged and Aid to Federally Impacted Areas) would be funded directly to local districts. Discussions in Washington of the Special Revenue Sharing package even suggest a significant mood for by-passing states altogether! This reflects the negative attitude toward state education agencies which exists in many quarters.

The implication is clear. State agencies, in concert with local school districts and other publics, will need to develop clearly defined priorities and coordinated policies in order to receive and allocate federal funds provided under this program. The best available information suggests that future federal funding will be dependent on state departments overhauling and measurably improving their planning and coordinating functions.

The Post Secondary Education Planning Commission (frequently referred to as the 1202 Commission), required under the Education Amendments of 1972, is further evidence of Washington's attitude that state agencies must be streamlined. What is clear is that the federal government is seeking a much greater and broader degree of coordination in educational planning and decision-making than exists at present in Illinois or any other state. In the area of occupational education, for example, it is looking for a level of planning that will involve the full span of educational institutions within a state, from elementary to graduate school. The message emanating from Washington is "coordinate" even if it requires painful and dramatic structural and organizational adjustments.

We should not be alarmed by these intrusions. Outside prodding is likely to result in some long-delayed housecleaning at the state level. What is alarming is that the states should have to be beaten into submission—that in the absence of incentives they appear to lack the ingenuity, initiative, and farsightedness to adjust to new realities. One of those realities is an indisputable shift in educational policy-making power from local school districts to the state. This shift, while not a planned one, is the result of an accumulation of factors which promise to allow the states at long last to assume a genuine leadership role consonant with their legal authority. The growing politicization of education, the gradual erosion of lay control of local school districts, and the growing involvement of the states in school finance resulting from various equal protection suits are forces tending to escalate educational policy decision-making at the state level. There is no guarantee, of course, that state departments will pick up the baton and run with it any better than is being done at the local level. Many departments continue to operate under an extremely constricted view of their purpose.

Of course, there are other internal and external constraints inhibiting the emergence of state educational leadership. Inadequate financial support has made it difficult for state departments to address themselves forcefully to new and critical needs. In general, financial resources have not kept pace with demands for new

services. That condition has been exacerbated by the failure of state
education departments to maximize their impact with available
resources. It is difficult to recruit and retain qualified personnel
who fear being trapped in a bureaucracy with all its attendant
rigidities and dullness. And finally, organizational inflexibility
(the inability to adapt to changing conditions and new realities)
and the lack of internal planning and development activities are
all factors which have diminished the effectiveness of state departments.

Constraints to Creative Educational Change

To better understand the situation in which state departments of
education as well as local districts find themselves today, one needs
to look more closely at both positive and negative elements. The
state system must do two things: (1) face and attempt to overcome
the negative aspects of constraints and (2) build upon those aspects
of constraints which, if properly dealt with, can contribute to constructive change.

First, the growing nationwide concern with educational accountability should be acted upon. Until a continuous system for assessing
needs at the local, regional, and state level is available, it will be
impossible to establish any "accountability system" on an objective
basis. The absence of reliable information regarding the status of
learners prevents communication with various publics and retards
their support for education. The tax-paying public and educators
simply do not know where they are and how they are doing.

Resistance to change exists in many quarters. There is an impulse,
not easily overcome, to perpetuate the status quo. The prevailing
conservatism is reflected in restrictive legislation and insufficient
financial support, and these factors prevent meaningful change.
On the other hand, a conservative climate can help insure a needed
element of stability in the change process.

Statewide educational systems have not institutionalized mechanisms for encouraging and nurturing innovation, demonstration,
and diffusion of successful educational practices. In those isolated
cases where research and development activities are occurring, they
are not adequately supported. It is reliably estimated that educational systems spend less than one percent of their total financial
resources on research and development whereas business and industry often spend between five and ten percent.

Because of the nature of educational systems in this country (i.e., local educational taxes and locally elected school boards), school districts often assume that their only responsibility is a local one. The "Macy's doesn't tell Gimbel's" syndrome which is all too prevalent in our educational system makes change difficult. A lack of coordination and cooperation hinders the institutionalization of modern practices on a regional and statewide basis. On the other hand, a local district's strong motivation toward meeting its own needs is a strength which a statewide system can build upon.

The unequal distribution of educational resources prevents widespread change from taking place. Wealthy districts often have the resources to undertake research and development and to implement modern educational practices while poor districts are faced with declining resources and find it difficult or impossible to maintain minimal program standards.

The lack of adequate dissemination of information must be overcome. Communication efforts on the part of educators are too often deficient, misdirected, and neglectful of relevant publics. The difficulties inherent in communicating effectively with the total community prevents the development of an adequate support base for bringing about change.

Finally, state departments and their subsystems have generally failed to integrate available community resources into the educational process. Participation in educational governance by all relevant interests is a precondition for reform. Inherent in this concept of participatory involvement is the need to establish mechanisms for resolving conflicts before they reach the crisis stage.

Characteristics of Educational Systems Which Support
and Facilitate Creative Educational Change

The variables which tend to inhibit state educational leadership are formidable, but they are by no means unyielding. There are no easy prescriptions, and yet the constraints themselves suggest the characteristics which must exist if a statewide educational system is to be viable and pertinent. A statewide educational system and its subsystems must:

- be accountable;
- be flexible, adaptive, and open;
- be relevant to the times;

- provide for equal educational opportunity;
- be humane;
- allow for methods of adapting to priority changes;
- provide for continuous training and retraining of professional educators in light of shifting priorities; and allow for
participation in planning and governance by all relevant
publics.

And in order to achieve these desired characteristics, the statewide
educational system must:

- have sufficient financial support;
- have qualified personnel and creative leadership;
- have the support of all relevant publics;
- develop sound information bases for decision-making;
- be sensitive to state, regional, and local needs;
- maintain effective liaison with and encourage coordinated
efforts among local, regional, and state educational agencies; and
- have "venture capital," i.e., resources for planned innovation and diffusion of educational practices on a continuing
basis.

These are the important components of state educational leadership. In Illinois these principles have been put to work, and by
making adjustments and by adopting, or altering, or abolishing
policies, positions and programs to facilitate the achievement of
the State's basic purposes, the state educational agency is beginning
to come to grips with the constraints referred to above. It has identified needs and problems. It is beginning to understand what must
be done about them, how it must be done, by whom, and by when.
    In Chapter II, a planning document entitled *Action Goals for the
Seventies* is discussed in some detail.[5] Compiled with the help of
thousands of citizens, this document spells out in specific terms the
direction in which public education should be moving for the
remainder of this decade. *Action Goals* represents a major breakthrough for ending the customary lethargy and aimlessness of
Illinois' statewide educational system. As a statement of goals, it
is broad, fundamental, long-range, and expressive of our loftiest
aspirations for education. As a statement of objectives, the docu-

ment is specific and relatively short-range. These objectives are clearly attainable, consistent with overall goals, and congruent with reality as well as the educational community's perception of what is possible.

Much of what Illinois is presently committed to achieving flows directly from this blueprint for action. Not only has this participatory planning given rise to purposeful courses of action, but it has allowed the state office for the first time in its long history to confront head-on some of the most fundamental and perplexing issues of public education. Among the most urgent items on the agenda are the following:

1. The reform of school finance.
2. The revision of teacher pre-service and in-service education programs, with greater emphasis on performance and competence.
3. The revision of recognition and supervision standards, so greater emphasis is properly placed on educational outcomes rather than inputs.
4. Curriculum reform, the foundation of which is increased individualization and the creation of more learning options.
5. The vigorous pursuit of equal educational opportunity, particularly in relation to school integration and special programs for disadvantaged, non-English speaking, and exceptional children.
6. The establishment of an educational assessment program to identify educational needs and measure educational outcomes.
7. The development of new and fairer standards to govern the organization of school districts.
8. Experimentation in various forms of local educational governance which reflect new and shifting power relationships among those publics having an interest in education.
9. The establishment of viable alternative educational models.

Subsequent chapters are devoted to a fuller consideration of these subjects.

This new activism on the part of the Illinois state office has generally been well received. On the other hand, there has been no lack

of nodding heads, raised eyebrows, and predictions of dire consequences. Such reactions were not totally unexpected, because
despite its inevitability change is never easy. If the notion of state
,educational leadership has not received widespread acceptance,
particularly in professional circles, the explanation lies in the fact
that such exertions by state departments are simply foreign to the
experience of most people.

So while there have been some uneasy moments in the life of the
present administration, conflict and confrontation should be
viewed as facts of educational life. They are valuable in the sense
that they provide a focus on problems for which solutions must
be found. The hard issues have to be faced up to. The state office
has often been counselled to play the waiting game in the hope that
pressing problems would somehow disappear. But, given the
dynamic character of education, it is futile to turn your back on
new realities or to defend zealously the status quo. Such a strategy
is clearly inconsistent with the leadership requirements of our
times. In education, as in other things, severe penalties await those
in positions of responsibility who choose to abdicate. Vacillation
has prompted the courts, for example, to interpose themselves repeatedly in matters relating to school finance, desegregation,
school district organization, collective bargaining and student
rights. While many people consider such intervention appalling,
it is obvious that the educational community has only itself to
blame for this condition.

Resistance to change has made the task of providing statewide
educational leadership difficult, but no more so than our fear of
failure. To be sure, mistakes have been made and others will be
made in the future. However, a fear of failure should not deter
educators from either a critical examination of problems or the
search for pragmatic solutions to them. As Dr. James Bryant Conant
observed a decade ago, "Too often educational leadership at the
state level—official and unofficial—has been open to the charge
that it was unwilling to examine public school needs critically."[6]
That, in large measure, is the root cause of the generally diffident
attitudes shared by both professional educators and lay citizens
with respect to state departments of education.

Therefore, it is not enough to honor excellence or even to demand
it of ourselves and others. Excellence is a condition which requires
not only hard work and purposefulness by state education depart-

ments, but a willingness to risk failure in the quest for excellence. Sluggish and apathetic educational systems accomplish little. Without a mission and the discipline and tenacity of purpose needed to carry out that mission, nothing ever changes for the better, nothing is renewed, nothing is healed.

The Issue of Local Control

The organization and diversity of most statewide educational systems militate against reform. The educational enterprise is comprised of hundreds of school districts, each of which is vested with the prerogatives of local government. And these prerogatives are jealously guarded, for as Ewald Nyquist, the chief state school officer of New York, has noted, local school control is "a minor branch of theology." So while few people would seriously suggest that the states actually operate the schools, clearly some understanding must be reached which will permit strong and purposeful leadership at both the state and local levels to coexist. A new partnership must be forged between the federal government, the states, and local school districts which vests in each partner sufficient authority to enable it to play an integral role in the educational process. This partnership must be based on two fundamental assumptions:

1. The kind of world likely to develop in the remainder of this century requires a new definition of "localism."
2. The state must invigorate its leadership role to prevent an excessive involvement of the federal government, on the one hand, and to strengthen local capabilities for leadership on the other.

To a world in which men can cross a continent in four hours, do transatlantic business in a day, maintain instantaneous communication throughout the globe, and watch men explore the barren surface of the moon, "localism" becomes a relative term. What is "local" depends, in large part, on where one stands. The incredible mobility of the country places great strains on the traditional views of localism. The world in which a family resided in one locale, raised and educated their children there, and lived to see the cycle begin with their grandchildren growing and marrying in the same location is a thing of the past. Thus, today in this country a person may be born in Chicago, marry and reside in Los Angeles, change job locations to Denver or Omaha, educate his children in two or three geographic places, see those children marry and reside in St. Louis and witness his grandchildren begin their mature lives in Wisconsin, New York, or California. Americans remain the most restless and mobile people on the face of the earth.

This, of course, raises serious questions regarding the traditional concept of localism in public education. Increasingly the needs and differences of one community are not very different from those of any other. Thus, it is of the utmost importance for all citizens concerned about public education to take a much more "global" view of education, to break out of the confines of a restrictive parochialism. The fact of the matter is that increasingly the quality of education in Oak Park, Illinois, cannot be divorced from the quality or lack of it to be found in Chicago, Rockford, or Peoria. The courts are now beginning to see this in regard to school finance, and this principle is likely to find even broader applicability in the future.

The second proposition is equally important. An active educational leadership at the state level can prevent an excessive involvement of the federal government in the area of public education. It is no secret that the United States Office of Education, as suggested earlier, has not always had the greatest respect and confidence in the abilities of the states to cope with major educational problems. And if the federal government has activated itself to an unprecedented degree over the past decade, it is only because the states have shown little initiative and capability, and have been unwilling to lead.

The most important results of a new state activism will be the renewed vigor it gives to local educational decision-making. At present the Illinois state education office, based on this philosophy, is deeply involved in a number of issues. In its efforts to desegregate the schools, revise recognition and supervision standards, reform the curriculum, and institute teacher education programs which emphasize performance, there is, as will be evident in the chapters which follow, one connecting thread: *the state must take the initiative to bring about needed educational changes; it must stimulate, encourage, and even at times threaten, but at all times the goal is the renewal and strengthening of local institutions and their capabilities for operating and directing their own schools.*

C. Northcote Parkinson once observed that "the central problem of our time—from which our other difficulties most stem—is one produced by the stagnation of political theory during an age of technological advance." The essential truth of this observation is obvious, but whether it can be fairly applied, as some have tried, to test the need for the continued existence of local school districts is quite another matter. There are some who believe that local school districts have outlived their usefulness. Most thoughtful people do not subscribe to that theory. Some months ago, a rather pessimistic article on this question was published in Illinois, an article written by the president of a local school board who seemed to question the need for local boards of education. This is what he wrote:

> Local control of education is a political theory. Judging from the discrepancies between what society wants and needs on the one hand and what education delivers on the other, we can conclude that local control of education is a *stagnating* political theory. Stagnation delays educational change in an era when everything else is changing. Delay . . . is the deadliest form of denial. How long will the American public be denied effective, relevant education? Not another 30 years, you may be sure. The question is whether the public will get what it needs from local school districts, from state and national districts, or from private industry. Local school districts still possess a virtual monopoly on childhood education. But countless local leaders strive for nothing more than the formulation of delaying policies. No one asks the most probing of questions: "Why not?"[7]

Despite this pessimism, there is a growing belief that state departments of education can help invigorate local boards of education and equip them to ask the right questions. Of course, there are limitations to local control; particularly when the interests and rights of children are jeopardized, state responsibility must be permitted to supercede claims to local prerogatives. The state cannot escape its overriding responsibility in education, a fact which the loudest proponents of local control refuse to understand. Recent court decisions dealing with segregated schools and with the inequities generated by our present system of financing education have consistently criticized the defendant—states and their respective educational agencies—for their failure to avert such conditions. States have been criticized even when they neither created the conditions nor were expressly empowered to prevent them. So it is not always easy to determine where state responsibility ends and local control begins, and given the shifting line of demarcation, there is only one certainty: we are undoubtedly headed for some testing periods before the issue is further clarified. However, the days when state education departments deferred consistently to the judgments and wishes of locally oriented educational interests are gone. The task now is to achieve a balance which is conducive to meeting the challenge relentlessly thrust upon the schools by the forces of change.

The Politics of Education

State departments of education can make a difference, if they are willing to play a leadership role. The quality of that leadership will depend on their willingness and ability to come to terms with change and with the various institutional constraints already discussed. The quality of leadership will depend, too, on the degree to which educators and other concerned publics understand that educational decisions are basically political decisions. The educational system does not operate in a vacuum; it is a creature and an extension of our political process. Reasonable men, of course, may disagree about whether this intimate association of politics and education is good or bad, but such a relationship does in fact exist. The real issue for state educational leadership is whether the political process can be made to work for public education.

Until very recently, school politics was peculiarly local in nature. It was within the nation's hundreds of school districts where the melding of politics and education was most pronounced. Boards of education are popularly elected, and, as is generally the case in a democracy, the tenure of board members is contingent on their being relatively responsive to community sentiment. The financial needs of school districts are satisfied largely by local property taxes, and up until a decade ago, 70 percent of the school tax referenda were being approved by voters. But as the cost of education has spiralled upwards and the demands for more and better schools have increased, that pattern has drastically changed. Not only are there 50 percent fewer referenda today than five years ago, but only 30 percent of them are receiving favorable treatment by voters. Perhaps more than any other factor, this diminishing capacity of school districts to generate cash has resulted in an evolutionary shift in both funding patterns and the locus of educational decision-making. Thus, the movers and shakers within the educational community must adapt to a new set of realities, for educational decisions are increasingly being rendered by representative government at the state and federal levels and less by electorates and their spokesmen within school districts.

So as a practical matter, new strategies must be devised to make the political system work for education. First, a coalition of educators, parents, and students is needed to operate collectively within the political process to influence educational policy-making; this coalition's orientation should be to the statehouses of the nation rather than local communities. State departments of education can play a catalytic role in coalescing interests to maximize the educational community's political influence with state legislatures and governors. There exists no more formidable barrier to state educational leadership than the failure of educators to understand how the political process works and how it can be made to work for education.

State legislatures and governors are constitutionally vested with broad policy-making powers which affect the operations and governance of public education. How those powers are used in the future will depend heavily on the willingness of citizens and educators to become involved in the political process and to provide direction and information upon which sound educational judgment can be made.

Legislative powers with respect to education are sweeping. State legislatures can determine who must attend school and for how long; appropriate funds for the operation of the schools and decide the level of funding and the manner in which funds are to be distributed; require curricular revisions; prescribe standards for the certification of teachers and other professionals; and create and recreate school districts to satisfy legislatively determined criteria. The political power of legislatures in the realm of public education is so vast that much of this legislative authority has been freely delegated to others, including the state superintendents and hundreds of local boards of education.

No less influential in educational matters are the nation's governors. Historically, they have not played a prominent role in educational policy-making, but their involvement has been inten-

sified in recent years. Whether or not a governor's party controls
the legislature, his powers vis-à-vis the legislature are considerable,
particularly in view of his control of the budgetary process and the
finality of gubernatorial disapproval and amendment through his
power to veto legislation.

The governor and the legislature represent major loci of power.
The manner in which power is used has a direct bearing on most of
the fundamental issues facing education. Most reforms relating to
the licensing of professionals, school finance, and educational
governance must first pass through the nation's statehouses. There
are very practical as well as legal limitations on what state departments of education can do on their own in these arenas. How well
then has this dispersal of power and authority worked? Considering how markedly conditions have changed this past decade, public
education, on balance, has fared rather well. However, it must be
admitted that the political system has failed miserably in some
respects. For example, it is generally acknowledged that state
systems for financing education are grossly unfair and inequitable
—that a fiscal policy which makes the quality of a child's education a function of the wealth of the district in which he resides
is a concept which is both obsolete and constitutionally suspect.
Despite repeated warnings regarding the probable consequences
of inaction, the political system has made few adjustments to rectify
the obvious inequities. The failure of legislatures to institute a
thorough-going reform of our school finance system does not suggest that the political system is inherently insensitive to the needs
of public education. What it shows is that the system must be
continuously jarred, pushed, and sensitized by outside forces.

Therefore, the overriding issue is this: how do we make the
political system more responsive to educational needs? First we
must finally dispense with the persistent myth that politics and
education do not mix. What is clear is that politics and education
are so totally and inextricably bound up together that it is virtually
impossible to tell where one ends and the other begins. James
Bryant Conant put this matter in perspective some years ago when
he remarked:

> If I were twenty years younger, and had the ideas I have now,
> I would go and sit in Albany as a lobbyist, and see to it that
> the bills to support public schools and reform teacher educa-

tion got through the legislature. Political action is what's needed.[8]

Second, the various components of the educational community must begin to close ranks. The problem quite frankly is that no one individual or organization can presume to speak for public education. It is essential that educators and concerned citizens forge a working coalition, submerge their minor differences of opinion and begin speaking as one voice on at least some of the vital issues.

The major impediment to realizing commonly shared goals is the intramural skirmishing of teachers, school administrators and school boards. A "give us all or nothing" attitude can only lead to divisiveness and self-defeat. Legislatures and governors will not become more responsive to educational needs so long as educators cannot agree on what is needed. If the education community remains a house divided against itself, the political leadership in our statehouses and in Washington cannot be expected to be sympathetic to cries for more help.

Educators must realize that the competiton for state and federal dollars is becoming more acute. Public aid, mental health, and highways are among education's principal competitors. And because the administration of these programs is highly centralized, they have a distinct advantage in their relationship to legislatures and governors in that they are able to do their bidding with one voice. Although public education enjoys no such built-in advantage, it is not powerless. Easily one quarter of the voting population of a state like Illinois, for example, is involved directly or indirectly in education. People, if they choose to, can make the political system work overtime for education.

Coalescing disparate educational interests will not be easy. However, it is possible, and clearly self-interest dictates that such an effort be made. If state educational agencies are to play a leadership role they cannot hope to operate autonomously and apart from the political process. Professional fragmentation has severely weakened the potential political leverage of educators, a condition which has made it relatively easy for some politicians to play one faction off against another.

Conclusion

The remainder of this book is devoted to an examination of some of the hard educational issues facing every state. Because the nature of these issues vary somewhat from state to state, it would be presumptuous to suggest that the approaches being used in Illinois could be employed in any other locality. Nevertheless, the Illinois experience is evidence that creative state educational leadership is still possible. It is important, however, that that leadership be used properly and creatively. Emerson hit upon the essence of true leadership when he said a leader is one "who shall make us do what we can." In other words:

> The education agency which perseveres in its commitment to change, which is willing to skip some of the details and take the broad view of educational problems, which is willing to accept the commitment and responsibility of accountability, and which actively seeks problems rather than seeking to avoid them, has by far the best chance of moving from its historic position of bureaucratic authoritarianism through its emerging stance of leadership, into its ultimate goal of educational statesmanship.[9]

That is the kind of educational leadership the state office has sought to provide in Illinois. It is not the kind which is bent on doing things *for* local school districts, but rather a leadership which can restore faith in local institutions by strengthening them.

Chapter II

Educational Accountability

The citizens of the state are concerned, and with justification, as to when, how, and why, their tax dollars are being spent for education.

Professor of Education

By rebuilding confidence in the schools a giant step will be taken towards securing the necessary financing.

Parent

Illinois is now without clear goals and priorities in public education. It has no defensible educational standards or requirements.

School Superintendent

People can accept the remoteness of government in an urban area in many of its operations, but we cannot let schools become remote from their clientele.

Concerned Citizen

"Accountability in education" is a curious concept. Over the past several years professional journals, professional meetings, the press, and the public have seemed to focus their concerns around the phrase. Unfortunately, more heat than light seems to have been generated. Each interest group seems to attach a different meaning to the term. And, often these different meanings have resulted in polarization of these educational interest groups.

There are several things that "accountability in education" is *not* and can never be. First, accountability is not new in education. People have always asked questions about schools, but the types of questions have changed from quantitative questions, from asking about the number of graduates to questions about the amount of learning which occurs in the schools. Second, accountability in education can never be achieved through the mere adoption of business practices. Numerous critics maintain that education should be "run like a business," measuring "inputs," "outputs," and "productivity" through "systems analysis." However, productivity in education remains to be defined. Until it is defined it can never be measured.

Third, accountability in education can never be achieved merely through greater infusions of dollars for measuring school outcomes, although greater investments in measuring school outcomes are needed. But, unless educators take some important first steps, these greater dollar investments could very well produce diagnoses of the wrong ailments.

Finally, accountability can never be a system for holding individual professionals directly responsible for learner performance. To maintain that a principal or a teacher should be evaluated on the basis of the reading and math scores of his or her students is nonsense and flies in the face of all we know about the many variables which influence learning.

If accountability in education is not or never can be any of the above, what then is it? An effective and equitable accountability system in education must be based on the following definition: Accountability is the responsibility of those in education to a) collect information about school processes and outcomes, b) to *act* on the basis of that information, and c) to determine how effective their actions have been. Note that this definition does not attempt to place blame or hold individuals directly responsible for outcomes. Rather, the crux of the definition centers on the *responsibility of educators to act* on the basis of information.

It is within this context that this chapter has been developed. The following pages discuss the Illinois approach to collecting information about the desired future directions and conditions of its educational system, the mechanisms for action based upon that information, and a long-range approach to assessing educational needs and determining educational progress.

STATEWIDE PLANNING AND PUBLIC PARTICIPATION

On June 21, 1971, in Rockford, Illinois, a little girl barely able to see over the podium walked confidently to the microphone and told the staff of the state office of education that she usually received good grades from teachers she liked and poor grades from teachers she did not like. She wondered why she could not have the right to choose her own teachers—a simple enough question, asked sincerely and in good faith that someone would be able to provide an answer.

That summer day was the beginning of a movement in Illinois public education which today is providing not only new directions for the education of every Illinois child, but a model for participatory planning across the country. A new chief state educational officer is invariably haunted by a basic question: How can a fundamental institution of this society, the public schools, be renewed to meet the needs of our times? In what direction should the educational enterprise be moving and for what purpose? There is a growing public impatience, a conviction among people that their schools are not working and that they are not receiving a fair ratio of success and benefit for every dollar devoted to education.

Coupled with the public's restiveness over the outcomes of education is the emerging realization that unprecedented social change has led educators at all levels to become increasingly bogged down in "crisis management" rather than the careful planning and management. The state office quickly concluded that what was desperately needed in Illinois was long-range planning to provide more comprehensive, less fragmented approaches to solving critical problems facing statewide educational systems. While business and industry have long seen the need for careful, systematic, long-range planning, the need for such activities in education is only beginning to be recognized. However, the increasing involvement of the private sector in formal education through performance contracting and the applications of modern technology to educational activities has provided some impetus for more systematic and comprehensive educational planning.

Planning represents one way of ending the aimlessness which characterizes public education and restoring public confidence in the schools. The courage necessary to test old assumptions and terminate, once and for all, outdated and unworkable programs is a necessary part of planning. No less important than planning itself, of course, is the need to involve people who hold firm convictions about what they want their children to gain from public education in that planning. No one in the field of education can presume to have a monopoly on answers and solutions, including, of course, any state office of education. If a meaningful consensus on educational goals and priorities is to be fashioned, educators must be prepared to consult with the people: community leaders, working men and women, school administrators, parents, teachers and students. The Illinois Office of Education did precisely that. It listened carefully to what people had to say, first at public hearings throughout Illinois and then at a statewide conference in Chicago. Almost 3,000 people participated in the process. The testimony, which was incredibly voluminous, confirmed what until then was only vaguely suspected: people are demanding educational reform.

Citizen involvement, while unprecedented in Illinois, is congruent with a personal belief that a strong dose of participatory democracy will help make the educational enterprise a truly public one. The public, heavily taxed and uncertain about the purposes of education, has an indisputable right to help chart the destiny of the schools. Furthermore, the public has an inimitable ability for bringing to bear on the decision-making process new sensitivities and insights which too frequently have been dismissed by professionals. Finally, without broad public support no significant and desired change in education is possible.

These were some of the considerations which led the staff of the state office first to Rockford and on six subsequent days to other Il-

linois cities. For eighty hours the staff listened, and more importantly learned what was wrong with public education and what might
be done about it. Two categories of themes emerged during the hearings: procedural and substantive. Substantive concerns related to
the form education should assume in the future—such philosophical
issues as more flexibility versus the return to the three R's, and the
need for individualized instruction rather than the lock-step patterns
of traditional educational programs. An impressive number of witnesses criticized present educational techniques and structures as
barriers to developing favorable attitudes toward learning. A kindergarten teacher summarized the views of many with this observation:

> I've worked with an early education class for the last couple
> of years and I have yet to see a child who didn't come to school
> excited and eager to learn. But all of us who have had chil-
> dren go through schools, all who have taught children,
> know that something happens to that eagerness and joy in
> learning by the time they reach the upper grades.
>
> School too often turns into playing the game. The teacher's
> game; the report card game; the pass the test game; the get
> into college game; and joyful learning is no longer associated
> with the formal educational process.

The procedural concerns of witnesses involved efforts to support
quality education, whatever form that education might take. Such
issues as the financial support level, school organization, the rights
of students, and the preparation, evaluation, and retention of teachers
were typical procedural concerns. Inadequate financing of the
schools was repeatedly identified as a major barrier to equalizing
educational opportunity. A common thread of testimony heard at
all the hearings was the need for the state to assume the primary
responsibility for financing schools. A United States congressman
attacked the present system:

> I must emphasize again that nothing will happen to improve
> our schools . . . they will only get worse . . . until we
> change the system of paying for public education.

The state office staff came away from these hearings knowing
something that was only vaguely articulated before. A massive out-

cry for schools to help students understand how to be human beings, as well as to train them to make a living and to survive had been heard. It was clearer than ever before that while reading, writing, and arithmetic are still important students are calling for much more. We understood more perfectly the extent to which the poor, disadvantaged, and minority people had been left out of the education picture.

The huge piles of testimony gathered at the hearings were carefully assessed and evaluated. And out of that process emerged a draft statement on educational goals and priorities. Compiling this material into workable form, then refining it into a cohesive program was an enormous undertaking. The witnesses, of course, had not been expected to present a detailed program of educational change from the podium. This was a task for the staff. The draft document was unique in that it was time specific. Unlike so many public reports, it did not call for reforms and changes at an unnamed future date, but attempted to place them within a time framework. Every action objective and most necessary steps contained a specific target date for accomplishment.

Furthermore, the document was unique because it did not seek to finesse the contentious and controversial issues. The program was not one that was likely to be universally applauded; some matters were certain to evoke dissent, anger, and strenuous protest. However, it was neither feasible nor in the best interest of school-age children to try to formulate a program filled with compromises to please everyone. It would have been easy, of course, to ignore the controversial issues such as student rights, school desegregation, teacher preparation, collective bargaining, school district organization, curriculum reform, and school finance, but these were and continue to be the issues that crowd the public agenda. Such controversial issues must be solved as quickly as practicable, although unfortunately they rarely yield to easy answers. Educational problems, painfully and emotionally charged as they may be, must be dealt with boldly and not permitted to paralyze an essential forward movement toward educational excellence.

With that underlying thought in mind, 1200 people—500 more than anticipated—gathered in Chicago for three days to consider the planning document. They came at their own expense from every corner of Illinois, representing the rich and poor, young and old, educators and lay citizens of the state. The conference had two purposes: (1) to clarify, redefine and seek some agreement on the goals and objectives of education; and (2) to establish and set into motion a mechanism to facilitate the achievement of those goals and objectives.

The participation was astonishing. No observer could fail to note the seriousness and concern of these citizens. There was no lack of heated discussion, but the prevailing attitude those three days was one of cooperation. People spoke of their concerns, and they listened carefully to one another. The conference slowly revised and strengthened the document. What was unworkable was made workable. A proposal that was good, but could be improved, was made better. The inflexible was made more flexible, the unclear clearer.

Despite the obvious success of this process, there were cynics who viewed the process as a charade, predicting that it would amount to nothing. The noise may stir the air, they contended, but it will fall on deaf ears. The skepticism was not completely unjustified. Reports have come and gone, and things have not changed appreciably. And to be sure, there was no ironclad guarantee that this particular plan would not join the infamous graveyard of public reports. As will be shown presently, a quite different fate awaited this report.

In March of 1972, after nine months of consultations with the people of Illinois, a report, entitled *Action Goals for the Seventies: An Agenda for Illinois Education* was made public. The report's foundation is the notion that no organization, including our vast system of public education, can long remain purposeful if in times of rapid change it is unwilling, or is unable, to renew itself; and this requires vitality, flexibility, vision, and creativity. It also involves taking risks and occasionally making mistakes. In short, the report was a call to action.

Action Goals for the Seventies is organized into two sections. First is a statement of substantive goals which specifies in broad language the desired eventual results of education. These goals are child or learner centered, long range in nature, and not locked into a specific time frame. Although the goals are not time specific, the aim is full accomplishment by 1980. To understand much of the material in this book, it is important to list the nine substantive goals:

Goal: The educational system must provide opportunities which help students master the basic skills of reading, communication, computation, and problem solving.

Goal: The educational system must provide an environment which helps students, parents, and other community members demonstrate a positive attitude toward learning.

Goal: The educational system must foster a feeling of adequacy and self-worth on the part of all students.

Goal: The educational system must provide opportunities for students to express the full extent of their creativity.

Goal: The educational system must provide experiences which help students adapt to a world of change.

Goal: The educational system must provide an environment which brings about appreciation for and positive attitudes toward persons and cultures different from one's own.

Goal: The educational system must provide equal educational opportunities for all.

Goal: The educational system must provide every student with opportunities in training for the world of work.

Goal: The educational system must provide experiences which result in habits and attitudes associated with citizenship responsibilities.

These goals can provide the basic framework for quality education. Once adopted, the goals can become the foundation for specific plans for educational reform, whether those plans are made at the local, regional or state level.

The second, and perhaps most important section of the report is a statement of *Action Objectives*. These objectives are program oriented, time specific, and product specific. They set forth in detail those specific actions and steps which must be undertaken, and by whom and by when. In all there are eighty-five objectives, covering a wide range of matters, including: surveying educational progress; equal educational opportunity; school governance; school finance; school organization; curriculum; professional preparation, certification, retraining, and relations with school boards; pupil services; and student rights. Illustrative of the action objectives which were adopted are the following:

Action Objective:

By the spring of 1973, prepare a plan for a pilot program to assess the attitudes and achievement of learners.

Action Objective:
> By 1975, all schools will provide a positive learning environ-
> ment for children of non-English-speaking backgrounds.
> These children should be encouraged to maintain and im-
> prove their language skills in both English and their home
> language. Cultural differences must be respected and de-
> structively discriminatory practices avoided.

Action Objective:
> By 1973, experiments in new or different methods of school
> governance will be established in at least two local school
> districts.

Action Objective:
> By 1975, to have encouraged experimentation with and
> evaluated the effects of the twelve-month school.

Action Objective:
> By 1975, a statewide network of schools will be established
> to test alternative instructional patterns and publish infor-
> mation on them.

Action Objective:
> By 1980, every school district in the State will have an in-
> dividualized instruction curriculum.

Action Objective:
> By 1974, all approved professional education preparation
> programs will include systematic procedures for assessing
> the candidate's attitude and competency throughout the
> preparation period.

Action Objective:
> By 1972, the State will adopt a collective bargaining act.

Action Goals for the Seventies is an effort to chart the direction in
which public education should be moving for the remainder of this
decade, but it is by no means a mandated master plan. Rather, it is a
useful device for airing controversies, resolving conflicts, and
fashioning a consensus on the crucial issues facing us. Quarterly

public hearings and annual revisions of the document are intended to encourage continuous discussion of the merits and appropriateness of its recommendations. In early 1974, the second edition of *Action Objectives* was issued, containing a progress report for each of the Action Objectives as well as specific examples of exciting local and state educational developments having some relationship to the objectives.

In relation to the internal operations of the Illinois state office of education, the impact of this planning process can be seen in three ways. First, it has had an impact on the budgetary process. Detailed operational plans for the accomplishment of the eighty-five goals have been prepared. These accomplishment plans include a description of the desired results, as well as the activities, staff, and other resources required for the completion of the goals. As a result, planning has significantly influenced the allocation and use of financial resources and evaluation of program effectiveness at the state level. All of the activities of the state office have been critically examined, and as priorities have emerged, appropriate shifts in the allocation of resources have followed.

Second, participatory educational planning has permitted the state office to identify four priority or central missions. Each is a matter of widespread public concern, and each has a direct bearing on the state office's overriding purpose, namely to provide citizens with opportunities for equal access to quality education. Briefly stated, these four missions are:

1. To insure the establishment of professional training and retraining programs which result in selection and retention of professional personnel who exhibit favorable attitudes toward all learners and who perform consistent with the high standards of the educational profession.
2. To insure that the schools provide a wide variety of learning opportunities for each learner. Central to this mission is the need to encourage learning opportunities which are humane and adapted to each person's style of learning.
3. To insure that every child attend a school which has financial ability to provide quality education. Inherent in this mission is the need to equalize access to quality educational facilities and programs regardless of geographic location or local socio-economic factors.

4. To establish standards for the recognition and supervision of
   schools that encourage them to offer quality educational
   opportunities through (a) strengthening the ability of
   those schools to assess local needs, (b) the specification of
   goals and objectives, (c) developing programs based upon
   local needs, and (d) continuously assessing the performance
   of the educational system in accomplishing goals and objectives.

Participatory educational planning has permitted the Illinois
state educational agency to move toward a system of program
planning and budgeting and to specify priority missions. It also has
permitted the agency to deal with the vexing issue of educational accountability. It has provided it with a mechanism for resolving
the most difficult question of all: What should the public schools
accomplish in the decade of the seventies? Education is under
attack from many quarters, because educators in large numbers
are confused about what they are supposed to be doing and to
whom they are being held accountable. Educational planning is
an indispensable key in answering the questions "Accountability
to whom?" and "Accountability for what?" Only when there is
some agreement as to what is to be accomplished in education, how
it is to be accomplished, by when, and by whom, can true accountability become a reality.

Educators have a tendency to communicate with their various
clientele on the basis of past experiences: the number of bond
issues that have failed, the number of teacher strikes that have occurred, the number of students who have dropped out of school, the
number of instances of student unrest which have disrupted the
educational process. Unfortunately, these facts standing alone tell
us little about the direction in which the schools should be moving
or how particular problems might be solved. Planning can reorient
education and compel educators to look the future straight in the
eye.

LOCAL PLANNING AND PUBLIC PARTICIPATION

Almost all state departments of education are charged by their
legislatures with the responsibility of supervising the public

schools and ensuring that they are organized, conducted, and operated as prescribed by law. In carrying out that task, state departments are not only required to apply legislatively determined
standards, but are often expected to establish reasonable rules and
regulations for recognizing schools. Typically, state departments
are authorized by law to enforce these standards by witholding state
financial aid from schools which seriously violate those standards
and fail to remediate unsatisfactory conditions. Generally, however,
the power to non-recognize a school and withhold state aid is
invoked only in extreme situations.

Traditionally, recognition standards have covered a range of
educational programs and services, including curriculum, teaching
and administration, and a school's physical plant, supplies, library
and maintenance. Despite the breadth of these provisions, it is no
secret that the recognition or non-recognition of schools has been
and, in large measure, continues to be based almost exclusively on
quantitative considerations. There is little likelihood today that
a school's status would be altered upon a showing that its students
were not learning to read or to write! If, on the other hand, the
plumbing of that same school were defective, the status of that
school would undoubtedly be in jeopardy.

Our preoccupation with educational inputs—with "things"—
has left unanswered the most important question of all: Are the
children of the state receiving a quality education? That question
will only be answered when educators begin to pay more attention
to educational performance than to educational conditions. That
question will be answered when they stop trying to measure the
performance of a school only in terms of the number of pupils per
square foot in a classroom, the cleanliness of lunchrooms, the
adequacy of a school's lighting, and the size of the library.

Obviously, the condition of school facilities, the diversity of the
curriculum, and the credentials of teaching and administrative personnel are important. But in relation to what young people should
actually be experiencing in the classroom, too much significance
has been attached to the more easily measurable conditions. This
concern with the presence or non-presence of tangible and visible
things has not permitted state educational agencies and professionals within school districts to move on to more important questions,
such as an examination of the efficacy of the educational process
within the districts, and the need to chart new and imaginative
courses leading to educational improvements.

If quantitative measures of performance are obsolete, a major shift in emphasis away from the inputs of education to the outcomes of education is necessary. An advisory committee, comprised of people representing all publics having an interest in education, studied this matter in Illinois for almost eighteen months. A proposal for evaluating, supervising, and recognizing schools was prepared in late 1972, and although revisions were made in the standards during subsequent months, the essential mission of the proposal remained intact.[1]

The central mission of the program is to develop and improve a local school district's capability for bringing about improvement in educational programs and services through comprehensive local planning and evaluation of educational programs and community participation in planning. The program permits school districts to operate with flexibility and encourages them to do so, but the community must be allowed to participate in the process of planning. In addition, the proposed recognition standards can become, through local initiative, a vehicle for establishing a clearcut system of accountability.

Perhaps the most significant requirement is that every district develop a written program plan. School districts have been asked to begin establishing a framework for continuous and systematic planning by completing five basic tasks:

1. School districts will establish long range, locally defined goal statements in two categories: (a) student goals and (b) system goals. The first set will be oriented to the desired general knowledge, skills, and attitudes of students. The system goals will state how a school district's educational and support programs can be used to accomplish the student goals. For example, the student goal of creating a "positive attitude toward learning" can be achieved in part through the system goals of "a broad range of relevant curricular offerings." System goals must address themselves to the following matters: district governance policy and practices; district administrative structure and practices; district policy regarding the rights and responsibilities of individuals; the instructional program; support services (transportation, food services, health services, facilities); and staff development and inservice education.

2. School districts will examine the needs of the educational system. Once a district has developed a clear set of goals, the next logical step is to ask two questions: "How are we doing in meeting these goals?" and "How much distance separates where we are and where we want to be?"

3. School districts will specify "system performance objectives" to satisfy institutional needs. On a longer range basis, districts will begin to develop learner objectives as a framework for curriculum planning. With the establishment of long-range goals and a written statement of needs, districts can proceed to develop performance objectives—a written statement of the specific, measurable results which are to be accomplished by when and by whom.

4. School districts will begin to develop and implement programs to achieve the desired results stated in the system performance objectives. After establishing the long-range student and system goals, defining system needs, and developing system performance objectives, districts will design programs to achieve the performance objectives. Whereas performance objectives define *what* must be done, a program design spells out *how* it is to be done.

5. School districts will develop an evaluation system. An evaluation program will provide local school board members, teachers, and administrators with information for determining the extent to which goals and objectives are being accomplished, and with a basis for revising local objectives and programs.

Such planning at the local level will not only help define the expectations of a school district and the responsibilities of school officials, but will strengthen local autonomy and encourage flexibility in the development of educational programs. If the citizens are concerned with where education is going, program planning at the district level provides a useful vehicle for moving ahead.

By assessing educational needs, a district will be able to determine the distance separating that point where it is in educational development and that point to which it aspires. The district will learn what it is doing well and what it is doing poorly. The strengths of school districts will be revealed and should be built upon. As for the weaknesses, they can be enormously helpful in indicating which programs must be initiated or upgraded if failures are to be remediated.

Once a school district knows where it is educationally, it can determine more easily where it should be going. The task then will be to specify who will be responsible for accomplishing what educational products. This process will allow schools to define the desirable outcomes of the local educational process in terms which are specific, and in terms of what students should be achieving at various levels of educational development.

In Illinois, no educational program is being imposed on the school districts by the state. The state's purpose is to enhance autonomy and flexibility at the local level. Program planning, however, will allow the statewide educational system to deal more effectively with a multitude of problems, the nature and intensity of which vary enormously from community to community. No state office of education has either the capacity or the desire to assess needs, to identify objectives, and to design programs for hundreds of school districts. Planning at the district level can only be done by people at the district level.

Guidelines for Local District Education Planning have been prepared to assist local school officials.[2] These guidelines were introduced in early 1973 at a series of twelve regional workshops for more than 5,000 superintendents, board members, and teachers, representing more than 90 percent of the districts of the state. Realizing that some districts may not be fully prepared in a technical sense to implement these guidelines, forty professional staff members from the state office have been assigned to provide fulltime assistance to local districts.

Community involvement is essential to success. Although the schools belong to the people, their advice or opinions seldom have been solicited, except at election time or when additional tax revenues are needed. Districts are being asked to maintain existing avenues or, if necessary, open new avenues of communication with the community.

Only those who share in decision-making can truly be held accountable. If citizens, teachers, and students are permitted to participate in reaching a consensus on local goals and objectives for education, a major step in developing a meaningful accountability system will have been taken. If educators choose not to involve these people, the risk of further isolating groups within our communities and inviting open conflict and confrontation among them becomes greater.

Community participation does not imply that decision-making powers should be exercised or even shared by anyone other than board members and administrators. Educators ought to listen to people, consult them occasionally, weigh their concerns, and consider their opinions. There is growing evidence that people in many communities are not being heard, and the consequence is rising levels of frustration and alienation. The symptoms are all too obvious: student unrest, teacher strikes, parents picketing or boycotting their schools, and incipient taxpayer revolts in communities throughout the country.

Few school boards, regardless of how they are chosen, can be fully aware of and sensitive to the shifting nuances of community sentiment regarding the schools. It would be presumptuous to believe that a state superintendent or anyone else in a position of authority had a monopoly on knowledge, i.e. had all the answers to all the problems. Establishment of community participation can be exasperating, time consuming, and sometimes inconvenient, but obviously the public interest is served by such a process and the benefits of bringing the people into the confidence of educators clearly outweigh the disadvantages—whatever they may be. Elected officials are obligated to serve everyone in their respective communities, not only those who may have voted for them, but also those who voted for their opponents and those who did not vote at all.

Although this matter of community participation has been discussed at some length because it concerns local school officials, it is not a design to usurp local prerogatives. How a school district involves the community in this planning process is a question which each district must answer for itself. There is no reason why this open and participatory process cannot be conducted within current governance structures.

Equally important is the need for professional involvement by teachers, administrators, and pupil service personnel. Avenues for professional participation are especially critical in the development of performance objectives, building programs, and in planning and developing evaluation systems. But again the specific avenues for participation must be determined locally.

Such planning at the local level will not only help define community expectations and the responsibilities of boards of education and professional staff, but can truly strengthen local autonomy, encourage innovation and flexibility in the development of educational programs and the utilization of resources. It can provide a framework for meaningful and realistic accountability. If carried out in an honest and open manner the planning process can make accountability an honorable pursuit rather than a system for placing blame.

One of the most obvious advantages of program planning is the impact it can have on the budgetary process, i.e. the allocation of resources. How the managers of a large enterprise, such as the schools, spend their money tells you what they think is important and what is unimportant. Program planning will aid educators to make such distinctions, and give reasons to de-emphasize and in some instances phase out altogether programs which are either an unaffordable luxury or unimportant in relation to the total educational program of a district.

The scarcity of financial resources, and other constraints, do not permit districts to do everything desired. And, of course, it is unreasonable to ask schools to do what is impossible. However, there is no reason why priorities cannot be examined more carefully. The school district which claims that it cannot afford to hire school counselors, but pours tens of thousands of dollars into programs or facilities which do not appreciably help all students meet their needs hardly deserves sympathy.

Program planning has not been initiated in Illinois on the premise that school districts have not been engaged in planning. The fact is much excellent planning continues to take place within local districts throughout the nation. However, in many instances that planning has not been well documented by the districts, and as a result, it is difficult for boards of education and professional staffs to communicate district plans and successes to their communities. The written plan can serve as a vehicle for improving communications within local districts. In addition, the state office of education will be able to improve its service and be more sensitive to local needs in conducting its recognition and supervision program. The documented local needs in the program plan will allow the state office to base recognition and supervision evaluations on the unique needs and plans of the numerous and diverse school districts of the state.

The amount of future state aid received by local districts will not be determined by how well districts achieve the objectives in their program plans. To repeat, this process will not be linked to levels of funding by the state. It would be unfair to allocate revenue to schools on the basis of student performance or some vague, but doctrinaire, definition of quality education.

Teachers fear that certification, licensure, and tenure decisions will be based on achievement by students of stated objectives. However, given the "state of the art" of measuring pupil achievement and attitudes, it would be unjust to tie teacher performance directly to learner performance. After all, teacher performance is only one of many variables responsible for the level of pupil achievement and attitudes. To assume that teachers are solely responsible for the quality of pupil performance is naive and overlooks research findings regarding relevant variables affecting student outcomes.

The new standards, when introduced in 1972, were greeted with skepticism and indignation in many quarters. Protests caused reverberations in the Illinois General Assembly. Several workshops designed to explain the standards were boycotted and in one instance even picketed. However, one newspaper, having reviewed the propriety of the state office's initiative and the possible infringement on local control of schools, concluded:

> We don't view Superintendent Bakalis' requirement as an erosion of local school board powers. It is equally in their interest as concerned citizens to have improved means of evaluating local school performances.[3]

By mid-1973 the storm had subsided. The mood alternated between passive acceptance of the standards in some school districts and genuine enthusiasm in others. The highly regarded *Illinois School Board Journal* summed up the attitude of many school people in a June, 1973 editorial.

> It makes no sense to resist an idea that is as worthwhile as school district planning. Rather, school boards should do their utmost to develop and implement the best possible program plans.
>
> Only when schools boards have their own houses in reasonably good order can they justifiably take to the bastions in defense of local prerogatives—when and if those prerogatives are threatened.[4]

Despite the criticism and fears engendered by the planning component of Illinois' new recognition and supervision standards, there is no question that such planning is an essential precondition to making the educational system accountable. *Action Goals for the Seventies* and local district program plans should enable educators to respond in time to those citizens who legitimately complain that they are pouring their money, and more importantly their children, into the schools and are never given an accounting of what happens to either. Planning alone, of course, does not achieve improvement or change, but if the process is honestly and seriously undertaken, it can help answer the questions which are uppermost in the minds of people:

- Where are we?
- Where do we want to be?
- What must be done to get there?
- How will we do it?
- How do we know how well we are doing?

INVENTORYING EDUCATIONAL PROGRESS

Although parents and taxpayers are demanding to know what the schools are accomplishing, educators are presently incapable of providing them with the information to which they have a right. Moreover, state legislatures are hard pressed to appropriate educational funds at levels which are commensurate with actual needs when those needs are imprecisely defined. Unfortunately, they are uncertain what students know or can do at various levels of development. As suggested earlier, with regard to recognition and supervision of schools, information about education is dominated by easily quantifiable matters, such as the size of libraries and classrooms, average level of education and attainment of teachers, and the number of schools with hot lunch programs.

It is easy to tell whether or not the money you paid for your new car was well spent—either the car runs well or it doesn't. However, when it comes to what students can do or the kind of educational progress they have made over a period of time, reliable data simply does not exist. The schools, everyone agrees, have a responsibility to teach children to read and write. But read what and write how well? Children should learn math, but to what level? They should know something about science and social studies, but what does "know" mean in this context?

Because of the educational community's inability to come to grips with these uncertainties, the rising demands for greater sums of money to operate our schools have been accompanied by growing demands by taxpayers that educators show evidence that existing resources are being spent in an effective and efficient manner. In effect school people are hearing: "Give us an accounting for the results achieved by the dollars you're spending. Then if we're satisfied with the results, we'll talk about giving you more money!"

It is not surprising that terms like "inputs" and "outputs" and "production" are rapidly becoming part of the educator's lexicon. However, we ought to be wary of an effort to draw a direct analogy between measuring the productivity of a business and measuring the productivity of a school; a simple parallel cannot be drawn between industry and education. Some argue that since the Detroit auto firms can be held accountable for their production, why can't the schools do the same? Unfortunately, educational accountability is not that easy. A child—who he is, and what he learns, values, and aspires to—is not a precisely measurable piece of machinery. Two schools, moreover, can have markedly different raw materials with which to work. These factors must be taken into account if educators are to build a meaningful accountability structure in the schools.

Much more than business or industrial models are needed; human and financial resources must be expended to develop new measures of the products of our educational systems. Current measuring devices which are culturally biased must be revised. For instance, tests ask children in the inner city to define *shrubbery*. Those who have never seen a stone more exotic than a hunk of pavement are expected to know the color of a ruby. Obviously, such tests are insensitive and do not measure the real abilities and knowledge of these children.

Some educators have concluded that it is impossible to measure the products of the educational system. The difficulties inherent in measuring educational outputs have for too long been used as an excuse for inadequate communication with the public. Now is the time to start down the difficult, but not impossible, road of educational assessment. Educators owe it to the citizens who underwrite the nation's vast system of public education, and to themselves.

Establishing any system for accountability is a virtual impossibility until educators assess "where they are" in terms of student performance, including attitudes toward learning as well as achievement in the basic skills of reading and mathematics. Many techniques beyond the traditional standarized tests are needed. The essential ingredients of an assessment system include analysis of dropout rates, interviews regarding attitudes toward school, and studies of the effects of factors such as socio-economic environment, various classroom techniques (lecture, small group work, individualized learning), and financial support level upon student performance.

The most ambitious nationwide attempt to answer the question "Are we getting our money's worth from our schools?" is the National Assessment of Educational Progress (NAEP). NAEP is a three million dollar per year project funded by the federal government and operated by an arm of the Denver-based Education Commission of the States, a cooperative that includes representatives of forty-four states and territories. After five years of planning under a Carnegie Corporation grant, actual testing began in 1969. A changing nationwide sample of about 100,000 people—groups aged 9, 13, 17, and 26 to 35—is tested each year. One test is given every five years in each of ten areas: art, career and occupational development, citizenship, literature, math, music, reading, science, social studies and writing. It will be years before a comprehensive body of information will be available since measuring changes in test performance over a period of years is a vital part of the program.

A key aspect of the NAEP project is the use of "objectives." Lists of detailed goals for all subject areas have been developed by committees of educators, consultants, scholars, and interested laymen. The reading committee, for example, has decided a successful reader should be able to comprehend what is read, use what is read, reason logically from what is read and have attitudes about and an interest in reading. These objectives have been subdivided and used as a basis for creating the reading test, and the test, in turn, has been designed to measure how well American schools are meeting those objectives.

The results and analysis published thus far in five of the ten subject areas have provided no great surprises. Those who have done poorest on the tests are people who are black, whose parents have the least education, who live in the Southeast and in inner cities. The NAEP has refused to break down its analysis into any narrower group than regions of the country—Northeast, Southeast, Central, or West. It has done so to avoid the inevitable furor that would follow school-by-school or pupil-by-pupil ratings. Therefore, as a practical matter the NAEP project cannot tell Illinois or any other state where it stands in relation to other states or specify the variables which account for differences in performance among Illinois and California students. The NAEP project may eventually provide a nationwide picture of education's successes and failures, and while that could be helpful, something more definitive is required within individual states.

Therefore, a statewide survey, called the Illinois Inventory of Educational Progress, is being planned, developed, and field tested by the state office of education. This development has been greatly assisted by the National Assessment of Educational Progress and the Upper Midwest Interstate Project, a consortium of states which is currently focusing on assessment and evaluation.

The Illinois Inventory of Education Progress is not intended to create a statewide curriculum, nor is it a statewide testing program in its traditional form. It is not intended to devise a single mold for all students or for all school districts. Rather than try to determine how many young people are above or below the national "norms" on standardized achievement tests (which would be a relatively simple task) the state office is seeking to provide information about what students specifically know, feel, and can do. Typical standardized tests reveal data about how a child stands in relation to other children or "norms." For example, analysis of standardized scores might reveal that sixty percent of the children in Illinois are above the national norm in reading. But this does not provide the public with specific information about the implications of this information. Furthermore, it is unclear what specific desired performance objectives form the framework for this kind of measurement. As a result of the inventory, the state will be able to describe, for example, the percentage of graduating seniors who can read and complete an employment application form or the percentage of children who can conduct a simple scientific experiment.

In addition, methods for determining children's attitudes toward learning are being planned and field tested. To attempt to make generalizations simply on the basis of standardized reading and mathematics scores (i.e., cognitive skills) does not provide a comprehensive picture of the status of educational progress. It may well be that children could score well on a standardized reading test, but at the same time have little desire or motivation to read on their own. Therefore, an assessment program must be carefully designed to avoid interpreting the responsibility of educators in a narrow manner. For example, if schools and teachers are given high rewards for improving reading and arithmetic scores, that is prob-

ably just what will occur, but at the expense of other developmental
tasks such as favorable attitudes toward the learning process. The
scores may improve, but the "kids" may hate school.

For instance, in one private school some rather drastic measures
have been used to improve student achievement in reading. In this
particular case the teaching methodology consisted of constant
badgering and even slapping the students. One mother remarked,
"Oh yes, I'm very happy. Johnny reads much better now." But almost as an afterthought she said, "But I do find that he's biting his
nails much more." The point is that if educators instill an aversion
to learning through an emphasis on achievement in the basic skills
to the exclusion of other factors, they are not truly carrying out the
complete mission of the schools. The unfortunate experiences of
some "performance contracts" in the schools (where private firms
contract to raise achievement scores) verify the complexity in building an accountability system for education. Because of their sole
attention to methods which were designed to improve achievement
in reading and mathematics, a U.S. Office of Education study found
among the contracts they studied that desired gains in achievement
were short lasting and, in some cases, did not come about at all.

So in addition to measuring learner needs and achievement in the
cognitive domain, student attitudes in reference to three broad areas
are being surveyed: the student's perception of his school environment and his role in that environment; his self-concept; and his
relationship to his peer group. This strategy also involves the development of an instrument for measuring learner needs in relation
to the components of the psychomotor domain, including strength,
impulsion, speed, static precision, dynamic precision, coordination, and flexibility.

What is being sought is a comprehensive picture of educational
progress through census-like data on the cognitive, affective, and
psychomotor performance of students. Methods are being developed
which will allow educators to measure the growth or decline which
takes place over time in selected aspects of the educational attainment of students. Eventually such data analysis will enable educators, among other things, to begin to identify the variables which
account for variations in student performance. Current findings in
this area are inadequate at best.

The assessment program will only use proven sampling procedures. Standardized testing will never constitute more than one-third
of the program. The students and school districts will participate

in the program on a confidential basis. The data will not be used to compare one classroom or one school district with another. Rather, the purpose is to develop a capability which will permit educators to inform citizens over a period of years of the strengths and needs of the educational system.

The initial planning and field testing of this program has been completed. In 1972, data regarding standardized achievement levels of more than 60,000 students were collected and analyzed. An instrument which measured attitude toward school and self was also field tested with 20,000 students. The purpose of this data collection and analysis was to determine some of the specific problems inherent in collecting, analyzing, and reporting data; it was not to make generalizations about the progress of the statewide system of education. Field test findings revealed many inadequacies in utilizing available achievement test data as well as a number of problems involving question construction, administration of instruments, sampling techniques, and costs involved in data collection and analysis. These findings have provided the state educational agency with direction in revising and refining its methods for the second round of field tests completed in the fall of 1973.

In conjunction with this project, advisory groups of teachers and other curriculum specialists have been convened to assist in the development of the program. These advisory groups are developing specific indicators of performance which would indicate achievement of the general "substantive goals" contained in *Action Goals for the Seventies*. As they develop the indicators, they are also analyzing different techniques for gathering performance information. This effort will be critical in providing a framework for our future inventory activities.

The Illinois state educational agency is also involved in the development of alternative strategies for measuring learner needs at the district level. The goal is to be able to provide local districts, upon request, with alternative methods of assessing learner performance in the cognitive, affective, psychomotor areas by 1975. Implicit in informing the local districts about field tested strategies will be an analysis of the implications of each alternative in the areas of data collection, analysis, and reporting findings, as well as the relative costs of each approach.

Finally, the experiences of other states which have implemented assessment programs are being carefully analyzed, in order to avoid many of their mistakes and borrow some of their successful techniques. In comparison with other states, the Illinois approach is unique in two dimensions. First, more than just cognitive or "achievement" information is being measured. When the inventory is implemented, answers to questions about student knowledge, skills, and attitudes will be sought. Second, three years of planning, development, and field testing will have taken place before the collection of data, upon which generalizations will be made, is undertaken. Only in this manner can educators hope to collect valid, reliable, and specific information which can be useful to decision-makers in pointing to the strengths of the system and to areas in need of greater attention and resources.

Assessment is controversial. Local school officials often fear that assessment is part of some murky plot to create a state or federally dictated curriculum, which, as one observer has noted, "ranks just above a return to the Ice Age on their list of unthinkable eventualities." Teachers, on the other hand, fear that student assessment will be used to measure their performance in the classroom—that a teacher's performance will be rated on a tangible but simplistic scale.

A statewide testing program in New Jersey in 1972 caused a bitterly emotional protest by teacher groups. *The New Jersey Education Association Review* called the testing "a straitjacket procedure that can only curb imagination and innovation among children and teachers in our classrooms." A suit was filed to prevent the state from releasing the test results, charging that to do so would be an "invasion of constitutional and statutory rights, as well as the right of privacy."[5] In Illinois, one point has been made repeatedly: the state educational agency does not propose to establish an assessment system which "places blame," but rather to design a system which collects information about school outcomes. The task then is to act upon that information in a positive fashion. Despite initial opposition to the program by the Illinois Education Association, fears of an assessment vendetta have largely dissipated.

Assessment should not be designed or ever used to place blame on teachers, administrators, or school boards. It must be used to determine where we are educationally and to consider where we would like to be in the future. A gap between these two points exists. After determining the magnitude of that gap and how it can be closed, concrete, specific plans for remediation can be undertaken.

Public Participation, School Management, and Accountability

The common man, it is frequently said, is a better judge of his own needs in the long run than any cult of experts. Given the technologically advanced society in which we live, this may be an extreme and exaggerated view. Illinois' experiment with citizen involvement in educational planning at the state and local levels has shown that it is possible to mesh the expertise of professionals and the expressed ideas and expectations of non-expert citizens. The process, however, has exposed three issues which educational policy-makers and managers will have to wrestle with increasingly in the years ahead.

1. Is it possible to operate public institutions, like the schools, in a participatory environment?
2. Is such a policy prudent from a public policy point of view?
3. Can participatory involvement in educational affairs be reconciled with established principles of management and public administration?

Because the schools are torn between the forces of popular participation and bureaucratization (a condition which is by no means peculiar to public education), it is not surprising to find varying shades of opinion on these questions. Much of the history of democratic institutions in recent decades has been devoted to a consideration of the tension between notions of popular control and professional autonomy, the tension between those who have assigned primacy to community opinion and those who for whatever reason consistently defer to professional and administrative expertise. History shows that once battle lines are drawn professional autonomy almost always triumphs.

Against that background, the new trend toward an authentic participatory or consultative democracy has become pronounced in recent years. In time the age-old struggle between elites and non-elites is likely to yield in favor of a struggle between two kinds of citizen participation, full or limited. As for the schools, citizen participation will become less ritualistic in the future; the citizen will do more than routinely vote in elections.

A strong and sustained dosage of citizen participation in educational affairs is needed. It may sound old fashioned and perhaps out of place in the space age, but the schools in this country still belong to the people, not only in theory, but in fact. So long as the people are the final and ultimate repository of authority in such matters, the essential direction of education should be decided through public agencies, chosen by and responsible to the people, and vested with sufficient authority to perform those functions which the public demands.

Over the years, however, schoolmen have successfully convinced consumers and public officials that their professional expertise qualifies them to control all aspects of educational policy, including budgets, curriculum design, personnel matters, and pupil policy. The result is that parents, taxpayers generally, and students too play a very small part in the debates over the hard issues facing the schools. The adversary relationship that exists today between teachers and administrators, between teachers and school board members, and between school board members and administrators has severely reduced the role of the lay public in school affairs. Increasingly, taxpayers are not calling the shots as they once did, but are merely spectators to a power struggle among insiders. Therefore, it is not surprising that public sentiment on the crucial issues facing public education is given little consideration.

It is time for an adjustment in the relationship of these various groups; an effort must be made to balance more evenly administrative efficiency and expertise with the feelings, desires, and perceived needs of citizens. But that adjustment will not be achieved so long as an attitude persists among professional educators that citizens are obstacles to the efficient functioning of the schools, because they are uniformly uninformed, self-interest oriented, and shortsighted.

Professionalism need not be abandoned to achieve a proper balance between professionalism and public participation in the policy process. Rather in the public sector, particularly in education, the profession of management must take on a new definition including skills in moving and managing in a participatory environment: skills in sensitive listening, in planning and organizing participatory mechanisms, in analyzing and synthesizing public expressions of concern, and finally in building a commitment to public participation on the part of professional educators. The development of these skills and attitudes must become an integral part of the training for educational matters.

Future managers of the educational enterprise must of necessity deal with the following characteristics of policy-making:

1. The taxpaying public has gradually grown impatient with a vast and costly educational system, in part because the public does not know what is happening in the schools and has been accorded few opportunities to participate meaningfully in the planning and decision-making process. Public support for education is diminishing and will continue to do so until participatory environments are created. Therefore, from the standpoint of public education, greater citizen participation is desirable and inevitable.

2. The attitudes and opinions of citizens should be regularly and systematically sought and weighed in the formulation of educational policy by administrators and school board members. Citizens have ideas and legitimate concerns, and they deserve to be heard. The cathartic value of public participation is no less important, for it is in the interest of educators to offset the feelings of helplessness, frustration, anonymity, and distrust which exist in most communities. However, citizen participation should be initiated only to facilitate decisions, never to delay or postpone them altogether.

3. Lay control of education must be firmly reestablished. This can be partially achieved by rescuing local boards of education from administrative trivia and by encouraging and preparing them to deal with the broader and clearly more important issues facing public education.

4. Enlarging the role of citizens in educational affairs does not require that school boards and superintendents surrender or even share their policymaking and administrative perquisites. It does require, however, that citizens be permitted real opportunities to influence the exercise of these prerogatives and the choices made by policymakers and administrators.

5. School administrators must broaden their concept of efficiency and traditional management values to accommodate expanding societal needs and citizen perceptions of program effectiveness.

6. Expanded citizen participation is likely to cause some professional discomfort and inconvenience—a necessary but modest price for a more effective and responsive educational system.

7. Educational administrators must be prepared and trained more effectively to navigate in participatory environments.

While familiarity with fundamental management concepts is necessary, education must become more action, value, and policy oriented.

One hundred and thirty years ago De Tocqueville made this observation:

> It must, I think, be rare in a democracy for a man suddenly to conceive a system of ideas far different from those accepted by his contemporaries; and I suppose that, even should such an innovator arise, he would have great difficulty in making himself heard to begin with, and even more in convincing people.

Illinois' experience with citizen participation is an effort to make it less difficult for people to be heard. It is an attempt to overcome the dilemmas created for school systems by our democratic ethos. How well a democracy functions can be judged in part by the level of popular participation it permits and elicits.

Anti-institutionalism has become more pronounced than at any-time in recent memory, and this is particularly true of political institutions. This despair touches our public schools which by their nature must operate in an environment of fragmented interests and tradition-induced inertia. Citizen involvement will increasingly become an essential tool in the schools' survival kit. It is also the key to forging a meaningful accountability system. The Illinois experience has shown that such participation can work, provoke useful change, and help restore public confidence in the schools.

Educational accountability is not an impossible task. Participatory planning at both the state and local level and a careful inventorying of educational progress are significant steps which can lead to a more intelligent use of public funds and genuine improvements in education. Someone once said, "Success is a journey, not a destination." The long journey to accountability will not be an easy one, but because the journey is difficult is no reason that action should be delayed.

Chapter III

EQUAL EDUCATIONAL OPPORTUNITY

The evidence is conclusive that by using schools as sorting devices, we reject, psychologically and physically, vast numbers of children whose potentiality is neither developed nor determined.

Community Leader

In beginning arithmetic, perhaps it is no longer enough to teach that 1 plus 1 plus 1 equals 3, but rather that one white child plus one black child plus one Indian child equals three children who ought to be friends, even if the discussion veers away from mere numbers.

Religious Leader

Spanish-speaking children should receive a fully bilingual program by right, not just as a temporary means of overcoming disadvantage.

Teacher

Testing of a destitute ghetto child with a test based on middle class experiences may mask the fact that his real obstacle to success in a middle class institution is his cultural difference.

Lawyer

And while I am reluctant to say this, among the first needing to develop sensitization to the needs and feelings of minority groups are members of the school boards.

College President

Racial Segregation

On May 17, 1954, nine men, sitting in the somber chamber of the United States Supreme Court, asked the rhetorical question:

> Does segregation of children in public schools solely on the basis of race, even though the physical facilities and other "tangible" factors may be equal, deprive the children of the minority group of equal educational opportunities?[1]

The high Court's answer was clear and unmistakable: "We believe that it does." In the long and difficult struggle for equality, the *Brown* decision was undeniably an historic milestone. Although the doctrine of "separate but equal" was legally buried, fourteen years later the National Advisory Commission on Civil Disorders warned: "our nation is moving toward two societies, one black, one white—separate and unequal." Today we are no less separate, no less unequal. Discrimination and segregation are still facts of life in America—realities which threaten our social fabric and the future of every American.

Racial division is not an unalterable condition. This nation and the democratic values it cherishes can be preserved and strengthened by the fulfillment of equal opportunity for all Americans. As a people, Americans have never subscribed to the proposition that all men are equal in their ability, their character, or their motivation. However, deeply embedded in the national faith is the belief that in the development of their character, their motivations and their ability all men should be given an equal chance.

The divisiveness which besets the nation will not be remedied by demonstrations in the streets. Nor will token moves and talk alleviate the crisis. Experience should tell us that those approaches only invite shame as well as violence. In this decade there is but one choice, and that is bold action—action that is long overdue—action that is founded on a sense of human decency, a sense of justice, and a sense of fair play.

Equal opportunity at all levels of our national life must become a reality or America courts national disaster. Anyone who is in a position of educational leadership knows that the absence of equal educational opportunity has resulted in incalculable waste. Talents have remained undiscovered; potentialities have been destroyed. The fact is that a black baby born in Illinois today, regardless of the section of the state in which he is born, has about one-half the chance of completing high school as a white baby born in the same place on the same day. This country cannot afford and must no longer countenance such waste.

The Supreme Court, since the *Brown* decision, has not deviated in the slightest degree from the holding and the constitutional underpinnings in that case, and subsequent federal court decisions have further amplified that holding. Undoubtedly, some progress in equalizing educational opportunity has been made since 1954, but that progress cannot begin to weigh in the same scale with the extensive segregation that stubbornly persists in school districts throughout this country.

A decade ago the Illinois General Assembly committed the state "as soon as practicable" to the "prevention of segregation and the elimination of separation of children in public schools because of color, race or nationality."[2] The evidence suggests, however, that despite the Armstrong Act Illinois schools are more segregated than they were in 1963—that between 1968 and 1970 they became more segregated than those in Mississippi.[3]

It must be acknowledged that the fulfillment of equal educational opportunity has not matched the promise despite the increasing evidence of the educational soundness of that commitment, and despite the steep price society is paying for its non-fulfillment. In the quest for new talent, new ideas, new brain power, new manpower, the responsibility is not being fully met. One would hope that those irrational barriers and ancient prejudices which serve to deny equal educational opportunity for all children would crumble quickly when the question of national survival is at stake.

The price being paid by children (black, oriental, Spanish-American, American Indian and white) is exorbitant. The evidence on the effects of segregation can no longer be disputed or ignored. The systematic separation of minority children from others of similar age and qualifications is capable of generating a feeling of inferiority that as the Supreme Court has noted, "may affect their hearts and minds in a way unlikely ever to be undone."

It is conclusively known that as a result of segregation the motivation of minority children to learn may diminish; their self-esteem and self-concept may be irreparably damaged, if not destroyed; their educational and mental development may be severely retarded. Also, for many minority children denial of equal educational opportunities impairs their access and contributions to the American mainstream. One need only consider the alarming dropout rate among black students attending all black schools and their failure to master the fundamental skills of reading and arithmetic to see these destructive forces hard at work. In short, the segregation of minority children can chill their passion for learning.

A resistant racism debilitates even the curriculum and day-to-day operations of many schools. The history and language of minority children are ignored and even deprecated. Teachers assigned to segregated schools are frequently the least prepared, the least experienced, and the least paid. These conditions are exacerbated further by the inequitable distribution of educational resources, not only between school districts, but sometimes between schools in the same district—a practice which almost invariably penalizes schools attended principally by poor and minority children.

Any child, white or black, who goes through his entire school career without ever meeting a child or teacher of another racial or ethnic background is denied the enriching potential which that culture holds for his own education and life. Segregated schools can only serve to nurture prejudicial attitudes among the young and to divide the American people further. A child who has been isolated throughout his formative years runs the risk of being educationally deprived. In a 1968 report, the National Advisory Commission on Civil Disorders concluded:

> We support integration as the priority education strategy because it is essential to the future of American society. It is indispensible that opportunities for interaction between the races be expanded. The problems of the society will not be solved unless and until our children are brought into a common endeavor and encouraged to forge a new and more viable design of life.[4]

Equality of opportunity for all children is an educational principle and a legal requirement. Segregated schools are the antithesis of both the principle and the requirement. The Constitution of Illinois is clear: The state is to educate all persons to the limit of their capacities—not some persons, not most persons, but all persons. Clearly, a chief state educational officer has an obligation to seek an end to those practices and institutional barriers which unfairly permit greater access to educational opportunity for some persons than others. The rulings of the Supreme Court require that he do so. State law and the Illinois Constitution require that he do so, as do the moral and educational imperatives which have come to bear on this issue in recent years.

Therefore, in November of 1971 the state educational agency filed with the Illinois Secretary of State administrative rules to govern the elimination and prevention of racial segregation in Illinois schools. These regulations provided the state office with specific procedures for the implementation of existing legal mandates for school desegregation. The rules set forth procedures which local school districts were to follow in preparing desegregation plans, and they insured that such plans would be uniformly directed toward quality education for all children.[5]

It must be stressed that the state office's objective is quality integrated education. And it must be emphasized, too, that in the 1970s mere physical desegregation, the mixing of bodies, does not constitute effective desegregation. While the mere removal of discrimination barriers may have been acceptable ten years ago, more is required now. In short, the essential task of a school district is to enhance the learning environment of all children and to promote more daily intergroup experiences so young people will come to accept one another fully as individuals regardless of race or nationality.

Requirements of a Desegregation Plan

A desegregation plan in this day and age is effective only if it is educationally sound and educationally relevant. In the final analysis, the measure of a desegregation plan's effectiveness will be determined by its meeting three requirements: first, an effective plan must conform to the specific requirements set forth by the Supreme Court; second, it must avoid undue disruption in school and community life; and third, it must achieve the positive goal of quality unified education for all students. The Illinois rules are entirely compatible with these three essential conditions.

First, as for the requirements enunciated by the Supreme Court, most recently in the *Swann* and *Detroit* cases, the ingredients for an effective plan can be summarized as follows: A desegregation plan will be effective (1) if a school system (district) is administered as a single or unified entity; (2) if there is no marked difference in the quality of facilities or the nature of programs at schools primarily attended by minority students; (3) if faculties are racially integrated; (4) if students are not assigned to schools or within schools on the basis of race, color, religion, or nationality; (5) if no school can be clearly identified as a "white" school or "minority" school because of differences in the composition of their faculties or programs; (6) if racial disproportionality of students assigned to schools is minimized so as to reflect, so far as possible, the racial composition of the student population in the district as a whole; (7) if students of the majority racial group in the district are given the option to transfer to other schools where they will be in the minority; (8) if school construction and abandonment policies are not used to perpetuate or reestablish racially segregated schools.[6] These factors which the Supreme Court suggested be taken into account in devising a desegregation plan are the factors which the state educational agency weighs in judging the "effectiveness" of desegregation plans filed with it by local school districts.

Second, no desegregation plan can be deemed effective if the dominant residual effect is the undue disruption of school and community life. The overall flexibility of the Illinois rules has considerably reduced the possibility of such disruption, for no school district under these rules has been compelled to adopt a plan that is not "administratively and educationally feasible." For that reason, it is essential that the community be deeply involved in the development of a plan, and also, it is important to recognize that each school district plan will be unique, for each community will present a unique set of problems.

Obviously there are certain developments which must and can be avoided. Polarization of a community or a school must be minimized. Most school districts engaged in desegregation have not experienced a rapid or massive withdrawal of students, a reduction of the public's support for bond issues and tax levies, a decline in the academic achievement of students, or a higher incidence of conflict and violence. If handled with flexibility and sensitivity, school districts can achieve quality integrated education while minimizing any potential negative impact which may ensue.

Third, a final measure of a desegregation plan's effectiveness is the extent to which it succeeds in the one thing that is really important: the achievement of quality integrated education for all students. If a desegregation plan is equitable, it will succeed. If students and personnel in the schools of a system are racially representative of the district's population, and if the burdens or inconvenience incurred as a result of desegregation are shared by all students, the plan will succeed. If an effective learning environment evolves—an environment which engenders personal and cultural respect as well as a positive appreciation for diversity—the plan will succeed.

However, care must be taken to avoid practices which tend to resegregate minority students within a nominally desegregated school, to discourage minority students from participating in extra-curricular activities, or to prevent their participation with other students in the decision-making process. Such practices would mark a plan for eventual failure.

Based on experiences in Illinois and elsewhere it is clear that desegregation can succeed. Commitment and leadership on the part of school authorities is a prerequisite; such commitment and leadership is known to exist in hundreds of school districts. In communities where desegregation is in effect, white parents have learned that their children do not suffer academically. While children in desegregated schools perform as well on standard achievement tests as white children in all white schools, poor and minority children who attend integrated schools perform at a higher academic level than their counterparts who attend segregated schools. Apart from academic considerations is the fact that students (be they black or white) are less likely to adopt racist attitudes in a desegregated setting, and such attitudinal changes represent a key to mending a racially polarized society.

Before discussing the operation of the Illinois rules, what these rules do *not* do should be understood. They do not require that all of the public schools be desegregated. Some schools in some districts cannot be fully desegregated, and some may not be able to be desegregated at all. The courts have recognized that while this may not be desirable, it is permissible.

The rules do not require that every classroom be desegregated to reflect a given majority-minority student percentage. This would be carrying numbers to an absurdity.

The rules do not require schools implementing desegregation plans to complete their task by any specific time—not within two weeks, not within seven months, not within one or two years. That differences exist within districts is recognized, and what can be accomplished in one district in one year may take longer in another.

Although the rules do not require that the schools reflect a fixed percentage of minority and majority children, it is recognized that some yardstick with which to work is needed: i.e. an attendance unit should reflect within fifteen percent, plus or minus, the racial composition of the district as a whole. Given the constraints of economic and administrative feasibility and educational soundness, the state has not insisted that every school within a cited district reflect the fifteen percentage range, for it is understood that we are not dealing with numbers on an adding machine, but with children. The foundation of the Illinois rules is the requirement that school districts adopt and maintain pupil assignment practices designed to eliminate and prevent racial segregation in the schools. School districts submit annually to the state office information upon which an independent judgment is made regarding the presence or non-presence of segregated schools. The same report calls for a detailing by local school authorities of the actions taken to date and those proposed to eliminate racial segregation and an assessment of the success of those actions.

Those school systems shown to be in non-compliance are then notified and asked to prepare a comprehensive plan to achieve compliance. The community on a representative basis must be involved in the preparation of the plan. The state office, if requested, provides technical assistance to such school districts.

In formulating a plan, a school district must satisfy the necessary conditions, enumerated earlier, for an effective plan as prescribed by the federal courts. School authorities must consider and employ all methods to satisfy those conditions which are educationally sound and administratively and economically feasible. School pairings, the alteration of attendance zones, the establishment of educational parks or magnet schools, pupil reassignment, and voluntary inter-district cooperative plans are just a few of the options available to school authorities in effectuating racial integration.

Once a plan is formulated and submitted to the state office a determination is made as to its acceptability in light of the rules. If the plan or parts of it are unacceptable, school authorities are required to make appropriate amendments or submit an alternative plan. Should this procedure fail, the rules then authorize the transmission by the state to the school authorities of an acceptable plan, together with a directive requiring its implementation.

The rules also delineate enforcement procedures. A school authority, refusing or failing to comply with the requirements of the rules, faces possible revocation of recognition, the loss of state and federal financial support, or appropriate legal action to enforce compliance.

Thus, the Illinois rules are *flexible*. The generous time frames, the provisions for judicial review, and various options open to school authorities for accomplishing desegregation give the flexibility required. The rules do not impose on the entire state one plan for desegregation, nor do they advocate a single method of desegregation. One must recognize, as the Supreme Court has, that "there is no universal answer to the complex problems of desegregation; there is obviously no one plan that will do the job in every case." Every community represents a peculiar set of problems and variables. Under the rules, the Illinois state educational agency deals with each community separately and differently.

The rules recognize, too, that *desegregation is a process*. It is not an event which must occur on a given day and hour for all school districts. It will occur in different places at different times, under widely differing plans.

It is important to stress this concept of desegregation as a process, because for too many the word itself means only one thing: the movement of black and white children for the purpose of having them sit next to each other in a classroom. This is not enough. It is possible for majority and minority children to be in the same classroom in the same school and still be, for all intents and purposes, segregated. School desegregation is a multifaceted, complex process of curriculum revision, attitudinal change, and careful education and preparation of all those who will be involved: the parents, the faculty, the administration, and the children as well. What the proper time, within reason, is for the sequence of community planning, education, assignment of faculty and pupils can best be determined by the local districts, not the state. But every district in the state has been required to address itself to this problem and formulate some concrete steps within a reasonable time frame for implementation.

In 1972, Illinois school districts submitted to the state office reports detailing actions taken and proposed to eliminate and prevent racial segregation in schools. Based on those reports, twenty-one districts were cited for non-compliance, including those in the large urban areas of Chicago and Rockford, as well as the state capital, Springfield. By early 1974, all but five of these twenty-one had made significant progress towards compliance. Chicago is the only large city district among the remaining five. The state rules require that the Department of Equal Educational Opportunity develop a comprehensive plan and order its implementation in districts refusing to act on their own.

It must be noted that litigation, actual or threatened, has played a role in the actions of several districts. Rockford, the second largest city in the state, developed and adopted a desegregation plan as a result of an order from a federal judge. In several other instances the courts, both state and federal, have by their actions lent legitimacy not only to the rules, but to the state's responsibility to eliminate segregated public schools.

To be sure, the desegregation of Illinois schools has met with varying degrees of success. In Chicago, for example, racial segregation in the schools had increased. The number of all-black schools has increased, and proportionately more white students are attending mostly white high schools. On the other hand, Park Forest, a suburb south of Chicago, has shown what can be done. The school board of that community has exhibited a deep sense of responsibility and involved the total community in the development of a desegregation plan which is working and has earned general community support. The actions and enthusiastic response of Park Forest have been duplicated in diverse communities throughout the state (Danville, Quincy, Alton, Freeport, for example) in response to the requirements of the rules. Several districts are notable for the positive programs undertaken prior to the adoption of the rules (districts such as Kankakee, Carbondale, Evanston, and Urbana). Despite these disparate outcomes and the attendant difficulties involved in the desegregation process, it is clear that Illinois has a unique opportunity to become a model for the nation. Reluctance to comply with the rules and regulations will inevitably result in the federal courts intervening and imposing on Illinois school districts stringent remedies from which there will be no escape. Such intervention can best be prevented by state educational agencies dealing with this problem forthrightly.

The Continuing Debate

Not surprisingly, the issuance of rules to prevent and eliminate segregation has prompted some lively debate in Illinois. Although the state educational agency had no choice if it was to abide by

federal law and court decisions, many people continue to dispute
not only the propriety of the issuance of rules but the essential cor-
rectness of school integration. Clearly, this issue is a more burning
one for Americans today than in 1954 when the *Brown* verdict was
announced.

There are a number of factors working in concert which have
helped sustain this nationwide debate. First, the character of the issue
has changed over the years, and as a result we are trying to cope
with problems today which were not clearly perceived twenty
years ago.

Second, those who are responsible for formulating public policy
in this country have failed to convince Americans that the quest for
school integration is a worthwhile undertaking, that it can succeed,
and that it can benefit all of us in terms of insuring domestic tran-
quility and saving untold human and financial resources.

Finally, the debate rages on because of politics—because of those
men and women in public office who have deliberately chosen to
play on black frustration and white fear, a game which Leonard
Woodcock has aptly described as a sort of "Russian roulette with
America's future."

What was perceived twenty years ago as largely a regional problem has become a national concern. Not only has the concept of
"separate but equal" been thoroughly discredited by the federal
courts, but the application of the ruling in *Brown* has gradually
been broadened so as to bring into question vestiges of racial segregation wherever they may exist in the public schools. The movement to integrate the schools is no longer focused exclusively on
the South, but focused on the nation as a whole.

It also is abundantly clear that the fundamental constitutional
issue considered by the Supreme Court in 1954 was somewhat
narrower than the question presently facing this nation. The *Brown*
case held that it is unconstitutional to force the separation of children in schools along racial lines. The question before the country
today is whether it is wise or necessary to compel the mingling of
children in the schools in proportions that reflect approximately
the ratio of blacks to whites within school districts. The rulings
of the federal courts on this second question have not only been
consonant with the *Brown* decision, but have repeatedly and com-
pellingly reinforced the Supreme Court's judgment that "in the
field of public education the doctrine of 'separate but equal' has
no place" regardless of the conditions which may have given rise
to the separation in the first place.

Once the crusade for integrated schools shifted in a northerly direction the issue assumed a distinctly national character. Gradually, the separate but unequal doctrine was applied not only to school districts whose practices intentionally reinforced patterns of segregation, as was typical in the South, but to school districts which did nothing positively to promote student integration, as is typical in the North.

The courts issued desegregation orders to school districts where school boundary lines have been redrawn with the intent of keeping schools segregated, where schools have been closed in racially mixed areas rather than permit integration, where optional school zones have been created to encourage white students to attend all-white schools, where sites for new schools have been strategically chosen with an eye toward keeping them all white or all black, and where the size of schools has been purposely limited so that they might serve only a limited geographical area and hence only one race. Federal Judge Stephen Roth's decision in Detroit is a case in point. Roth concluded that the Detroit schools had encouraged segregation by drawing its school boundaries North-South rather than East-West, by the small size of some schools, and by the use of transportation to perpetuate segregation. In the Detroit case, as in the Richmond case, the courts have uniformly found that the primary responsibility for dealing with segregation in local school districts lies with the state.

The question of school integration has become one of the preeminent social and political issues of our times. The emotionalism surrounding it is exacerbated by the federal courts' proper insistance that segregation be remedied speedily, even if such remedies prove "administratively awkward, inconvenient and even bizarre in some situations." No domestic issue in recent American history seems to have generated so much heat and so little light. As a result, confusion and bewilderment abound in the land. Fear among some of our citizens has spread like a contagion, stirring up old anxieties, hardening latent hatreds, and even fomenting acts of violence. However, it is doubtful that all of the emotionalism surrounding the issue of school integration is attributable exclusively to a resistant racism in America.

Although no one can fairly dispute either the existence of racism or its potential influence on those who shape public policy in this country, Americans, for the most part, are people of good will: generous, eminently just, and possessed of a deeply ingrained belief in the principle of equal opportunity. Therefore, it is reasonable to conclude that the underlying source of discontent is the failure of policy-makers to communicate and the failure of the public to understand the purpose which integration is intended to serve.

Many people remain convinced that the Supreme Court is simply engaging in speculative "contemporary social justice" when it declares that the segregation of white and minority children, whether such separation is a matter of design or accident, has a detrimental effect upon all children. The fact is segregation is capable of inculcating a sense of inferiority among minority children which in turn adversely affects the motivation of these children to learn. What critics claimed was sociological hyperbole in 1954 is now increasingly being supported by evidence, namely that schools isolated on the basis of race or lower social and economic status may be decidedly harmful to the academic achievement of these students.

It is ironic that those who most ardently oppose integration cannot escape defraying part of the enormous costs to society of public education's failures. Too frequently the person who is a public aid recipient, or who is unemployed or unemployable, or who is incarcerated in a prison or a mental institution was an underachiever in school and possibly a dropout, and to some degree such underachievement was the result of being relegated to a school and to classrooms with lower social and economic status children. When the walls which segregate children on the basis of race can be torn down, the cycle can be broken once and for all.

Perhaps it was with Woodrow Wilson's observation that democracy "releases the energies of every human being" in mind that a somewhat less reticent President declared in 1970 that "racial isolation ordinarily has an adverse effect on education . . . desegregation is vital to quality education—not only from the standpoint of raising the achievement levels of the disadvantaged but also from the standpoint of helping children achieve broad-based human understanding that increasingly is essential in today's world." Such an assessment of the importance of integrated education is no less valid today. It is not sufficient to warn people of the dire consequences of segregation; they must be shown that school desegregation is workable, and that it is, in fact, working in thousands of communities in this nation.

Recent studies of numerous school integration programs substantiate the positive effects of integration.[7] These programs have generally facilitated the educational development of minority students while white students continue to make their usual achievement gains. Even when lower-status students are transferred to schools with predominantly upper-status students, the evidence suggests that continued residence in a lower-status neighborhood will not interfere with the achievement gain that is to be expected as a result of attendance in the school with predominantly upper-status students. If the American people are provided with demonstrable evidence—proof that school integration can produce such dividends—one would hope that the stridency which characterizes much of the current debate will gradually diminish.

The case for desegregation should not be overstated. It is by no means a panacea for all of the problems facing our society. As Christopher Jencks has pointed out in his controversial book, *Inequality,* those who view education as an instrument for pervasive social reform operate from certain basic assumptions about the schools, most of which, in Jenck's opinion, are suspect, if not clearly erroneous:

1. Social and economic differences between blacks and whites and between rich and poor derive in good part from differences in their cognitive skills.
2. Cognitive skills can be measured with at least moderate precision by standardized tests on "intelligence," "verbal ability," "reading comprehension," "mathematical skills," and so on.
3. Differences in people's performance on cognitive tests can be partly explained by differences in the amount and quality of school they get.
4. Equalizing educational opportunity would therefore be an important step toward equalizing blacks and whites, rich and poor, and people in general.[8]

While equal educational opportunity is important and necessary, it is nonsense to argue that equal educational opportunity will result in equality. Those who argue from that premise make a rational consideration of the issue more difficult, because such expectations have no relationship whatsover to reality. It is Jencks' position that "differences between schools have rather trivial long-term effects, and eliminating differences between schools would do almost nothing to make adults more equal."[9]

This suggests that variations in student performance and in levels of success among adults are more attributable to variations in environment than to variations within schools. In other words, the success of a school and its students depends largely on the characteristics of the entering children rather than other inputs, like financial resources, the quality of teachers, or school policies. While total elimination of racial and socio-economic segregation in the schools might reduce the test score gap between black and white children and between rich and poor children by 10 to 20 percent, and that would not be an insignificant development, Jencks insists that such a development does not guarantee that black and poor kids will be appreciably better off economically and socially as adults.

As is often the case, Jencks' research has been unfairly seized upon to justify segregated schools, financial disparities among schools, and other inequities. If equal access to quality education is not defensible in terms of insuring the economic and social mobility of graduates, why, the critics ask, should we agonize over such conditions. Obviously perturbed by such reasoning, Jencks clarified his position in the *New York Times*.

> . . . the research we reported does not justify cutting school expenditures, abandoning desegregation, or giving up efforts at school reform. It has always been a mistake to assert that equality of educational opportunity could eliminate problems like poverty and injustice in America. Our research suggests we should stop making such claims but the fact remains that American schools badly need improvement and this effort ought to continue.[10]

Even if equal educational opportunity will not produce equality among adults, equalizing educational opportunities can be justified on broader grounds. If desegregation and equal financial expenditures do not *significantly* reduce differences in student performance or economic success in later life, why should those policies be pursued? To state the case simply, public policy requires that public money be equitably distributed, even if such a policy has no enduring effect. With regard to desegregation, it is Jencks' view that such a policy should not be justified primarily on either academic or long-term economic grounds. The issue at hand is really much simpler. If we want to live in a segregated society, then the schools and all other public facilities ought to be segregated. If we want society desegregated, then the schools should be desegregated. These are the considerations—rather than any fancied, imagined, and illusory hopes—which must be carefully weighed in formulating public policy. "Solving these problems," Professor Jencks correctly points out, "will not make much dent on poverty among adults, either now or in the future. But it does not follow that we should sweep the problems under the rug, or use the fig leaf of social science to claim that they are not important."[11]

The schools cannot and should not be expected to solve deep-seated social problems which they did not create in the first instance. The schools, however, like other important institutions in this country, have a role to play in tearing down the barriers which artificially divide people. If significant progress is to be made, fundamental reforms in our economic institutions also will be needed. It is clear, for example, that economic inequalities between blacks and whites are attributable less to segregated schools than to white employers' hiring and promotion practices. Therefore, it is arguable that if desegregation gradually reduces racial hostility and, as a consequence, if employers' attitudes also change, blacks will in time end up in better paying jobs. One need only look at the South and the remarkable impact the destruction of the Jim Crow system has had on that region's social and political mores. Such a transformation two decades ago would have been unthinkable. Although differences in average reading scores among whites and blacks have not been eliminated, such differences have been reduced and, more importantly, southern blacks are more socially and economically mobile than anyone might reasonably have thought possible in 1954.

Quality integrated schools, therefore, can help create a more congenial state of mind and an environment in which the possibilities for a better life among poor and minority people become more promising every year. This fact is often either obscured by the scholarship in this area or by those who misinterpret the scholarship. As Harold Howe II, former U.S. Commissioner of Education, has observed:

> . . . so much recent research and argument has been devoted to whether or not integration produces better reading scores or better mathematic scores or fewer dropouts among minority-group children. Without denying the value of such studies and debates, I contend that there are vastly more significant considerations: the intangible effects on individual

children of being segregated or integrated and, even more
significant, the influence of education upon the nature and
values of society.[12]

Howe is correct, but experience tells us that school desegregation
can have a more salutory impact on personal values if it is part of
a larger and more pervasive effort to transform relations between
blacks and whites in this country. The schools cannot and will not
do that job alone.

The Issue of Busing

Although school busing represents the great non-issue of the
continuing fight over school integration, it has, unfortunately,
become the centerpiece of the debate. It is unfortunate, because in
Illinois alone 700,000 students are bused daily from home to school
and back. For young people compelled to attend school, busing
has become a cherished convenience. And for those who earnestly
seek a quality education busing has become an indispensable
necessity.

Few people today would seriously propose that busing be dis-
pensed with altogether. Yet there was a time not many years ago
when in the name of educational excellence thousands of tiny
school districts throughout the nation consolidated. The proposed
abandonment of hundreds of one room school houses and the
"forced" transportation of students to larger and more modern
educational facilities provoked years of noisy protests and emotional
misapprehensions. For a decade after World War II the issue of
school district consolidation and the attendant issue of busing
students to achieve reorganization seriously divided communities.
Ranged against the promise of superior and more diverse educational advantages for young people were the arguments of those
who zealously opposed change. A massive program of student
transportation, the critics warned, would be too expensive, too
dangerous, or too inconvenient; it would mean sacrificing neighborhood and community schools, and of course, local control.

Looking back at that period, it is obvious that many people
never grasped the real issue—or perhaps the issue was never well
defined for them. Obviously, busing was not undertaken for the
sake of busing nor for the transparent purposes of closing small
schools or depriving citizens of control over the educational pro-

cess. Busing was simply a tool which made consolidation logistically possible, and, more important, made the pursuit of the twin goals of American education—quality and equality—easier and more manageable. In the final analysis, the real issue in the 40's and 50's was the genuineness and depth of society's commitment to guarantee equal access to quality education for all children regardless of cost or inconvenience.

In the past twenty years, the number of school districts in Illinois alone has been reduced from 8,000 to 1,083. Four times as many students are bused today within those districts than were bused in 1952. Expensive? Yes. Inconvenient? For many, yes. However, the price of improving educational opportunities, options, and economies has been a modest one—so modest, in fact, that no one could seriously advocate retreating and abandoning the buses without threatening to bring hundreds of school districts to a grinding halt.

Unfortunately, the hard learned lessons of those years, and the history of that period, have largely been forgotten, thus depriving citizens of a valuable bridge to the present and a guide for shaping the future. Daniel Webster once noted that "when a mariner has tossed for many days in thick weather, and on an unknown sea, he naturally avails himself of the first pause in the storm, the earliest glance of the sun, to take his latitude and ascertain how far the elements have driven him from his true course." Webster's observation has special meaning for our time, for once again this nation is caught up in a storm involving the most divisive domestic issue in decades. The hysteria, fear, and confusion generated by the question of busing has once again driven Americans from their true course.

To weather the current tempest, the nation must be willing to focus on the real issues, for just as busing itself was not the fundamental issue twenty years ago, it is not the fundamental issue today. What is at stake once more is the kind of education we want our children to have, and as Father Theodore Hesburgh has written, that means weighing "the firmness of our resolve to redeem the nation's pledge of equal rights for all, and, in the final analysis, the kind of society we want our children to inherit."

Little can be gained by agonizing and temporizing over busing to the exclusion of more basic issues. The basic issues which the American people, including their leaders, must face up to are school desegregation and quality education, and this necessarily involves a larger question which only Americans can answer for themselves. Are Americans willing to continue the difficult struggle of transforming the illusion of equality into something more befitting the promise of the national experience? The question is whether Americans shall mold an abstract principle, their professed belief in equal opportunity, into a meaningful reality for all.

The hysteria over busing has obscured the fact that student transportation is only one of many remedies for overcoming school segregation. Unfortunately, those who fiercely attack busing, who advocate eliminating it from the list of remedial options open to school districts, are attacking, unwittingly perhaps, the entire process of equalizing educational opportunities itself.

A moratorium on busing could eventuate in a moratorium on desegregation, for a successful assault on one method of achieving desegregation could inevitably invite attacks on the remaining available methods. In recent years, for example, legislation has been considered in Illinois, which if enacted by the General Assembly could have the effect of repealing state law regarding the prevention of school segregation. History, if it tells us anything, is clear on one point: well-motivated, but ill-conceived, tamperings with the rights of some people may result in an irreversible erosion of the rights of all. That is the very real danger which has been unleashed in recent years by those who instead of talking sense about the issues prefer to peddle cheap and easy answers.

The subject of using busing to help achieve racial desegregation of public schools is so complicated and so fraught with emotion that it often defies rational discussion. Several factors should be kept in mind: First, from even before the beginnings of the Republic, but especially since the turn of the present century, the transporting of students has been an absolutely essential method of achieving equal educational opportunity for children of all races and economic groups. This process was alluded to earlier in relation to school consolidation. It is clear that the general quality of American schools would deteriorate markedly if busing to create more equal educational opportunities were to be prohibited.

Second, if racial desegregation of the schools serves to equalize educational opportunities, then busing students *when necessary* is an appropriate and essential method for achieving that end. There are school districts in this country where housing patterns are so strongly segregated that busing may be the only means to achieve desegregation. In such cases, the prohibition of busing would effectively stop desegregation, dash any hope of equalizing educational opportunities, and preserve the racial hostilities and misunderstandings now frozen into our segregated residential patterns.

Third, although busing should be available to achieve racial desegregation, children should not be transported to a school that is significantly more dangerous or violence prone, significantly more dominated by students from lower-income households, or demonstrably inferior educationally, than the area in which those children live. Most of the current hue and cry against busing is directed neither against transporting children to school in large motor vehicles nor in a desire to preserve the so-called neighborhood schools, despite all the protestations to the contrary. Any opposition derived from sheer racism must be denied any legitimate standing in the shaping of public policy.

There are parents who legitimately fear that busing may result in their children attending schools that have higher levels of violence and lower levels of academic achievement than local schools. To the extent that these fears are legitimate (and frequently they are) they must be carefully weighed in designing a desegregation plan. That such conditions may exist, however, is not reason enough for abandoning desegregation. Rather the task is to ease parental anxieties by creating within each school those conditions conducive to personal safety and optimum academic performance.

While the evidence would seem to suggest that the alarm and concern over increased violence in a desegregated school is largely unjustified, it is not easy to dismiss the concerns of parents who care for their children's safety and want them to enjoy the fruits of the social and economic status they have worked so hard to attain. The schools can help achieve that goal while simultaneously using busing and other techniques to enable poor and minority children to enjoy middle-class educational conditions. Equalizing upwards is a better basic policy than equalizing downwards in most situations—and this is one of them.

It is worth noting that while desegregation may require increased student transportation within some school districts for other districts desegregation can result in a decrease in the number of students transported. For years in Illinois, as in the South, students have been transported, often unnecessarily, to avoid attending desegregated schools. To date, only a small percentage of the students bused in Illinois are bused for purposes relating to desegregation.

Finally, the burdens of desegregation must be shared ones. "One-way" busing cannot be regarded as desirable. If desegregation is of mutual benefit to blacks and whites, then the attendant inconveniences and hardships ought to be borne jointly by the beneficiaries. On the other hand, one cannot blindly dismiss the fears of parents who envision their children being transplanted in schools which are in fact appreciably inferior and, in many cases, hopelessly beyond retrieval. So while one-way busing may not be desirable, it must be permitted in those instances where it is educationally prudent, and seriously considered where community resistance could only hasten the enactment of laws or constitutional amendments which explicitly forbid busing or make it practically impossible.

It may be painful to concede that our worst schools cannot be salvaged and transformed into model laboratories for learning. But then this is only one of the harsh realities that must be coped with if the process of desegregation is to enjoy any continued public support. Obviously, the long range goal must be to make every school, wherever it is located, a center of excellence and opportunity. However, busing alone cannot do the job. Yet, if what a student experiences at the end of a bus ride is incomparably better than what he leaves behind—then busing, even if used as a temporary expedient, is an option that school people ought to be free to exercise until equal opportunity is possible in every school. In judging the appropriateness of busing students or not busing students, this must be the final standard.

It is ironic that in the search for alternatives to busing, proposals have been made for the greater use of magnet schools, more emphasis on redrawing attendance zone boundaries, and the construction of new schools—alternatives which more than likely would require in our larger cities an actual increase in the number of children bused to school. It is not so ironic, on the other hand, that those who once countenanced busing to maintain racial segregation should now be opposed to busing to achieve desegregation. For the segregationist, vindication and redemption must seem very near.

One important point should be restated: busing is not an end in itself. At best, it is an artificial and inadequate instrument of change. Imperfect an instrument as busing may be, it should not be abandoned if it results in resurrecting a dual system of racially segregated public schools.

What is especially depressing is that in all of the frenetic posturing over busing policy makers have lost sight of the child who is all that really should count. If this society truly believes in the educability of all children, then its first concern should be children, the kind of schools they attend, the quality of their teachers, the climate of their classrooms, the quality of their education, and whether each child has equal access to those opportunities.

Summary

The problems of achieving equal educational opportunity are wide-ranging and basic. They touch on all aspects of society and government, the rights of individuals and communities, the personalities and experience of all concerned and the physical facilities available. There is no easy answer.

Studies on the impact and results of costly compensatory education programs are so contradictory and inconclusive that only one conclusion is possible: money alone cannot guarantee equal access to quality education. Equal educational opportunity is not a commodity which can be bought and sold at will. Compensatory programs should not be precipitously discontinued, but given their ambiguous value they can never be an adequate substitute for desegregation. As one educator recently observed, "if you spend money properly it can help, but" he added, "it can help more if you integrate."

Children of different races can and do attend the same schools without jeopardizing their well-being or academic growth. More important for our collective future, young people are less likely to adopt racist attitudes in a desegregated setting, and that is the key to mending a racially polarized society. However, that key may rust with disuse if school districts are not permitted to utilize the option of pupil transportation for achieving school desegregation.

The debate over school integration is not likely to end anytime soon, and, given the fundamental issues involved, the debate ought to continue. There is no reason for fear so long as the debate is presided over by strong and purposeful leadership, both locally and nationally—leadership which will move boldly to calm fears, talk sense, and appeal to the best instincts of the American people.

It was the concern for the children themselves and their equal access to educational opportunity, not taking the public's pulse, that prompted Illinois' educational agency to issue its administrative rules in 1971. Those same concerns prompted its opposition to a proposed federal constitutional amendment prohibiting busing. After all these years, we, and our children even more so, deserve something more enduring than one nation, divided—or, to put it in another way, two nations, quite divisible, one white and one black, with liberty and justice for some.

Only by reaffirming our faith in an educational enterprise that is unfettered by unnecessary constitutional amendments and moratoriums of dubious constitutionality can we continue to expand freedom's domain. Should we succeed, and there is some basis for optimism, this nation will have put the divisive and self-defeating issue of race behind it once and for all.

Educating Non-English-Speaking Children

A decade ago President John F. Kennedy unveiled a plan intended to give expression to the noblest goals of society. The Alianza Para El Progreso—or as it is popularly known, The Alliance for Progress—was to be something more than a doctrine of development; it was an untested, but desperately needed, strategy for transforming the Western Hemisphere into a vast crucible of revolutionary ideas and efforts. It was a call for self-help as well as American help, for ending injustice as well as poverty, for reform as well as relief.

Throughout Latin America a revolutionary fever was quickly spreading, and the challenge, as the President saw it, was to chart a course for dealing with those who in making peaceful revolution impossible were making violent revolution inevitable. The task was to defuse a gigantic bomb by bringing to bear the resources and ingenuity of an entire hemisphere on such human problems as a rate of infant mortality four times our own, a life expectancy less than two-thirds of our own, an illiteracy rate of fifty percent, a lack of schools and sanitation, shocking slums in the cities, and squalor in the countryside.

Meanwhile a similarly dangerous and incendiary situation was revealed in America. Edward R. Murrow and his film *Harvest of Shame* dramatized the miserable plight of migrant workers, and the American conscience was momentarily pained. Author Michael Harrington then introduced Americans to the *Other America*. And finally, a nation was shocked into the uncomfortable realization that in this wealthiest of nations easily one-fifth of our fellow citizens were ill-fed, ill-housed, and poorly educated.

Those millions of "other Americans" were largely composed of thousands who monthly streamed into New York from San Juan, and thousands of others, mostly Mexican-Americans, who migrated to the American Southwest, to California, and to Gary and Chicago seeking a new lease on life for themselves and for their children. What awaited the new and unsuspecting immigrant was what he had sought to escape: poor schools, urban barrios, unemployment, discrimination, political manipulation, ridicule, and chastisement.

There is something uniquely American about forging and unveiling policies to remake the world when at home serious and debilitating conditions go unattended, conditions which threaten to tear apart our own social fabric. One would hope that in the past twenty years Americans might have learned some important lessons regarding the implications of their own unfinished work on their international standing.

One lesson we should have learned is that efforts to insure economic progress and social justice for the people of Latin America can never succeed so long as economic progress, social justice and equal educational opportunity are denied the twelve million Latin Americans who have chosen to live in this country. It is time the Alliance for Progress, quietly interred some years ago, was resurrected, but this time as a domestic alliance. What is needed is a far-reaching plan to begin to ameliorate the uncertainies and hopelessness which plague the lives of the good and proud people of our Spanish-speaking community. The initiative need not come from Washington; it can begin at the state level.

The serious educational problems facing the Spanish-speaking community, and especially the thousands of young people for whom English is virtually a foreign language, must be faced. There is a passage in Studs Terkel's book *Division Street America*, in which a seventeen-year-old Mexican-American, Frankie Rodriguez, comments on his school experience. He says:

> I wasn't learning nothing in this school, nothing at all . . .
> just sit back, watch the teacher say something, and what not.
> He never asked me to say anything. He never told me to do
> nothing. Just as soon as the bell rings, go to another class.
> That was it.[13]

Frankie Rodriguez is a dropout. There are thousands of children
like Frankie Rodriguez on the streets today, living evidence of one
of the most massive and shameful failures of modern education.

The dropout rate for Spanish-speaking students alone ranges
between sixty and seventy percent. Is it any wonder? Such students
cannot speak or understand English; their native language and
culture is deprecated; there are few bilingual teachers and fewer
bilingual counselors and school psychologists to whom to turn for
help; their intelligence and achievement is measured by tests which
are culturally biased; and they are relegated in large numbers to
classes for the mentally handicapped based on tests which are
administered in a language which is foreign to the students. Furthermore, schools are often so overcrowded that classes are held in
poorly lighted hallways, unventilated washrooms, or unheated
auditoriums.

Under these circumstances, who could possibly retain a healthy
attitude toward learning? These youngsters are not really dropouts
—they are pushouts, refugees from an educational system that is
failing. Unfortunately, there is no place else for them to go. The
result is immeasurable waste reflected in functional illiteracy (not
just in one language, but in two), in unemployment which for
Latins in Chicago is six times the city-wide average, in the destruction of pride and self-respect. Few Spanish-speaking students go on
to college and, therefore, few enter the professions.

What Is Needed and What Is Being Done

One of the earliest actions of the Illinois state education office in
1971 was the establishment of a Bilingual and Migrant Education
Unit. This unit is responsible for bringing order out of the chaotic
negligence that has long reigned at the highest level of public
education. Its charge is to coordinate and supervise all activities
within the state educational agency relating to programs for the
Spanish-speaking. It works closely with all other state and federal
agencies which may be engaged in similar work. The Unit's staff

consists of men and women who are bilingual, bicultural and who possess the technical skills necessary to do the job.

The activities of the Bilingual Education Unit are intended to augment five goals to which the state office of education is committed.

1. All schools will provide a positive learning environment for children of non-English-speaking backgrounds. These children should be encouraged to maintain and improve their language skills in both English and their home language. Cultural differences must be respected and destructively discriminatory practices avoided.
2. Teachers of students with non-English backgrounds will be trained in understanding the student's language and cultural background.
3. Schools with students of non-English-speaking background will provide special programs to meet their needs.
4. All agencies and organizations involved in the education (preschool through adult) of the non-English-speaking will have a well-established means of communication and coordination through the use of interagency committees and advisory councils.
5. The number of non-English-speaking graduates completing high school will increase substantially and vocational counseling and training will be provided to those who wish to discontinue formal schooling. Colleges and universities will substantially increase enrollment of non-English-speaking students.

The Bilingual Education Unit has made some progress in achieving these goals and on other fronts as well. For example, it has started consultations with other educational agencies and testing services in this country and in Latin America to identify reliable and culture-free intelligence and achievement tests, to validate them through field-testing, and then to disseminate them for use throughout Illinois. If such instruments do not exist or cannot be found, the unit will seek to develop the instruments. If this cannot be accomplished within a reasonable period of time, the state office will consider ordering a moratorium on all such testing until such time as fair instruments of measurement can be developed.

In California, where Chicanos constitute nineteen percent of the school enrollment, thirty percent of so-called mentally retarded students are Mexican-Americans. Although accurate data is not available, the pattern is certainly not markedly different in other states. The practice of penalizing Spanish-speaking youngsters and other minority or low socio-economic children through faulty diagnosis and hasty referrals into special classes must end.

In Illinois legislation has been enacted which requires that no student whose language is other than English be placed in a class for the mentally retarded or handicapped without first being examined by a school psychologist who speaks the student's language and understands his culture. There are, of course, few bilingual psychologists and counselors in Illinois. A thorough review of certification requirements is being made to determine the feasibility of altering those requirements to permit the use, on a provisional basis, of professional psychologists in the schools. They must, of course, be bilingual and bicultural.

The Bilingual Unit has developed and stated in measurable terms objectives for programs related to bilingual education, migrant education, and Teaching English as a Second Language (TESL). Despite the existence of such programs, there has existed until recently no acceptable or accurate method of measuring the effectiveness of these programs, no adequate method of determining the extent of success or failure, no method of insuring accountability or fixing responsibility for mistakes and misjudgments.

Of course, without bilingual teachers, existing and planned programs for the Spanish-speaking cannot possibly succeed. There is a surplus of teachers in this country, and yet there is a critical shortage of bilingual teachers. Because there is only one Spanish-speaking teacher for every 223 Spanish-speaking students in Chicago, the state office of education has started negotiations with several state universities, exploring the feasibility of establishing advanced degree programs in TESL, bilingual education, and counseling for minority students.

In this connection, the State Teacher Certification Board has assessed and will possibly alter its requirements for prospective bilingual teachers so that the schools can begin utilizing a vast reservoir of immigrants from Latin America who, while having university degrees, are precluded from teaching because of our narrowly drawn and applied licensing standards.

All teacher training institutions have been asked to include in their professional preparation programs experiences and course work to sensitize all teachers to the educational problems of minority, culturally different, and economically disadvantaged children. This has been coupled with a comprehensive pre-service and in-service program for local school districts involved in bilingual and migrant education. These programs are being supervised by the state office and are being staffed by specialists in bilingual and bicultural education.

Finally, there is the question of money. Illinois has made a dramatic turn-about since 1970. Most programs for the Spanish-speaking in Illinois were either funded by the federal government or to a lesser extent by local school districts. For school year 1972-73, more than $2 million in state resources were appropriated by the legislature for either the initiation or continuation of a total of forty-five bilingual projects. That appropriation jumped to $6 million in 1973-74. Illinois is presently financing and developing programs and services for non-English-speaking students on a per capita basis at a level unmatched by any other state.

The state's involvement became necessary, in part, because of federal funding practices for bilingual education. For example, although Illinois has the fifth largest concentration of Spanish-speaking people in the nation, it has consistently received a disproportionately small share of the funds provided under Title VII of the Elementary and Secondary Act. In fact, among the states receiving such funds, Illinois has consistently ranked twentieth, despite the enormous growth in its financial commitment to bilingual education.

This condition has been compounded, at least for non-English-speaking youngsters, by narrowly drawn criteria which severely limit the use of Title I ESEA resources for such purposes. One Title I program is TESL (Teaching English as a Second Language). Title I funds, including those available for TESL, can only be used in those schools where there is the greatest incidence of poverty, measured either in terms of personal income or participation in public aid programs. Given the high cost of educating the economically disadvantaged child, this policy is justifiable.

For Spanish-speaking children, however, this policy has tended to reinforce rather than solve their problems. When funds are divided among eligible schools, which have been ranked according

to poverty, the result is that thousands of Spanish-speaking youngsters are denied remedial programs. It has been estimated that only
one-fifth of the students in Chicago who need the TESL program
are receiving it.

It would seem self-evident that a child who cannot speak English
is impoverished and disadvantaged whether his family earns less
than $3,000 a year or $15,000 a year. Yet, the latter is not eligible to
participate in Title I, because his family is not poor enough. Federal funding of education is undergoing some very substantial
changes. Congress would be well advised with regard to TESL and
similar programs to formulate guidelines which will permit expenditures where they are needed without regard to artificialities like
poverty criteria. Spanish-speaking Americans are proud and hard-
working people who are anxious to stay off welfare rolls. So while
programs for the poor should not be tampered with, the federal government should not penalize those children who are culturally and
educationally disadvantaged rather than economically disadvantaged.

Effectiveness of Bilingual Programs

Do bilingual education programs work and are they worthwhile
from the perspective of social integration? The state office recently
completed an evaluation involving 156 Spanish-speaking first-
grade students in three school districts over a four-month period.
This preliminary study is the first phase of a much more extensive
longitudinal study on the effectiveness of bilingual programs.
While the findings are necessarily tentative, the data gathered to
date dramatically underline the positive impact that instruction
in the child's first or dominant language has in the development of
cognitive skills in first-graders of Spanish-language background.[14]

There has been some controversy over bilingual education programs arising from the legitimate fear that instruction in languages
other than English would arrest fluency in English and hinder
entry into the mainstream of the American educational system. The
study results dissipate this fear and instead highlight specific
academic gains with no accompanying loss of fluency in English
among the children participating in the bilingual program. That
is, while the children in the bilingual program were exposed to less
English than their Spanish-speaking counterparts in the regular
school program, the former did not learn any less English. In fact,

the children in the bilingual program learned more English in the same period of time.

Nor was achievement in English the only gain for the children in the bilingual program. In all of the language arts and mathematics areas tested, the children in the bilingual programs made greater mean achievement than their counterparts in the regular school program. This was true whether achievement was measured in English or in Spanish.

Furthermore, it is clear from the results of this study that children from a Spanish-language background who are not in a bilingual program are losing their fluency in Spanish, while similar children enrolled in a bilingual program are increasing their skill in both English and Spanish. At first glance it may seem that the replacement of Spanish by English is desirable if integration into the mainstream of United States life is to come about. Further examination, however, identifies at least three reasons why this is not so.

First, mobility. Many of these children will be returning to either Puerto Rico or Mexico; other parents have hopes of returning to Cuba when political circumstances change. Successful achievement in these countries by students of modest economic means (and most of the children in this sample fall into this category) requires them to compete in Spanish, not English. Many Puerto Rican students, for example, arrive in Illinois only to flounder in a curriculum taught in English. Then, about when they are making the transition to the American system, they return to Puerto Rico only to discover that they had neglected their Spanish-language skills and are once again floundering in school.

Second, self-esteem. Children who enroll in a school to find that there are only negative penalties for all they have learned at home suffer devastating damage to their self-esteem. When the language of a child's home is deemed worthless as a vehicle for learning, and when many of the family (i.e., cultural) conventions only serve to exacerbate hostility in teachers, the child is forced to the painful and erroneous conclusion that he is not worth as much as an English-speaking child. Little wonder that as many as seventy percent of Spanish-speaking children in Chicago drop out of school before high school graduation, and that one Illinois district outside of Chicago listed over 700 Spanish surnamed children in the elementary schools and 43 in the district secondary school.

Third, in the mid 1960s Congress formally declared bilingualism to be in the national interest. Millions of dollars were subsequently appropriated to rescue the alarming loss of fluency in languages other than English, a loss at least partially the result of an anti-intellectualism which equated patriotism with an ignorance of one's ancestral language. The most economical way to maintain the nation's reservoir of linguistic talents is for children who come to school already fluent in a language other than English to continue to grow in their first language as well as in English. Besides the worth of bilingualism in terms of the country's international economic and political interests, knowledge of another language carries with it many well-known social and professional advantages which afford the bilingual individual a great deal of affective satisfaction.

Many of the problems facing the non-English-speaking community in this country can be remediated through formal education, but education cannot be expected to do that job alone. Progress will come much faster if an alliance of common interests and concerns can somehow be forged—an alliance which brings the resources and creativity of this nation to bear on human problems which no free society can afford to tolerate for very long.

There are some encouraging stirrings within the Spanish-speaking community; people are getting themselves together. There has been a rebirth of pride in their beautiful language and rich history. This pride is reflected in the slogan *La Raza* that says to all: this can and will be a multilingual and multicultural society, and America will be better and stronger for it. Spanish-speaking people are entering the political arena, lobbying in Washington, at statehouses, at city halls, and with boards of education. They are learning, as so many others before them have learned, that even in this country you don't get anything for nothing. You must demand what is rightly yours, including social justice, economic progress and equal educational opportunity—or you may never get it.

EDUCATING MIGRANT CHILDREN

In *The Grapes of Wrath,* author John Steinbeck observes that "man, unlike any other thing organic or inorganic in the universe, grows beyond his work, walks up the stairs of his concepts, emerges ahead of his accomplishments." This rather cheery view of mankind cannot be easily applied to migrant workers. Once an individual is caught up in the migrant stream it is difficult to escape its potential inhumanity. Sub-standard housing, sub-standard health care, sub-standard wages, and sub-standard education are the bitter fruits many migrants harvest. And for the migrant young, there are few opportunities to grow beyond their work. Scarcer still are the opportunities to emerge ahead of their accomplishments, for accomplishments do not come easily in the migrant's world.

While some progress has been made in recent years in educating migrant children, there is little basis for optimism. Among the public schools' failings, this is the saddest, because no group has been more neglected and shortchanged than migrant children. For thousands of these young people, poverty, segregation, and alienation are a way of life.

The task of educators is to do everything in their power to arm youngsters (and particularly such neglected groups as migrants) with the self-confidence, independence, and self-direction required to break out of their vicious cycle. Whether educators can ever do enough to remediate those conditions must remain an open question. However, there is little to be gained in applying a Band-Aid to a wound which requires surgery. If it is true that a migrant child has one chance in a hundred to graduate from high school, then new strategies must replace old and unworkable ones. If the Illinois experience with migrant education is at all typical, then major surgery is necessary.

Educators must either sharpen up current approaches to the problems, or they must radically depart from them, if educational opportunities for migrant children are to be appreciably improved. First, who are the migrant children in this country? Interminable quibbling and hairsplitting over a precise definition of the migrant child ought to end in favor of seeking out all children who need and deserve help. Precise information through the record transfer system on the number of children being served by federally funded migrant programs is just beginning to come in. Until methods of identifying migrant children are upgraded, migrant education programs will not receive their fair share of federal funds.

Second, educators must seek to involve those thousands of youngsters who are not presently reached by migrant programs. In Illinois, easily one-third of the eligible migrant students never set foot in a classroom. Almost ninety percent of migrant students are in grades K through 6. Present offerings for pre-schoolers are few, and the holding power of available programs for junior high and high school youngsters seems to diminish with each passing season.

If economic necessity requires older students to work in the fields or to babysit for younger brothers and sisters, strategies must be devised that will enable education to compete economically. Such incentives may include economic assistance, work-study programs, a more relevant curriculum, more prevocational and vocational programs, and earmarked scholarships to colleges and universities for migrant youngsters. Money must be appropriated, too, for day care centers, transportation, and food and clothing when necessary. Money alone cannot solve the problems, but funding for migrant education ought to be sufficiently generous to offset the economic forces at play.

Third, the improved use of the record transfer system is necessary. Migrant children begin arriving in Illinois, for example, as early as March, and some remain as late as October. Depending on planting and harvest schedules, somewhat less than half of these youngsters are in the state for a period of between one and five weeks with the remaining fifty percent here for five or more weeks. Given the ebb and flow of the migrant stream, quick access to student health and academic records is necessary. Occasionally, migrant projects do not secure these records at all, or when they do, they are too late to be of any use. The result too often is the arbitrary placement of a student in a grade, which, if carelessly done, can chill a child's desire to continue.

Fourth, individualized instruction deserves more attention. Children who move frequently from school to school are likely to develop peculiar and highly personalized needs, but a rigid curriculum and a lockstep routine is not the answer in such cases. Educators must learn to diagnose quickly the individual interests and needs of migrant children and to provide immediately learning experiences which are relevant to them.

Finally, the future fortunes of migrant education will rise or fall depending on whether the whole effort seems worthwhile. So few procedures exist for evaluating and monitoring current programs that it is hard to determine whether educators are succeeding or failing; such an admission at a time when accountability is being demanded throughout public education does not auger well for the future. Presently most evaluation is self-evaluation, and while that procedure may often lack the objectivity desired, reports of Title I in Illinois raise some very serious questions about success and failure. Despite the probable unreliability of the data, it is evident that the greatest gains by migrant children are personal and social rather than in the domain of work-study skills. Improving a child's self-image, his personal adjustment, and his classroom behavior and cooperativeness should never be deprecated. However, if a child cannot read, or communicate, or compute, or solve problems, the educational system has failed that child totally, and in the process has helped consign him to the fateful cycle of poverty, eventual escape from which will require more than sociability.

How can migrant children be offered more effective education? The litany of problems is unending. Funds are inadequate, and the untimely allocation of what funds are available make it difficult to hire top-notch teachers. Materials are not always available. Teachers are not always prepared to deal with the special needs of migrant children, particularly if they are bilingual.

These problems are only compounded by the "plantation spirit" (i.e. the patronizing attitudes and uncooperativeness) of some local administrators. Ways must be found to demonstrate to the migrant child and his parents that we as educators and as people regard each child as a unique person, that what the child has learned at home and in his travels is of value, including the way he has learned to speak and to act. The child has not come to school as a *tabula rasa* for educators to mark on at will.

These problems face many states. As a result of activities within the state office in Illinois, more individualized attention is being given to the special educational needs of migrant children. Children in full day programs now receive free lunches. A resource mobile unit has made possible the availability of special materials and equipment, consultative services on special linguistic and cultural problems, and the recruitment of both staff and students. A teacher-exchange program permits Illinois-based teachers to understand the environment and educational programs of the migrant student's home base. The Illinois State Legislature, as noted above, has appropriated special funds which now make it possible to offer non-English-speaking children, including settled-out migrants, programs in bilingual education.

Despite these and other activities, it is not entirely clear whether the problems or those who are steadfastly seeking to solve them have the upperhand. Efforts in any state alone will make little difference in the final analysis; without a far-reaching national strategy, little can be done at the state level to turn things around. Solutions to the severe educational problems of migrant children are not to be found in the *ad hoc* and uncoordinated development of programs by individual states and local school districts.

The futures of several hundred thousand children are involved. To the extent that state and local political considerations and other provincial interests prevent meeting the needs of these children, they must be swept away. Forty-eight separate strategies will no longer do. Only national leadership and planning can prevent further chaos and confusion. Only a national strategy will enable us to find the migrant child wherever he is and meet his needs whatever they may be.

With regard to a national strategy, two approaches should be considered. First, the present status of the curriculum for migrant children is disastrous. The job of reforming the curriculum is much too big for any one state to handle; national coordination is necessary to provide some articulation. The development of weekly student performance-based learning units should be considered. Under national supervision, the task of producing these units could be parceled out among the states which provide migrant education. One state, for example, might develop brief units for math instruction on the early elementary level, if this is an area of strength and interest, while another state might develop science units on the high school level. Illinois could work on an early childhood project, such as skill and concept development in Spanish and in English.

Second, greater use should be made of information contained in the data bank in Little Rock. The amount of helpful information provided by the standard tests reported on the national migrant student transfer forms is minimal. As a first step toward making sense out of the reported scores, test data in the bank at Little Rock should be studied to establish national norms for migrant children. A second step is to retest samples of the Spanish-speaking children with Spanish versions of some of the standardized tests. It should be noted that none of the fifteen tests identified on the migrant records is in Spanish, yet, in Illinois for example, many of the younger children are more fluent in Spanish than English.

Although a national strategy is required, it can be argued that public education should do nothing to help preserve a farm labor system which too often preys on powerless people by paying them inadequate wages and providing indecent working and living conditions. The farm labor system should be dismantled; after all, it is the root problem. The best guarantee that migrant children in the future will get a decent education would be to bring the migrant stream to a grinding halt. But until that happens, bridges for continuous and uninterrupted educational experiences must be provided those children who remain in the stream as well as those who eventually settle out.

EDUCATING EXCEPTIONAL CHILDREN

Society's duty is to educate all persons to the limit of their capacities, not just the young, the affluent, or the so-called normal. A strategy of excellence will not permit any less.

If mediocrity is to be the standard in education, then we must be prepared to live in a mediocre society. The final measure of this nation's greatness will be determined not by what it did for those who are richly endowed with a healthy environment, a healthy body, and a healthy mind, but by what it does or fails to do for millions of Americans for whom hope and opportunity have long been luxuries—the poor, the disadvantaged, the physically, mentally, and emotionally handicapped.

Regrettably, there remains a lingering notion in this country that those who are handicapped by retardation, poverty, race and color are a drag on society. Of course, most thinking people reject that notion. However, a rhetorical commitment to excellence in education must now be matched with actions—actions which give meaning to our steadfast belief that every child has worth and dignity and that every child is potentially productive.

Educators can point with justifiable pride to the progress made in special education. In Illinois, for example, the General Assembly has passed legislation which has placed the state in a position of leadership in services to handicapped children. School districts are required to provide special education programs to *all* children whose needs cannot be met by the standard program, including children with mild and unnoticeable handicaps as well as those whose handicaps are severe and obvious. Recent regulations developed by the state office require preventive and supportive services in addition to those aimed at rehabilitation.[15] Other states throughout the country have modeled their developing services on the pattern found in Illinois.

However, pride in what has been done should not obscure the real work that remains to be done. Consider, for example, the fact that less than one-half of the nation's school districts have special classes for handicapped children, and that only about 1.5 million of the more than 5.5 million of our school-age handicapped children are currently receiving special educational services. Two and one-half percent of the 3 million students in Illinois are Educable Mentally Handicapped (EMH), and another one-half percent of that total are Trainable Mentally Handicapped (TMH). A large majority of students, once placed in EMH and TMH classes, will never escape from them; the discouraged and downhearted among them will either drop out or be pushed out of school at any early age.

The public schools in this country do not yet have sufficient diagnostic personnel to define the problems of educationally troubled students. In addition, the number of psychologists, social workers, and others who are responsible for evaluating handicapped children is, in many parts of the nation, completely inadequate to meet the need. In too many cases teachers have simply given up referring their children because of the backlog of cases to be evaluated.

While the schools are serving most of the children who have some degree of mental impairment, there are still large numbers of other handicapped children for whom services are unavailable. This is particularly true for children whose problems are not readily visible, such as the hard of hearing; for children whose problems occur infrequently, such as the blind; and for children whose problems are very severe, such as the autistic.

There is little doubt that special education programs are more costly than the standard program. When schools are faced with curtailments in other areas, it is difficult to find the resources to expand services to handicapped children. However, those services must expand if the schools are to meet their obligation to all.

A unified system of educational services for the handicapped does not exist in most states. The division of responsibility among a number of agencies inevitably results in some children "falling between the cracks." Too often, the child most in need of help has nowhere to turn.

In the coming decade, educators must not be afraid to question methods and techniques, and even basic assumptions about special education. A major breakthrough will not come unless educators experiment and take chances, make judgments on imperfect knowledge, and occasionally make mistakes. Mistakes are sometimes painful, but they are the essential price of growth.

Basic questions must be asked: in what directions should the schools be moving with respect to special education? What should the *role of special education* be in our society? Traditionally special education has been considered as a series of self-contained special classes which serve the severely handicapped and which have little relation to the so-called regular program of the school district. This concept must be abandoned, and in its place emphasis must be placed on appropriate education for all children. The use of the terms "handicapped" and "exceptional" must be abandoned. It is far better to consider each student as having certain educational or educationally-related needs which may or may not be met in the standard program. If the student has "exceptional needs" that cannot be met in the ordinary course of affairs his program must be adjusted or changed accordingly. He should not be automatically labeled as different or be isolated from his peers.

When *special services* are introduced to assist the child, these services should range along a continuum with, at the furthest point, a special program for the most severely involved children. Before that, however, the schools should provide such things as modified textbooks, consultation to the teacher, alternate curriculums, special services like speech therapy and part-time specialized instruction by a resource of itinerant teacher. Evelyn Deno's "Cascade of Services" and other similar models reflect a growing attitude that, insofar as possible, the schools should attempt to meet the exceptional needs of students within the mainstream of the system. The distinction between "education" and "special education" has always been artificial; it should now be eliminated.

A primary goal for the education of handicapped students must be social and occupational competency, which can result if the capacity of handicapped students to think critically and to act independently is properly developed. What is required is a basic survival curriculum with emphasis on skill development, with the remainder of the academic program supportive to this central thrust. Continuity and progressivity in programming is needed, as is an end to the tedious repetition of the same instruction at each level. Only in this way can a student be expected to develop progressively through various levels of classes. However, as stated above, once a student's strengths and weaknesses have been clinically determined, those strengths should be developed as fully as possible within, not apart from, the mainstream of the educational system.

What are the methods and problems of determining a student's strengths and weaknesses? *Classification* through intelligence tests carries with it, as former Education Commissioner James Allen has noted, a "surplus meaning which is threatening to parents and detrimental to children." Therefore, judgments must be made with great care, and not on the basis of a child's race and economic condition, his clothing, or his inability to speak English. Nor should a test or a battery of tests be the final arbiter, for educators are finally realizing that the tests they administer are more related to their world than to the students' world. In many cases test scores are of dubious value. Normally ghetto children would not be expected to score high on intelligence tests, and yet it has been customary to equate low scores with retarded intellectual ability. Such a practice only serves to compound further the disadvantages under which a poor child must live and learn.

The process of evaluation must go a step further. School psychologists and teachers must go into a child's home and into his neighborhood and assess his behavior there. If the home behavior of the child is not consonant with his low test score, it is a serious mistake to label him mentally retarded, though it may be evident that additional educational treatment is warranted.

The Illinois office of education has completed a revision of the rules and regulations under which school districts administer special educational programs. These new regulations emphasize the need to evaluate a child in a variety of dimensions so that a complete profile of his abilities and problems becomes evident. Labels are eliminated, although recognition is made that children do have certain characteristics which interfere with their educational progress. Thus, the state educational agency is attempting to change the focus from the "retarded child" or the "blind child" to "the child with mental impairment" or the "child with visual impairment." Even these characteristics are based on their relationship to the child's educational development.

It is hoped that such regulations will contribute to evaluations which are more appropriate and more meaningful. Further, it is hoped that the system of labeling children will be abandoned. However, regulations cannot singly achieve this goal; attitudes and behavior of those who work with children must be refocused.

There is also a need in special education to *involve the parents* of handicapped children. All too often parents are unaware that their child is having difficulty until he is placed in a special education program. The new Illinois regulations require parental notification and involvement, but to be effective, the rules must be translated into activities which make use of parents' concern. Parents must become partners with the school.

There must be *accountability*. People want to know how their tax dollars are being spent, and expect a fair ratio of benefit and success for every dollar spent—special education is no exception. The day when educators could take comfort from the mere establishment of programs for the retarded has passed. Now the burning question is: "Are the programs working, and if not, why?"

On the question of accountability, Dr. Wilson Riles' conclusion is pertinent: "there are no dropouts; there are pushouts." The educational system, as we know it, is calculated to eliminate those who don't succeed within the system. This problem has traditionally faced the handicapped and the retarded. For the future, schools must be turned around; educational needs of the individual student cannot be ignored and programs must have relevance to each student's particular aspirations and learning problems. This is what accountability is really all about.

An in-depth evaluation of special education programs in the schools of Illinois has been initiated by the state office. Teams of professional peers and parents of handicapped children are visiting special education programs and determining how well these programs are serving the children involved. Such external evaluations will be made on a regular basis and will promote program development as well as ensuring accountability. However, it is also hoped that this external evaluation will not be the only method of program assessment. Each school district should be responsible for continuously reviewing the methods and programs being used with handicapped children, and for determining their success or failure.

The public schools have not been adequately equipped to educate all of the physically and mentally handicapped. Private institutions, with the State's encouragement and financial help, have sought to fill this void, and in many cases private schools are performing admirably. However, there is a need to generally upgrade these institutions. Complaints and on-the-spot investigations have revealed that in some schools accurate and up-to-date records are not maintained, that the curriculum is haphazard, that textbooks and equipment are inadequate, that some directors and teachers have little or no formal training in special education and, in some cases, do not have degrees.

Private schools, receiving public financial assistance, should be expected to provide children with more than mere caretakership. Like the public schools, they have a duty to educate every child to the limit of his abilities. Therefore, the state office has recently prepared new educational standards and guidelines for the operation of private schools.

Preschool and early education programs for handicapped children are desperately needed. Some preschool services have been provided to the deaf/hearing impaired, blind/visually impaired, and physically and multiply handicapped since 1969. However, these programs are not widespread, and legislation such as the 1972 Illinois law, would permit all children with handicapping conditions or potential learning problems to be provided special education programs and services between the ages of 3 and 21.

If early education can accelerate the social and mental development of handicapped children, it is a mistake not to provide it for children diagnosed as handicapped at birth or shortly thereafter. To do nothing between the ages of 3 and 5, the critical years in a child's life, is to waste two valuable and irretrievable years. No longer can educators afford to stand by hopelessly as opportunities for a head start toward adjustment in school and society slip slowly away.

Recent studies have concluded that half of all growth in human intelligence takes place between birth and age 4, thirty percent occurs between the ages of 4 and 8, and the remaining twenty percent takes place between ages 8 and 17. In other words, half of a child's growth in intelligence takes place before the school ever sees him, and eighty percent has occurred by the time he has completed the third or fourth grade.

Why have educators failed until recently to recognize the importance of preschool programs? Perhaps they have been so awed by complex psychological constructions of learning and cognition that some of the simpler principles of human development have been overlooked. It is important to intervene early and educationally in the life of the physically handicapped and mentally retarded before motivation has ebbed, when readiness to learn is high, and when the parent is still enthusiastic about the child's learning potential. By not making full use of early learning years, frustration will result, and the child, treated as handicapped and unable to contend with his handicap, will become more handicapped.

The most enticing feature of early education is its corrective and preventive potential. Early education can help prevent secondary emotional handicaps. A youngster can easily feel inadequate, unworthy, or even persecuted, because of his own reaction to his handicapping condition and because of reactions of people around him. The tragic result is frequently an emotional disturbance more severe than the initial handicap.

Eighty percent of the mentally retarded young people in Illinois come from backgrounds of economic and cultural deprivation. No child can be expected to learn satisfactorily in a hostile environment in which discouragement is a way of life and in which the infectious diseases of apathy and disinterest interfere with normal educational growth and development. For children who are undernourished, who live in deteriorating housing, who are easy prey for rats and contagious disease, life itself is a constant struggle; while most are not retarded organically, these youngsters will almost all be functionally retarded. Early childhood education can help transform impoverishment to enrichment by ameliorating the conditions which retard intellectual curiosity and growth.

A four-year experiment by the Institute for Research on Exceptional Children at the University of Illinois has conclusively shown the potential value of early education. For four years the Institute has been working with preschool-age children (and their parents) who come from poor and culturally deprived homes and who show evidence of retardation. The results have been astounding. Not one of the youngsters upon entering the primary grades has been placed in an EMH class; all are functionally involved in the classroom. Adverse conditions can make academic achievement more difficult, but what is more important is the realization that such conditions do not automatically preclude academic success.

Several matters of concern have been touched upon, but there are, of course, a host of others, including the need to upgrade teacher training and retraining, the need for greater parental involvement in program planning and implementation, and the need for increased financial support. The essential tasks facing educators in this area can be briefly summarized as follows:

- To develop services to handicapped and gifted children to assure each child educational programming appropriate to his needs.
- To develop improved procedures and techniques for identification, diagnosis, and prescriptive teaching of exceptional prekindergarten children.
- To incorporate experiences in all professional preparation programs to sensitize the prospective teacher to the educational problems of all children including those classified as exceptional.
- To require a mandatory program of periodic testing and examination of students classified as handicapped.
- To train thousands of persons to teach handicapped preschool children, students with learning disabilities, social and/or emotional disorders and hearing disorders, and students diagnosed as mentally retarded.
- To permit parents whose children are recommended for classes for the handicapped easy access to all information pertaining to such recommendations and the right to a hearing and appeal.

The basic problem with which the handicapped continue to do battle is public opinion. An insensitive public, perhaps more than its schools, has, to use Charles Silberman's phrase, "mutilated the spirit" of many of our handicapped youngsters. It has unintentionally "mutilated their spontaneity, their joy in learning, their pleasure in creating, their sense of self."[16]

Society must be reminded repeatedly that concern for the individual, regardless of his economic, physical or mental disability, has been, and must continue to be, one of the central themes of our history. Citizens must be reminded that their task today is to create an atmosphere which will permit them, their children, and their children's children to experience perpetual self-discovery, perpetual reshaping to realize one's best self, to be the person one could be.

EDUCATING THE UNDEREDUCATED

In the report entitled *Action Goals for the Seventies: An Agenda for Illinois Education,* one goal calls upon the state to make available by 1975 to all its citizens, regardless of age, a free foundation level education. This commitment is the outgrowth of a remarkable piece of legal draftsmanship: the Education Article of the 1970 Illinois State Constitution.

While the wording of Article X is specific in relation to the overarching goal of public education in Illinois, the new article, unlike its century-old predecessor, is sufficiently flexible to permit the state to meet the largely unforeseen and future educational needs of people. Three features of Article X are pertinent to any consideration of adult and continuing education.

First is the declaration that "the paramount goal of the state is the educational development of all persons to the limit of their capacities." The words "all persons" are especially crucial to this discussion. The second is the article's declaration that "education in public schools through the secondary level shall be free." And the third is the article's declaration that "the state has the primary responsibility for financing the system of public education."

The significance of these provisions in relation to adult and continuing education is to be found in the clear and unmistakable meaning of their words. In its report to the Constitutional Convention, the Education Committee emphasized the vital role of education in our society; it was thought that there would emerge in Illinois a system of public education which would encourage the enhancement of vocational skills, lift the cultural levels of its people, and enlarge the abilities of all citizens.

Of particular significance was the Convention's recognition

that basic education should not be the exclusive domain of young, healthy, and normal children between the ages of 5 and 18, as had been the case under the 1870 Constitution. The objective now was to provide each person with equal opportunities to progress to the limit of his ability, regardless of age or circumstance. That proviso was intended to apply with equal force to those educable persons who suffer from either physical or mental handicaps. It was also intended to apply to adults who, in countless instances, need, deserve, and can obviously profit from expanded educational opportunities: i.e. to provide for the free education of those who have not completed high school insofar as the programs are established within the public school system.

Another provision has implications for adult and continuing education and refers to the authority vested in the General Assembly to provide by law such other free education as it may deem necessary. In order to cope with the knowledge explosion and ever-increasing technological capacities, the legislature may determine in the future that free education should be extended beyond the secondary level to include some part of the collegiate experience or to include retraining, enrichment, and public service programs, any or all of which could in the legislature's discretion be tuition free.

So in Illinois the constitution is clear: the state must guarantee a free foundation level education for all of its citizens. But more is involved here than constitutional imperatives. One would have to say that sheer necessity—educational, economic, social, and political necessity—requires that adult education programs become more universal. Seventy-five percent of today's young adults have a high school education. That figure represents an increase of almost forty percent over the graduation rate a decade ago. We can take pride in that success. However, educators must still live with the uncomfortable realization that in Illinois fifty-five percent of the adult population has never completed high school, and this condition exists throughout the nation. Furthermore, ten percent of this country's population is functionally illiterate, 21 million adults lack reading skills at a "survival" level, and millions are unable to read a telephone book or complete a simple job application.

It is difficult to assess the real cost to individuals and to society of inadequate education. Recently the United States Senate's

Select Committee on Equal Education Opportunity commissioned Henry M. Levin of the Stanford University School of Education to conduct a study of this subject.[17] Based on a study of 3.18 million American men between the ages of 25 and 34 who have failed to graduate from high school, the Levin Report estimated that the cost to these individuals in lost personal income will be $237 billion and the cost to federal, state and local government in lost tax revenue will be $71 billion. Senator Walter Mondale, the chairman of the Select Committee has observed that:

> For the individual, educational failure means a lifetime of lost opportunities. But the effects are visited on the nation as well, for society as a whole pays for the undereducation of a significant segment of its population.[18]

Low levels of educational achievement are known to be prime contributors to unemployment and underemployment. Reductions in earning power inevitably result in less tax support for government at all levels. And yet, public budgets, rather than personal resources, are being increasingly relied upon to pay for food, housing, health services, job training, remedial education, income maintenance and other services. Government is expected to do more in the fight against poverty—but with diminishing resources.

Furthermore, the correlation between a low level of educational achievement and crime is well documented. Of the inmates in the Illinois State Penitentiary System, nearly three-fourths have less than a 12th grade education, and only 400 of nearly 8,000 inmates have had any educational experience beyond high school. Scarce public resources are being expended on crime prevention programs and expanding judicial and penal systems, with the return, in terms of national and individual income, almost non-existent. Based on his limited sampling, Levin reports that $3 billion of the nation's annual welfare expenditures and at least $3 billion of the annual cost of crime are attributable to inadequate education.

Perhaps the most significant finding of this educational economic research is the potential return which could be generated by a more intensive and sustained investment in public education. Higher educational attainment and achievement is not only helpful in reducing juvenile delinquency, adult crime, and economic dependency, but, according to the Levin study, each dollar invested in public education is likely to result in a six-fold return on our national investment in terms of income production alone. Every $4.00 devoted to providing a minimum of high school completion will generate $7.00 in additional tax revenues to federal, state, and local governments. To elevate the educational levels of the 3.18 million young adults studied by Professor Levin would cost the nation approximately $40 billion dollars—but in time, government revenues derived from this investment would exceed this original expenditure by more than $30 billion.

So it is clear that persons who receive insufficient education, in a society which rewards individuals according to their educational attainment, suffer in comparison with those who have received a better education. And of course, the magnitude of the cost to the nation resulting from the undereducation of a large segment of its citizenry is enormous. While other variables—including differences in ability, effort, and luck—can and do influence the competition for rewards in our society, education plays a paramount role. Whenever society fails to provide a child (who is legally compelled to attend school) with a quality education, society eventually pays for that failure. And if the adult, who in his youth dropped out of school or who failed for some reason, is prevented from easily returning to the classroom and perhaps succeeding where once he failed, society's failure is compounded.

Those who contend that adult and continuing education is an unaffordable luxury cannot themselves escape the prodigious social costs of poor education. Children whose parents have been handicapped by poor education will themselves generally complete fewer grades of schooling and will show substantially lower performance in standardized academic achievement. The cyclic nature of the problem represents the most persuasive argument for expanding and upgrading adult education programs.

For years the public school system and the colleges and universities, in Illinois as elsewhere in this nation, have ignored the older adult student whose employment or family responsibilities have prevented him from attaining the education he desires and has the ability to complete. While it is true that in 1971 thirty million adults participated in part-time educational programs sponsored by adult educational agencies in this country, only six percent of that total number were adults with less than eight years of schooling. Clearly the challenge of providing adult education opportunities to the less advantaged citizens of this country is not being met, and in our larger cities the failure is particularly acute.

This is true even though, in Illinois for example, millions of state and federal dollars are being spent annually on basic adult education programs. Thousands of adults are participating in various Americanization, high school equivalency, and credit programs. These programs, which presently operate in 52 counties and 103 school districts, are designed to help adults learn English as a second language, to prepare them for citizenship, or to provide them with elementary and secondary equivalency classes, or prepare residents over the age of nineteen for the G.E.D. (General Educational Development) test—which, if passed by a student, attests to his educational maturity and competency.

In a cooperative but very complex arrangement, involving the federal government, the State Department of Public Aid, the State Department of Labor, and the state office of education, thousands of welfare recipients are being provided adult basic education programs which include G.E.D., high school equivalency instruction, and occupational and vocational training.

The adult basic education program (ninety percent of which is federally funded) seeks to provide instruction for adults in speaking, reading, and writing English at less than a high school level of proficiency.

Under the Work Incentive Program (WIN) the Illinois Department of Labor has selected hundreds of individuals, all welfare recipients, to participate in special educational and training programs. The Department of Labor specifies the type, nature, and duration of the program for each WIN trainee. The state office of education then enters into individually negotiated agreements with schools and agencies for the training of these adults in accordance with predetermined specifications. Once a trainee has completed the WIN Program, the Department of Labor is responsible for placing him in a job.

The issue is whether these programs, as they presently operate in Illinois, are of sufficient quality and scope to conform with the state constitution's directive that the state provide a free foundation level education for all citizens. Measured by almost any standard, it is clear that the state is not meeting that mandate. After all, less than 100,000 citizens were served by reimbursable adult education program in Illinois in 1972. This pattern persists in other states.

Two other indices, the steadily rising crime rate and the burgeoning public welfare budget, provide some measure of the exorbitant cost resulting from inadequate education; the cost of lost opportunities and destroyed potentialities is ultimately borne by all.

As has been shown, adult and continuing education is an investment in human resource development which benefits the community as well as the individual. Because it is important that an adult discover new opportunities for himself and because of the nation's continuing need to expand and refine its human resources, state departments of education should initiate a multifaceted program which dramatizes the seriousness with which they view this matter.

First, recognizing that competent and full-time adult educators and adult education program administrators are urgently needed throughout the country, state departments of education should make financial grants to universities for the development of graduate programs in adult and continuing education.

Second, state departments should fund the development and testing of curriculum materials and techniques appropriate to adult programs. The success of adult education programs will depend to a large extent on the adult teacher's understanding and use of effective instructional procedures, such as adult-oriented methods that encourage the participation by both teacher and learner in program planning and in the teacher-learning transaction.

Third, state departments should develop consumer education curriculum materials for use by local adult education programs. These materials should be designed to teach reading and consumer education simultaneously.

Fourth, state departments should pilot test programs to determine the feasibility, as well as the potential cost, of teaching reading for illiterate and semi-literate adults by means of computer assisted instruction.

Fifth, state departments should work closely with state departments of corrections to insure the establishment of a sound and viable educational program within our penal institutions.

Sixth, state departments should work closely with community colleges in areas having high concentrations of non-English-speaking citizens and, when possible, fund full-time coordinators in those colleges to develop and administer bilingual adult basic education programs.

Seventh, state departments should design a curriculum to help prepare adults of Latin descent to take the Spanish language versions of the G.E.D. examination.

A number of states are making such efforts to provide adults with opportunities for equal access to quality education. In 1972, the Illinois Department of Corrections and the state office of education cooperated in the establishment of a statewide school district for the adult correctional institutions. Through this new district— one of the first of its kind in the nation—inmates now have available to them a comprehensive education program, including offerings in basic literacy skills, high school equivalency, and vocational training.

An overall strategy to govern adult education in this country is long overdue. Adult education programs are presently administered by a rather complex mixture of private and public, national and local organizations, all of whom operate under the law of supply and demand. Regrettably, the result of this uncoordinated, often nondirected, effort has been a tendency to confuse means with ends, to become protective of vested interests, and to needlessly waste resources and duplicate efforts. There are communities in Illinois where the local high school, an area vocational education center, a community college, and a university are all providing adult education programs, trying to serve the same clientele, and each drawing on funds from different sources.

On the other hand, adult education programs are having a difficult time getting off the ground in other communities. There are high schools which simply do not want to deal with welfare recipients, community colleges which see their mission as being something more exalted than mere service to the community, and area vocational education centers which admit adults reluctantly and with a fee required. Clearly, educators need to look at adult education in its totality. They must find ways to combine and make better use of resources; they must clarify the mission of the schools at every level, because adult education is the proper business of all educational institutions.

There is truth in Justice William O. Douglas' observation that "the way to establish an institution is to finance it." If adult education is to survive and prosper, then states must find ways for fully funding a system of free foundation-level education. At present, adult education funds are essentially categorical in nature; they must be used for specific target populations. No state fully supports foundation level education for persons beyond the compulsory school age, but that is precisely what is required. State departments of education should determine the feasibility of incorporating the cost of adult education through the secondary level as a factor in their school aid formulas, with payments being computed and made to local school districts on an average daily attendance basis.

To require, as Illinois does, that a high school dropout pay tuition to finish high school is constitutionally suspect and, from the point of view of social policy, shortsighted. A way must be found for increasing and stabilizing financial support for adult education. Only then can the necessary planning, staffing, and programming get under way in earnest.

We should be concerned not only about the millions of Americans who are under-educated, but with those Americans who are educated, possessing marketable skills, and overwhelmed with leisure time. Also those people who believe they have a right to terminate their education—to rest smugly on their degrees and positions—are a concern. In an age in which our knowledge doubles every five or ten years, new competence is demanded of all people: lawyers, doctors, teachers, plumbers or electricians. Competence can be maintained by re-education on a continuing basis. Ideally, education should be a life-long experience, not merely a twelve-year interlude in a youngster's life.

The essential task facing the educational system is the creation of an environment which permits students, parents, and other community members to become imbued with a positive attitude toward learning. In short, the speed and economy with which an individual can adapt to continual change must be increased. The desired outcome is a society in which any adult who wants to do so has the opportunity to learn about any topic, at any time, without unnecessary restrictions.

The notion of continuous learning has been lionized throughout history. It was Thoreau who observed that our education should "not leave off . . . when we begin to be men and women." He said it was time "that villages were universities, and their elder inhabitants the fellows of universities with leisure . . . to pursue liberal studies the rest of their lives." It is the educational system's responsibility to begin transforming the ideal of continuous learning into something which is real and meaningful. The nation ought to make an in-depth inquiry into ways and means by which to make continuous learning a reality in the foreseeable future. We need a far-reaching strategy which involves the university community, labor unions, the business community and other interested publics.

If educators are serious about adult and continuing education, they must focus their attention on the community and its needs, begin the arduous task of laying the foundation for an enduring education system which is relevant enough, flexible enough, efficient enough, and human enough to meet the continually changing demands of a complex and relentlessly advancing society. Then, and only then, will the quest for equal educational opportunity bear fruit.

Chapter IV

CURRICULUM

The question is: what kind of individuals do we want to graduate from our public schools? If we want obedient, non-creative young adults who will follow orders, but not necessarily think for themselves, then we will want to continue classes set up for obedience training where all children regardless of interests or abilities will follow the same lessons each day, listen attentively to the teacher and return the information given out by the teacher on a written or oral test.

Parent

Most importantly, educators will have to understand that education is an individual thing, not a group effort. Each child must be approached in the way which affords him the most chance for success.

Concerned Citizen

Positive action must be taken to develop a comprehensive education program which elevates career opportunities to an equal status with the traditional academic program.

Businessman

Instructional processes should be shifted from the pattern of assign-drill-memorize-test to patterns in which students inquire, discover, identify, classify, analyze, generalize, hypothesize, and predict consequences.

Teacher

WHAT SHOULD BE TAUGHT? HOW SHOULD IT BE TAUGHT?

Ninety-eight years ago the *Illinois State Register,* a Springfield, Illinois newspaper, strongly criticized the public schools on the grounds of unwarranted expenditures, too extended a curriculum, and general mismanagement. The newspaper called for a sweeping revision of curriculum:

> The only way to save the public school system from extirpation as a nuisance is to reform it. If the General Assembly will pass a bill restricting the studies in all public schools to the English branches, excluding all the singular flub-dubs and fribbles . . . it will be a grand reform.

The editor went on to charge that the high schools were "taxeating monopolies" and "instead of being schools to furnish all children a good common school education they are quasi-colleges, where dead and foreign languages are taught, and children are turned out expensive blockheads without even the rudiments of a common school education."[1]

The debate over curriculum has not subsided in over a century. Curriculum remains the one battlefield in education on which the most fundamental questions about the schools are repeatedly raised.

What is education for?
What kind of human beings and what kind of society do we want to produce?
What methods of instruction and classroom organization, as well as what subject matter, do we need to produce these results?
What knowledge is of most worth?

These are the questions which have often constituted the central concerns of men and women who have been in the vanguard of curriculum reform movements in this country. These are the issues which prompted the inclusion of curriculum revision as one of the priority concerns of Illinois' state educational agency.

The answers to these basic questions still seem inadequate. Educators continue to live with the uncomfortable realization that children today remember little of what they are taught and are taught much that is not worth knowing. Charles Silberman's sweeping indictment of contemporary curriculum is strikingly similar in tone to the charges lodged against education by the Springfield editor a century ago. In assessing the failures of educational reform, Silberman has made this observation in his book *Crisis in the Classroom:*

> The great bulk of students' time is still devoted to detail, most of it trivial, much of it factually incorrect, and almost all of it unrelated to any concept, structure, cognitive strategy, or indeed anything other than the lesson plan. It is rare to find anyone—teacher, principal, supervisor, or superintendent—who has asked why he is teaching what he is teaching.[2]

Historically, two contending and extreme ideals which have tended to obscure the true nature of the educator's mission have dominated the debate over curriculum. The one ideal has held that education is simply a question of "mastering" subject matter. The other has held that education is a process of meeting the "needs" of children. And, of course, this dualism, namely that schools must either be child-centered or subject-centered, inevitably influenced the curriculum—what students were taught and how they were taught. The ascendancy of one concept or the other invariably lead to dogmatic extremes in curriculum development which almost always left unanswered one central question: What is education for?

Educators have frequently had to choose between either a curriculum which was highly structured, traditional, and academic in character or a curriculum which, in its extreme form, was loose, *avant garde,* and of passing interest only. This either/or approach has frustrated reformers from Horace Mann to John Dewey. It was Dewey, who in exasperation, observed that the reformers of his time could "conceive of no alternative to adult dictation save child dictation." These contending forces, of course, are still very much in evidence. It is Silberman's position that in the 1960's subject matter was emphasized while the needs of individual children were ignored.

The question confronting educators is whether or not they are capable of interfering with this cycle; whether or not they can stop the pendulum from once again swinging convulsively in one direction or the other. It may be true that history is prologue, but educators' increased understanding of the learner and learning process and their more acute sense of what the future will demand will hopefully permit them to by-pass the mistakes which often have characterized past efforts at curriculum reform.

One of the obvious stumbling blocks of the past has been the notion that curriculum involves only the quantity of subject offerings—the development of skills and the teaching of facts through rather fixed and immutable course sequences. This traditional and one-dimensional concept of curriculum is gradually giving way to an expanded concept which places equal importance on the process of education. In other words, how a student learns and how a teacher teaches is just as important as what is learned and what is taught. Education will be revitalized when learning is equated with living and curriculum is recognized as the acquisition of skills plus the interaction of individuals.

Obviously a redefinition of curriculum does not begin to tell us what is or is not a good curriculum. Such judgments require new standards. In his enormously influential book, *The Process of Education,* Jerome Bruner has suggested a criterion for measuring the adequacy of a curriculum. The question educators ought to ask themselves, according to Bruner, is "whether, when fully developed, [the subject or material] is worth an adult's knowing, and whether having known it as a child makes a person a better adult. If the answer to both questions is negative or ambiguous, then the material is cluttering the curriculum."[3]

Bruner's formulation can be restated as follows: the curriculum of the future must permit a student to master the basic skills of reading, communication, and computation; it must provide him with a foundation of knowledge which will equip him to solve problems, to engage in continuous learning, and to adapt to the world of work and to a world of ever-accelerating change; it must facilitate the transfer of those values and habits consonant with responsible citizenship and essential for an appreciation of the cultural and racial diversity of this nation and the world beyond; and finally the curriculum must be able to adapt to the individual student's style and needs so as to bring out the very best that is in him. A curriculum or the elements of a curriculum, including teaching methods, which do not serve these ends should be shelved once and for all.

Most people would probably not disagree with this philosophical concept of the type of curriculum needed to produce the kind of young people society needs. The challenge quite frankly is to translate the rhetoric of curriculum reform and innovation into workable strategies which will effect not only the content of subjects taught but the methods by which they are taught.

The curriculum of the future must take into account more fully the potential for learning derived from the process of interaction between teacher and learner. While that interaction is a process which is not yet fully understood, it is more precisely understood today than a generation ago. It must take into account the nation's values and ideals, and, more importantly, the characteristics, lives, and personal social needs of young people. And, of course, the curriculum should reflect the fact that we live in a world where rapidly shifting social, cultural, and political conditions are likely to alter the mission of the schools and of those served by the schools. It is against all of these factors which today's curriculum must be judged, and that, as most people know, is not an easy task.

While the implications of this process for both learning and teaching has been a matter of inquiry and speculation for years, a point has been reached where ideas are beginning to take root and have an impact on curriculum design. For example, there is nothing wrong with a student knowing that the Boston Tea Party took place in Boston. Unfortunately, that fact, standing by itself, serves no useful purpose other than to equip a student to play more ably the examination game. It would be preferable to see students grasp the importance of the revolutionary period in relation to the total American experience and to the issues and ideas of our own time. For such understanding, a student needs to do more than memorize isolated and unrelated facts or events. Both the teacher and the student, in turn, need to understand what some people would call the fundamental structure of American History, or any other subject the schools choose to teach.

The role of structure is central to both useful learning and good teaching. We live in an age when the volume of our knowledge is multiplying at an incredible rate. And, therefore, the capacity of a student to use what is learned in the classroom and to bring that knowledge to bear on future problems and events both outside and inside the classroom will be conditioned by the extent to which he understands the fundamental structure of the subjects taught.

It is the mindless practice of pumping students full of facts about a subject rather than the general underlying principles of a subject which has excited the often heard charge that much of what is happening in our schools is irrelevant—especially when measured against the identifiable needs of students and the anticipated demands and uncertainties of the future. As Henry Adams once observed: "Nothing in education is so astonishing as the amount of ignorance it accumulates in the form of inert facts." So it is of the utmost importance that current efforts at curricular revision reflect the importance which attaches to structure.

Furthermore, in fashioning the curriculum, generous allowances must be made for our growing knowledge of how a child learns. The fact that the process of learning varies with each child is now supported by incontrovertible evidence. If educators truly believe in the educability of all children, as Jerome Bruner does, that "any subject can be taught effectively in some intellectually honest form to any child," then methods of teaching must increasingly make room for individualization. The subject matter embraced by a curriculum, regardless of its breadth and sophistication, does not lessen the need of most students to have educational programs tailored to their learning needs and their characteristics as learners. This applies not only to students who require special or remedial assistance, for individualization is equally useful to all students.

When educators talk about instructional methods, such as team teaching, individual pacing, independent study, modular scheduling, or schools without walls, they are referring to procedures which permit a teacher to give a student individual attention, which permit him to respond to a student's questions, to check his progress, and to offer him help. This is not to suggest that group-teaching is altogether inappropriate. There are numerous occasions when assembling and teaching students in different sized groups is highly desirable.

The establishment by the end of this decade of an individualized instruction curriculum within every school district in Illinois is one goal of the state educational agency. The validity of any future curriculum will depend, in large measure, on the degree to which the concept of individualization has taken root in teaching methods. If a student's mastery of a learning task is linked to objectives which are well-defined and measurable in relation to that single student, educators can begin to resurrect the joy derived from learning for the student, because mastery will mean that he can retain and use what he has studied and that his success will increase his motivation to learn, as well as enhance his belief in himself and his abilities.

Of course, the leap from philosophical concepts to actual implementation is a difficult one. Those two stages in curriculum planning are like two cliffs; many well-intended efforts at reform have fallen irretrievably into the gorge which divides them.

In Illinois all unit and discipline areas have developed materials in individualized instruction, and alternative models for curricular delivery systems have been established. These models are intended to assist local schools with planning, programming, definitions of goals and objectives, needs assessment, and evaluation. The supervisory duties of the Curriculum Development Section of the state office have been reorganized. The services of a curriculum specialist are being made available to all school districts in the state. The curriculum specialist is prepared to offer assistance in program planning, individualization of instruction, and curriculum design. Further, each school district will be able to utilize this specialist as a resource person. Also, the Instructional Services Section of the state superintendent's office has been restructured to provide services and materials for individual subject areas.

Flexibility is desperately needed in the area of instructional programs so that schools can serve both general and individual needs of students. Therefore, the new recognition and supervision standards, discussed in Chapter II, seek to relax those limitations which have inhibited the development of a broad academic program in the past. Wherever possible, specific time allotments for instruction have been removed. And, of course, individualization is encouraged, as are other specific areas of concern like vocational and career education programs.

Integrated with those provisions which list legislatively mandated curriculum offerings, are those areas not mandated but generally considered essential to a comprehensive and balanced curriculum: English, science, mathematics, foreign languages, vocational education, and the fine arts. By offering an expanded curriculum, the options available to students for purposes of meeting their individual needs will be increased. The state educational agency is also exploring with the General Assembly a number of proposals designed to relax the curricular mandates under which the schools presently operate, thus according districts even more flexibility to meet local needs.

The development of a new program known as the *Illinois Network for School Development* (INSD) will provide educators with a unique opportunity to test and refine some of the concepts related to curriculum developments. Although alternative schools, demonstration schools and renewal centers have produced many fine individual programs across the country, experience has shown that such programs have failed to achieve a new level of educational quality on a statewide basis. Some of these efforts have not focused on the entire educational process, and most have not generated any meaningful impact beyond the students directly involved in such efforts. The result has been short-lived programs helping only small numbers of children and having no enduring results.

The Illinois Network for School Development represents a unique device for combining state and local leadership resources to initiate carefully planned comprehensive educational improvements which in turn will be diffused into other schools within and surrounding local districts. In 1973, ten districts were chosen as the first affiliates of the Network and each was awarded a planning contract.

While INSD affiliates are not directed to undertake specific programs, considerable weight is given to proposals relating to individualized instruction, career education, program evaluation, and equal education opportunity programs. The potential for significant educational change is evidenced by the commitment of the affiliates to "impact," i.e., to develop specific methods and to spread proven practices to surrounding schools. By 1977, INSD is expected to have forty-five affiliate members. Together they will offer alternative models for improved educational programs to at least 117,000 students from prekindergarten through high school. Benefits of the network system will be extended to all Illinois school systems by providing them with complete information about successful new programs and techniques.

The Illinois Network for School Development has obvious implications for curriculum design. The program should help end the frustration regarding the value of innovation by showing that existing rather than new financial resources can be redirected to achieve educational renewal.[4]

What the state office does not want to do in this process is to create a curriculum which will be uniformly imposed on every school district. The purpose of the program is to strengthen the capacity of local districts in this area. Any curriculum must be adapted to local realities. There must be due regard for student populations and school settings which vary greatly from community to community.

Needless to say, the teacher has an integral role to play in this process. Some educators argue that curriculum design is not really important, that the educational enterprise stands or falls with the quality of the teacher because teaching goes on in individual classrooms, and it goes on regardless of curriculum organization or suggested course content. But again, this should not be treated as an either/or proposition.

To be sure, a good curriculum design alone does not insure that any teacher can achieve optimum results, but a poorly conceived curriculum design can hinder the talented and enterprising classroom practitioner. In short, both a sound curriculum organization and good teachers are needed, for only through the joining of these two components can the schools hope to extend a student's range of experience, help him understand the underlying structure of material, and dramatize the importance of what he is learning. Should curriculum reform proceed satisfactorily, a likely result may be the demand for more and better teachers.

Efforts to overhaul the system by which teachers and other professionals are prepared is intended to complement and reinforce curriculum revision. The traditional view of a teacher as a mere dispenser of knowledge must yield in favor of a new role in which the teacher is truly the director of learning experiences. Therefore, teacher preparation and curriculum design are two processes which must move ahead hand in hand. To refine one process and not the other is to undermine the quest for educational excellence.

Although most people understand that times are quickly changing, change for the sake of change makes no sense, and such impulses should be resisted by the public and the profession. The practice of embracing whatever is fashionable at the moment in the way of ideas should be discontinued. On the other hand, many people today, including many educators, are simply overwhelmed by the prospects of change. There is an impulse to strike out at it, to try to flee from it. Difficult as it may be to face, the fact remains that change is a constant and unalterable condition. Whether one is talking about schools without walls, modular scheduling, or team teaching, each innovation in education is an effort of sorts to keep pace with the changes relentlessly thrust upon society by shifting circumstances. That is why curriculum reform is so important. The challenge is to fashion a curriculum which will enable public education to impart more perfectly to young people what Alfred North Whitehead declared "is an intimate sense for the power of ideas; for the beauty of ideas, and for the structure of ideas, together with a particular body of knowledge which has peculiar reference to the life of the being possessing it." That is the task facing educators.

Most educators know that the schools often foster bad strategies, raise children's fears, and produce learning which is often fragmentary, distorted, and short-lived. John Holt is right when he says children fail because they are afraid, bored, and confused. The curriculum and some current approaches to teaching have tended to kill the natural curiosity and urge to learn of young people. In his book, *How Children Fail,* Holt summarizes the problem this way:

> We break down children's convictions that many things make sense. We do it, first of all, by breaking up life into arbitrary and disconnected hunks of subject matter, which we then try to "integrate" by artificial and irrelevant devices. . . . Furthermore, we continually confront them with what is senseless, ambiguous, and contradictory; worse, we do it without knowing that we are doing it, so that hearing nonsense shoved at them as if it were sense, they come to feel that the source of their confusion lies not in the material but in their own stupidity. Still further, we cut children off from their own common sense and the world of reality by requiring them to play with and shove around words and symbols that have little or no meaning to them. Thus we turn the vast majority of our students into the kind of people for whom all symbols are meaningless, who cannot use symbols as a way of learning about and dealing with

reality; who cannot understand written instructions; who, even if they read books, come out knowing no more than when they went in; who may have a few new words rattling around in their heads, but whose mental models of the world remain unchanged and, indeed, impervious to change.[5]

This criticism is much harsher than the prescription. A partial solution is to be found in a curriculum which can satisfy rather than stifle a child's curiosity, which permits a child to develop his abilities and talents, pursue his interest, and acquire from those who are around him, including adults, an appreciation for the variety and richness of life. That is what curriculum reform ought to be all about.

ETHNICITY AND EDUCATION

Social historians several hundred years from now will record that one of the two or three truly notable achievements of this era was the creation of a nation on the North American continent made up of widely diverse nationality groups. Perhaps they will note too that the American educational system in our time made a commitment to impart to students an understanding and appreciation for the cultural and racial diversity of the nation, and in so doing, reinforced each student's sense of self-worth and adequacy regardless of his race or national origin. We hope they will be able to say that once that commitment was made, the schools of this nation ended their traditional attempts of making children more American than their parents and of molding the descendents of immigrants into unhyphenated citizens.

The notion that somehow America was ever intended to be a vast melting pot will undoubtedly be dismissed by future historians as a curiosity of a by-gone age. Curious, too, will be the reaction of future generations which may stumble on Zangwill's play *The Melting Pot,* and read its memorable exhortation:

German and Frenchman, Irishman and Englishman, Jews and Russians—into the crucible with you all! God is making the American. . . . The real American has not yet arrived. He is only in the crucible. I tell you—he will be the fusion of all the races, the coming superman.[6]

Today, those lines evoke disbelief if not outright laughter. Most people would agree that any prediction of a grand amalgamation of peoples is, at best, pretentious fantasy. And yet despite the fact that the "melting pot" concept has been largely discredited, our schools persist in their efforts to assimilate the young, persist in compelling many students to believe that they are what they are not, and probably never can be. An educator of Italian descent, reflecting on his years in school, put it this way: "We were becoming Americans by learning how to be ashamed of our parents."

Such an attitude has no place in the schools. To deprecate, in the name of Americanization, a student's culture, or his language, or his history is to risk crushing his self-esteem and pride so as to affect his heart and mind for life.

America can be a multilingual and multicultural society, and be better and stronger for it. While the reasons are not entirely clear, the process of assimilation has gradually slowed down. The long-expected decline of ethnicity has not taken place as was predicted. Instead, emerging out of the peculiar experiences of life in America, recent years have witnessed an incredible burst of ethnic and racial pride. On balance, this development is a welcomed one, because it is in so many ways an outgrowth of the brutal racism and ethnocentricity which has made entry into the American mainstream a virtual impossibility for millions of people.

The person who believes that *he is somebody* need not view the future with trepidation. The schools have a responsibility to help young people discover who they themselves are and understand more perfectly who other people are. Although it is illusory to believe that the world will ever be free of prejudice and discrimination, the young who must face those harsh realities can be reinforced by equipping them to overcome mindless slurs and stereotypes.

If homogenization is out of the question, what then should the schools be striving for? The goal should be a nation of racial, ethnic, and religious diversity—what Kenneth Gipson calls "a mosaic of pluralism where each contributes what is unique, where each knows and honors his own roots and can, therefore, be secure enough to honor what is different in his neighbors." Judging people against ethnic standards which are essentially Anglo-Saxon in origin and placing some people on probation and excluding others from consideration altogether, are practices which are at long last yielding to a reborn appreciation of the unique racial and ethnic pluralism of America.

The schools can and must help students adapt to the reality of diversity. Ethnic studies have a place in the classroom for three basic reasons. First, ethnicity in America is important. Ethnicity has always been and is likely to remain one of the most pervasive influences in our politics and culture.

Second, America is just a small part of a racially, culturally, and linguistically diverse world, and that world is increasingly shrinking on account of population growth, urbanization, industrialization, and communication. Therefore, our existence on this planet may become utterly intolerable unless we rise to new levels of understanding about the human species. Adlai Stevenson once suggested that we ought to try to make the world safe for diversity. Can we afford to do anything less in our own society?

Finally, ethnic studies in the classroom can help reveal the *truth* to young people about themselves and others whose origins, customs and values may differ from their own. The pursuit of truth has always been one of the principal functions of education. However, if the multi-colored and multi-cultured children of this nation are not permitted to get to know one another as individuals, then mythology will surely triumph over truth. To be ignorant of what makes people both similar and different is to invite the predictable penalties of living in an uneducated society. The distorted treatment accorded our minorities and their place and contributions to this country's development is well documented. Such insensitivity has helped create and perpetuate myths, and a myth, perhaps more than the deliberate and contrived lie, is the greatest enemy of truth.

An Ethnic Studies Section has been established within Illinois' Office of Education. It is developing curriculum and instructional materials designed to foster an intellectual and emotional acceptance by young people of diversity and the growing interdependence of mankind. The objective is to heighten every student's perception of his place and his relationship with others in the scheme of things.

Anything which would serve to enhance ethnocentricity or the polarization of American society must be avoided. The critics charge that ethnic studies will only divide us further, but what the critics fail to recognize is that ethnicity is not only a fact of life in this country, but, in all probability, a permanent condition.

Many of the so-called failures of education stem from our inability to accept and come to grips with diversity. Many teachers, particularly those who are suddenly thrust into urban settings, are intimidated by students who are Afro-American, Mexican-American, Puerto Rican, Appalachian, and poor, because they simply do not know how to cope with products of the culture of poverty. In the suburbs, the experience is often equally excruciating because of the spinoffs generated by affluence—the drug-culture and the counter-culture.

Much of the chaos attributed to inner-city schools is rooted in the difficulties historically associated with intercultural communication. That condition is frequently exacerbated by teachers and administrators who do not understand these cross-currents, and whose behavior is interpreted, often mistakenly, as insulting, hostile, autocratic, and sometimes racist. Obviously offerings in Afro-History will not remedy this situation alone, but the emerging interest in ethnic studies ought to be a factor spurring us on to reform our teacher preparation programs. Training in pedagogy, subject matter, history, philosophy, and psychology of education constitutes the whole of most teacher preparation programs. Clearly more is required if teachers are to communicate effectively with students and if they are to succeed in raising the level of communication among students of differing racial and ethnic backgrounds. Today's teacher desperately needs:

> an acquaintance with culture, that system of commonly communicated behaviors, beliefs, and values which exist in all social groups. When teachers are assigned to work in situations which involve them with people culturally different from themselves, they should be selected with an eye to their suitability for work in the culture or cultures which they will be engaged. They should be taught to speak and understand the language of their students, when and where that is necessary, and thoroughly trained in the culture of the community in which they will serve.[7]

Although it is possible that the current demand for ethnic studies will soon dissipate, there is more reason to suspect that the demand will continue. In any event, its implications for teacher training and educational research are rather obvious. Clearly, more and better ethnographic studies are needed. Such data can help teachers as well as students understand "that behind all the apparent confusion and disorganization of human behavior there is order, . . . that any culture can be understood because it is at bottom both orderly and systematic."[8]

ART AND EDUCATION

We live in an urban age thrust upon us by science and technology. It is an age marked by incredible movements of people. No migration in our history can compare with the movement since 1940 of thirty-one million people from farm to city.

These people, most of whom were poor (the blacks of Mississippi, the whites of Appalachia, the Mexicans of Texas, the Indians of the Dakotas) have sought no more than a better life for themselves and their children a share of the American dream, a share of her abundance.

For too many, these legitimate aspirations are being denied. The ugly fact that easily one-fifth of our population is ill-housed, ill-fed, and poorly educated is some measure of society's failure. And for these people, the city is really their final refuge. There is no place else for them to go.

Of course, the perils of the age touch all of our lives. Crime rates rise; schools fail; water is polluted; and the very air we breathe is contaminated. But for millions—especially the poor and the powerless—life has become a constant struggle to survive, a precarious existence devoid of the meaning, beauty, and the happiness all cherish.

The child caught up in this urban milieu cannot help but feel anonymous, lonely and confused. He cannot help but feel bewildered and resentful of those forces dividing blacks and whites, the poor and the rich, the old and the young. Gone is an essential sense of community, that age-old need to depend on one another.

And in this age of plenty, any child's unfulfilled expectations can only excite new frustrations and anxieties. This is especially true of the poor urban child, for while he can see and touch those visible manifestations of the good life, he learns at an early age that he may never enjoy them himself. Those who try to escape this tedium and fail frequently turn to violence or temporary palliatives like drugs.

This process of dehumanization does not end here, for the disadvantaged child—be he black, brown, or red—is constantly reminded that his heritage, culture and language (those few things which are his alone) are inferior and, thus, unacceptable. Because what he is is not an object of pride but of shame and opprobrium, he often tries by adapting to the dominant culture to become what he can never be. This perhaps is the most tragic aspect of his dehumanization.

We are witnessing across this country, not only in our cities, what Walter Lippman has called a "disintegration of hope." Is there still a moral commitment in America to equal opportunity and the eradication of poverty? Such a commitment requires that our vast technology be used to promote human interests, needs, values, and principles. It means that all of our institutions, public and private, must seek new answers to old and persistent problems, and engage in self-renewal. Nowhere is the need for self-renewal more pressing than within the educational community itself.

The objective must be to educate every child to the limit of his capacity. This will require that education become less de-personalized, and more humanistic by applying values to knowledge and releasing the creativity too often stifled in the classroom.

Society's preoccupation, even in education, with money and things must yield to a renewed emphasis on the importance of man, his nature, and his central place in the universe. Teaching a child that all persons, including himself, have dignity and worth is as important as training the intellect.

As described by Alfred North Whitehead: "There is only one subject matter for education, and that is life in all its manifestations. Instead of this single unity", he continues, "we offer our children algebra, from which nothing follows; science from which nothing follows; a couple of languages, never mastered; and lastly, most dreary of all, literature represented by plays of Shakespeare with philological notes and short analyses of plot and character to be in substance committed to memory."

It is this sort of de-personalization which has made the pursuit of excellence in education so difficult and has hindered the unleashing of our children's more creative and more human instincts. It is this approach to education which has helped nourish the divisiveness and despair of our urban era.

It is time for an educational renaissance in this country; the arts can play an integral role in this process. Literature, drama, music, dance and the visual and applied arts can help young people to relate to one another and to the world around them. "The arts", as President Nixon recently noted, "have the rare capacity to help heal divisions among our own people and to vault some of the barriers that divide the world."

If the arts are so valuable a medium, recognition of the fact is not enough; implementation is needed. Perhaps what is needed will be made clearer by a discussion of what is not needed. For instance, a program that asks no more of a child than that he make holiday decorations by coloring-in the mimeographed lines of a turkey, rabbit or Santa Claus, or a program that permits only brief encounters with the arts (museums, the symphony orchestra, and theaters) can give no genuine understanding of the arts. What is needed is direct experience involving the use of artistic media.

It should concern us that some black children still paint their self-portraits in pink or white and depict landscapes and houses which are clearly suburban, upper middle class. An art program that fails so completely in enhancing self-identity and self-confidence is not a worthwhile program. The arts, indeed the entire curriculum, must do much more if there is to be a renaissance in education.

For the student, art can be a way of realizing self-actualization, of proving to himself that "I exist," that "I am capable of creating," that "I have worth." Farmers can more easily experience self-actualization than an inner-city dweller, and therefore it is in cities that children desperately need opportunities for productive action, opportunities to feel the satisfaction derived from achievement. City children must learn that they too can be creative persons capable of reaching out to others, sharing with others, and influencing others.

The child must be stimulated to think about himself and other selves and things and experiences and to say something about all this in a way no one else can do it. Because of its emphasis on creativity, self-expression, perception and awareness, art can give children opportunities to become inventive, searching and daring.

The arts can and must be a medium for developing a healthy self-concept. Like a heavy fog, a sense of inferiority and helplessness has seeped into the lives of too many children. The youngster who cannot believe in himself or his people will not be able to relate well to others, a phenomenon which has serious implications for society.

The traditional emphasis on Western art must give way to the growing consciousness within the Black, Indian, and Spanish-speaking communities. This consciousness should be reinforced and augmented to make the inner-city child aware of the contributions to art made by his people and its importance to the total community. Pride and self-respect can be a powerful antidote in an environment which conspires against a disadvantaged child's desire to learn and get ahead.

And finally, keep in mind Bernard Shaw's observation that next to torture, art persuades fastest. That is a fact which should not be forgotten. A child's simple picture frequently describes more eloquently his condition and his innermost feelings than any words he might have at his command. Art can be a medium of communication between those who have so much and those who have too little. It can prick the collective conscience of society and rouse it to action. The wall paintings and murals seen increasingly in the inner-city are hardly instances of art for art's sake. Beyond their aesthetic value, one is struck by their social, economic and even political overtones. They are powerful statements by people who for too long have been powerless. They represent a call for action; a silent, but eloquent, protest against racism and bigotry; a protest against hunger and all those conditions which rob life of hope and vitality, and a warning, too, of impending crisis should promises go unfulfilled.

Some may argue that it is inappropriate for schools to kindle social consciousness and political awareness. I do not agree with this view. The artistic expressions of the inner-city·(and all disadvantaged) should be encouraged. They ought to be enshrined in museums, art galleries, and public buildings across this land as a reminder that this nation has a rendezvous to keep with those who are disadvantaged, poor, or handicapped. As Robert Henri recently wrote in his book *The Art Spirit,* "where those who are not artists are trying to close the book, the artist opens it, shows there are still more pages possible." An art program must be designed to give a child in an urban setting an opportunity to realize self-actualization, to improve self-concept, and to develop a social consciousness. And in so far as it is possible, these same objectives should be supported not only by the arts, but by the total curriculum, and by extracurricular activities, too.

Experimentation is essential. "The artist in the school" program should be fully developed. An artist in residence can explore creative ideas and alternative approaches with students, including the origins and contributions to art made by the students' own community. This program allows professional artists to come into our schools to share with students their skills and perspectives on life. And there are benefits for the artist, too. Arthur Mitchell, the founder of the Dance Theater of Harlem, has noted: "I love working with kids, and every time I work with them I learn more. Through teaching I'm also learning and growing . . . it enhances my dancing (and) makes me much more aware."

More must be done to help the classroom teacher who all too frequently is not self-confident himself. He should not be expected to be an art expert with one or two college level courses. But he should be expected to establish a non-threatening environment so that art can happen. Curriculum guides have been too general and ambiguous to be useful for the classroom teacher. In Illinois efforts are underway to make the guides more practical; new and creative art instructional materials are being prepared for the classroom teacher. The task is to back up the classroom teacher with specialists and with in-service training—to impart knowledge which will permit him to be more creative and enable him to assist that second grade child to paint himself black, red, yellow, brown or white, the color he is and wants to be.

The John D. Rockefeller 3rd Fund has made grants totalling $346,000 to a pilot project in University City, Missouri, to prove that the arts can be integrated into a school system from top to bottom. The goal: to involve all the children of this community in all of the arts: dance, theater, drawing, music, architecture and all the rest. English, social studies, and the language arts have become vehicles for heightening student interest and involvement in the arts. Central to the program are rich resources provided by museums, orchestras, theater and dance companies.

In one unit, "Redesigning the Community," students worked with architects in planning a large playground complex. They served as actual clients in deciding about costs, construction, and site. Today the recreation area stands, the result of student exchanges with architects and builders. There is no question that such experiences can have a profound and positive impact on the personal development of young people.

In May 1971, the state education office unveiled in Washington, D.C. an art exhibit, consisting of 125 works submitted by students at more than ninety public and private agencies. The artists in this case suffered from mental retardation, emotional disturbances, or physical handicaps like blindness and deafness. One discovers from their art that despite their disabilities, these kids are just kids; they love ponies, ice cream, dogs, story books and painting brightly colored pictures. They enjoy forming, changing, manipulating, controlling—in short, calling the shots on their own creative productions.

In many ways they are not unlike the youngsters in our inner-cities. Art is and must increasingly become a media which allows young people the total freedom of expression. It gives them the ability to say things they could never otherwise say, and each one has something important to say. Art is a means of drawing attention to the problems of these youngsters, a way of showing that they have creative talent just as other children do. When they are finished, they have something they alone created. They have become what we desire all our children to become: contributing members of society.

There is a lesson in all of this for educators and concerned citizens. To develop the capacity of every child to learn to the fullest extent of his ability, we must seek to meet his individual needs. We are only now beginning to understand the limitless potential of the arts for meeting those needs.

VOCATIONAL AND CAREER EDUCATION

Increasingly one hears the complaint that the schools are failing to prepare young people for a productive life, that after four years of high school few students have a marketable skill, and that at best high school graduates have been prepared for college where they will get more of the same. There is substance to this charge.

The problem, of course, is an historical one. In the nineteenth

century, and for a large part of the present century, the schools
were intended to satisfy the insatiable needs of a burgeoning industrial society. However, in recent decades, the elementary and
secondary schools of this nation have been marching to a different
drummer. Until very recently, over eighty percent of the students
enrolled in high schools were participating in either college pre-
paratory or general education programs to ready them for college.
This pattern has persisted in large measure despite the fact that in
the decade of the 1970's less than twenty percent of available jobs
will require a college degree. Is it not reasonable to conclude that
when eighty percent of our students are getting ready to do what
only twenty percent will do, something is seriously wrong with
American education?

This anomoly is seen in the fact that more and more Ph.D.'s are
out of work simply because there are so many Ph.D.'s being churned
out by colleges and universities. These same individuals, now in
surplus, are being forced to turn back to a world for which their
academic training has not prepared them. The fact that teacher
preparation institutions in Illinois alone turned out in 1971-72
more prospective teachers than there were teaching vacancies in
the entire nation suggests that there is much to learn about the
planned use of human resources.

It would appear, at least on the surface, that educational development in this country has proceeded in a vacuum. There is little
recognition that we now live in a post-industrial society where
the production of services is increasingly outweighing the production of goods. The need for unskilled labor is disappearing. If
people are going to need special skills in order to be productive,
the schools must become an instrument for the acquisition of those
skills. Too many students see no relationship between what they
are being asked to learn in school and what they will someday do
to earn a living. This realization becomes all the more acute when
one considers the 750,000 high school students who drop out annually and the hundreds of thousands of students who, though
they survive school, do not know why they are there.

The issue is whether or not the schools are capable of preparing
students to live a life as well as earn a living; there is little choice.
The future economic well-being of the nation and of those whoare
enrolled in school argues for a change in educational orientation.
By 1975 one-quarter of the nation's population, ages 16 to 25, is

expected to flood the job market; what responsibility do the schools have to insure that the entry of young people into the world of work is successful and personally satisfying? First, the schools, in addition to providing education for personal enrichment and fulfillment, should be responsible for preparation and career guidance of every student, regardless of a student's ability, life-style, and occupational inclination. Second, the schools should offer career training programs specific enough to meet the needs of students seeking jobs following or during high school and broad enough to match the wide range of the interests and abilities of young people seeking post-secondary education. When one surveys developments across the country, it is clear that expectations for career education have little relationship to what is actually happening in the schools.

The challenge, quite frankly, is to dispel the popular but mistaken notion that career and vocational education is the exclusive province of dull and unexcelling students. Once that is done, it will be much easier to garner greater resources and public support for work study programs, vocational schools, and training for dropouts. All graduating high school seniors should possess a salable skill whether they are college bound or not, but that will not begin to happen until basic education and career education are bound together to form a unity. In Illinois, this integrative process has been difficult to achieve because the actual administration of vocational programs has been performed for years by an agency which operates largely independent of the state office of education. Such organization has helped foster the prevailing attitude that vocational education is demeaning and reserved for the unpromising student.

One of the objectives of the state office is to provide by 1975 occupational information for elementary school pupils and career education programs for all students in high school, post-secondary schools, and four-year institutions. The state educational agency hopes to achieve this objective by taking three basic steps. First, vocational education is being broadened in each institution by developing a sequential career education concept which includes career awareness, exploration, orientation, and preparation. Second, instructional materials related to the teaching and enrichment of career education programs are being developed and made available through local and regional media centers. Third, comprehensive career education programs are being developed at all institutions, through joint agreements with other public and private institutions, participation in area vocational centers, or the development of self-contained programs.

Exposure to the world of work cannot take place too early in the life of a young student. If authorities on developmental guidance are correct in their assertions that career development begins in childhood, then clearly occupational experiences are as essential to elementary school children as they are to high school and post-high school youth. Such programs can help youngsters at an early age discover their talents and interests and relate them to the world of work. Occupational experience-oriented activities, however, can and should be integrated into a school's regular curriculum. Some schools in Illinois are using a multi-media approach to present occupational information in the elementary schools.

Much of the present enthusiasm and impetus for career education has been stimulated by the United States Office of Education. The federal government is prepared to spend millions of dollars on career education experiments. A large share of these funds is destined for the nation's community colleges on the condition that they adopt as their overriding mission the preparation of students for useful employment. The Office of Education has not only succeeded in stimulating a national dialog about career education, but it is developing models that can be tested and validated for adaptation or installation in schools and adult training centers. It is extending exemplary projects already operating under state plans. And it is developing K-14 instructional programs for fifteen broad career clusters, from construction to public service, that represent the more than 20,000 career options available in this country.

One cannot disagree with the appropriateness of these activities. Unfortunately, in education, as in other fields of human endeavor, enthusiasms easily come and go. Very often well-intentioned strategies are suddenly abandoned because certain variables and dangers were not anticipated and dealt with in advance. This could prove to be the case with vocational education. What are some of these variables and dangers?

Vocational programs and funds must have a strong positive correlation with projected manpower demands. If educators are left to the mercy of an economy which cannot be accurately read and interpreted, then vocational education could become a perilous venture. The business community and the government must find ways to project employee needs. There is one indisputable economic trend: employment increases in goods-producing industries are becoming marginal while other sectors of the economy are absorbing a larger share of the available and employable labor force—our society is moving from a goods-producing to a service-producing economy. Vocational programs must reflect the change.

Current data, however, reveal that the forces of supply and demand are not sufficiently influencing the outputs of vocational programs. For example, in Illinois in 1972, 62.4 percent of the vocational education output was in bookkeepers, secretaries, stenographers, typists, auto mechanics, body and fender repairmen, metal workers, carpenters, other craftsmen and farm workers. However, the anticipated labor market demand for this group was only 23.6 percent of total demand. In the actual distribution of federal and state vocational funds, eight-two percent is provided to local schools for applied biological, agricultural, business, marketing, management, and industrial oriented occupational clusters. Only eighteen percent is expended for health, personal and public service occupations. This allocation is in conflict with projected labor demand, and unless a shift in emphasis takes place the future value of vocational programs will remain in doubt.

New concepts and directions are needed for both in-service and pre-service education for occupational administrators and instructors. Data collected in Illinois suggest that a large number of teachers and counselors do not satisfy the minimum 2,000 hours occupational experience mandated by the state. In fact, a significant percentage of these professionals appear to have limited, if not insignificant, occupational experience. Clearly there is a need to review certification standards to insure that talented craftsmen and other experts are not arbitrarily prohibited from providing high quality vocational programs.

The continued segregation of women in vocational education programs is also a concern. Career programs, as they operate today, tend to promote the traditional concept of the woman's role in the world of work, and, thereby, contribute to the continuing sexual discrimination in the occupations. The success of vocational education will depend to a very large extent on the degree to which we come to grips with this discrimination. Keep in mind that nine out of ten women will work at some time in their lives. About thirty-two million women are in the labor force; they constitute thirty-eight percent of all workers. Women compose three percent of the craftsmen, seventeen percent of the managers, forty percent of the professional workers, fifty-seven percent of the service workers, sixty-one percent of the retail sales workers, seventy-six percent of the clerical workers and ninety-seven percent of the private household workers. Unfortunately, women workers are concentrated in low-paying, deadend jobs. Vocational education, if properly conceived, can help break down this cycle and the disparities between men and women with respect to income levels and employment opportunities.

Finally, it should be observed that vocational education ought to be viewed not as an end in itself, but as one of several ways by which young people can develop personal meaning. There has been so much talk in recent years about the erosion of the "work ethic" in America that one gets the uncomfortable feeling that the promoters of vocational education are motivated by a thinly disguised politics. To conceive of the schools as places which blindly and efficiently supply workers for the private sector would be a serious mistake. What happens or does not happen in the schools should not be solely determined by corporate America, with its emphasis on high productivity, large scale organizations, automation, spiraling wages, and technology. American society cannot afford to promote status and financial power at the expense of the arts and the humanities. To fashion the curriculum, including vocational offerings, in the belief that young people are only achievement-driven and security-conscious is to close our eyes to the pervasive influence of contemporary social realities in American life. Many young people are not concerned about earning an abundance of money. Others are challenging the moral validity of an expanding economy which desecrates the environment and dehumanizes its workers. So while it is important that the educational system provide every student with opportunities in training for the world of work, this task should not be approached uncritically.

SOME THOUGHTS ON PRIVATE BUSINESS AND VOCATIONAL SCHOOLS

Related to the issue of career education is the existence in this country of more than 7,000 proprietary vocational schools. Only a small minority of the students attending such schools can rely upon their parents or personal savings to pay for their entire schooling. Therefore, most students work full or part time to finance educational costs. The clientele is incredibly varied. There are high school dropouts with no occupational training and high school graduates who lack any specific preparation for employment. Others are preparing for a licensable occupation. Some students are college dropouts or even college graduates, who desire an otherwise unavailable course such as computer programming. And finally there are those thousands of persons who while they have several years of employment experience are either currently unemployed or finding it difficult, for physical reasons, to remain in their present occupations.

When one considers employment forecasts for the remainder of this decade, and particularly the estimate that the demand for technical workers will increase by about forty-five percent in this decade, it is clear that proprietary schools can play a unique role in meeting national manpower needs. And the success ratio is astounding: of the more than 1.5 million students participating in such programs nationwide, seventy percent complete their training as compared with only thirty to forty percent of community college entrants and sixty percent of college entrants.[9]

In Illinois more than 500,000 persons are enrolled in private business, vocational, and technical schools. The attractiveness of these schools is, in large measure, attributable to their ability to respond quickly to changes in the manpower needs of local business and industry. They offer a wide variety of courses in practically every imaginable occupation category—about 1500 separate courses. Because these schools are not encumbered with red tape and interminable procedural delays, they are uniquely equipped to tailor courses quickly to meet the needs of non-English-speaking students and handicapped students. Generally, marginal students who have never experienced academic successes can proceed at their own pace and successfully complete courses aimed at developing practical techniques rather than theoretical knowledge.

At a time when a great deal is being said and written about the need for diversity in American education, the growth of proprietary education should be encouraged. Historically, however, private business and technical schools have constituted part of the educational periphery; they have been neglected and their contributions have gone unrecognized. There is both room for and a need for many kinds of educational institutions in this country. Proprietary schools, by virtue of the valuable services they provide, must be increasingly viewed as an integral part of the educational system.

Proprietary schools obviously represent a gigantic business venture. In Illinois alone, thirty million dollars are spent annually by students in such schools. Until very recently, the licensing of proprietary programs was perfunctory; it amounted to granting a permit to do business in a given state. Licensing signified that safety and minimal commercial standards had been met; however, it was not necessarily an endorsement of the educational content of programs. Those who have responsibility for licensing proprietary schools have had to re-examine this *laissez-faire* relationship. In Illinois the state educational agency has had to initiate legal proceedings against some schools which have refused to upgrade business practices and programs. It has had to issue rules and regulations to protect innocent citizens; these rules and regulations have become a model for the nation.

While proprietary schools have a significant role to play in providing opportunities for continuing and career education, there can be no room for unscrupulous practices which serve to victimize and cheat good citizens. Regulation is not intended to intimidate the industry. Even the reputable schools realize that it is in their own self-interest to clean house.

One area of concern is deceptive or fraudulent advertising. For example, because out-of-state schools have not indicated their locations in the past, students have often been misled into believing that training was available in their own communities, even though the school might be 1,000 miles away. Advertisements must now reveal the actual location of a school. In addition, they may not guarantee a prospective student a job upon completion of a course.

Pursuant to the Illinois regulations, contracts have been simplified and clearly labeled. Students now know what they are signing and are less likely to be misled. And in the interest of equity, proprietary schools operating within Illinois have been compelled to overhaul their refund policies. It was not unusual in 1970 for students who signed contracts, but withdrew before the start of classes, to be held liable for as much as twenty-five percent of the total tuition. Now if a student withdraws within five days of entering into a contract, regardless of whether or not classes have commenced, the school may not keep more than twenty-five dollars. For the student, savings may amount to more than $800.00.

Proprietary schools are now also more accountable for their physical plant and equipment. They must submit annually building inspection reports, proof of liability insurance, floor plans, and inventories of equipment. This is all intended to protect consumers from back-room operations which are more concerned with the fast-buck than providing quality educational programs and services. In addition, placement and curriculum lists are submitted to the state office of education to determine the relevance and need for program offerings. This procedure has permitted the state office to weed out needless courses, with the result that students are spared the disappointment of having completed a course at great personal expense and then discovering that for their acquired skills there is no market.

The regulations have had a salutary effect on upgrading the proprietary school industry. In the area of student refunds alone, students are recovering several thousand dollars a month. The severity and number of complaints from citizens have been reduced. And although the state is not in the business of closing schools, some of the more questionable and valueless schools have simply ceased operations. At least sixty to seventy schools in 1971-72.

Nationally, the situation is complicated by the fact that sixteen states have no regulations at all regarding proprietary schools. Therefore, several states have begun exploring the need to work toward uniformity of laws, regulations and contracts pertaining to the operation of private business and technical schools. Recently Minnesota and Illinois entered into a bi-state compact. The provisions of the compact—the first of its kind—call upon the two states to mutually strive for uniform legislation and rules and regulations with respect to proprietary schools. Other states have shown an interest. in participating in such inter-state agreements. Such agreements will help facilitate the joint recognition of schools and the inter-state resolution of complaints and conflicts.

Proprietary education is a growth field. The emergence of high quality private trade and technical schools in the country is welcomed. That growth, however, should be controlled to the extent that the consumers of such programs are assured of receiving a reasonable ratio of quality service for every dollar spent. Educators and public officials who dismiss proprietary education are simply not aware of its potential for meeting special educational needs. It is providing new opportunities for thousands of people and filling a void regrettably left by too many public schools.

EARLY CHILDHOOD EDUCATION

> Nobody starts off stupid. You have only to watch babies
> and infants, and think seriously about what all of them
> learn and do, to see that, except for the most grossly re-
> tarded, they show a style of life, and a desire and ability to
> learn that in an older person we might well call genius.
> Hardly an adult in a thousand, or ten thousand, could in
> any three years of his life learn as much, grow as much in
> his understanding of the world around him, as every
> infant learns and grows in his first three years.[10]

This observation of John Holt is pertinent to the growing controversy over the provision of early educational experiences for children
age five and under. Our increased understanding of the rate of
intellectual development of young children has added an element
of urgency to this debate. It has been estimated that fifty percent
of a 17 year old's intellectual development takes place between
birth and age 5, thirty percent between ages 4 and 8, and about
twenty percent ages 8 and 17. What this signifies, of course, is
that the single greatest increment of growth takes place before a
youngster ever steps into a classroom. In theory at least, pre-school
education may be as important, if not more important, than four
years in college. The question then is whether early childhood
education programs should be promoted, and if so, why?

Support for primary education is not new. It has been encouraged
by educational theorists since the 16th century: Martin Luther,
Comenius, Rousseau, Montessori, Piaget, Hunt, and Bloom. The
names span centuries and all have emphasized the importance of
a child's early years in relation to his future success.

Early childhood education does not imply a closed and structured
classroom but rather an environment in which children have an
opportunity to acquire the skills needed to cope with the world in
which they live. This requires experiences which will enable pre-
schoolers to meet and fulfill their immediate developmental need
as well as help them make sense out of these experiences. It requires
experiences which will help youngsters acquire in their formative
years a sense of self-worth.

At best, growing up is neither simple nor easy. And the modern
world has complicated that process at the same time it has expanded

opportunities for the individual. In his early years, a child needs to begin to broaden his world, needs group relationships so that he can develop social skills, and needs stimulating and enriching experiences so that his potential can be developed and used most fully. Because the early years are the most malleable ones, this period represents an opportunity to either enhance or inhibit a child's optimum development. If nothing else, pre-schoolers could benefit from an early assessment of learning problems, and this is especially true in regard to handicapped children.

Much of the impetus for the present debate over early childhood programs is to be found in society's concern with either the welfare problem or the shifting role of women in society. Each year, an increasing number of women who are mothers of pre-school age youngsters and public aid recipients are seeking either employment or special training. Others are rebelling against the traditional role of homemaker, because it is stultifying and unrewarding. For purposes of this discussion what is important to keep in mind is that an increasing number of women are veering away from their traditional roles, and they are doing so for a multitude of reasons. So while some may argue for tradition and the sanctity of the home, the demand for day care programs is growing while the debate continues over whether or not day care should be expanded.

It is no longer realistic not to provide for the needs of children under five. It is also unrealistic to hope that family structures, as we may have known them in childhood, will reemerge any time soon. It is equally unrealistic to withhold day care programs from families in the belief that such familial structures will necessarily reappear. What is realistic is an honest assessment of emerging trends in American society and planned programs to meet those needs.

Those needs are obviously being inadequately met at the moment. For example, the number of day care facilities in Illinois increased sixty-three percent between 1966 and 1971. However, only 70,540 children or six percent of the state's children age 5 and under, were being served by such programs. However, more critical is the absence within most of these programs (most of which are privately operated and licensed by the state) of any redeeming educational content. Less than five percent of the country's fourteen million youngsters in the 1 to 5-1/2 year age bracket are enrolled in day programs, and a very small percentage of those programs are developmental in nature. A proliferation of day care programs which are merely custodial and caretaking operations is not needed.

Should day care programs be child development oriented and perhaps school-centered? During the Congressional deliberations on the Comprehensive Child Care Act of 1971, much of the debate centered around the merits and dangers of "universal day care." Of serious concern was the suggestion that early childhood or pre-school education be provided like other educational programs, through the present school system. Opponents of this proposal have countered that pre-school education, if provided in this manner, would simply become prey to the severe inadequacies of the present school system, with the result that a child's potential for development may be even further stunted. On the other hand, some child development experts have argued that such a scheme might just have the opposite effect. That is, early childhood education and child development oriented learning could influence and serve to upgrade the curricula of kindergarten and first grade programs.

Although the Comprehensive Child Care Act was vetoed by President Nixon, the debate over child development programs is not expected to subside but rather to intensify. Educators should be experimenting more with school administered child care programs to determine their efficacy. California provides a notable example of day care services provided in conjunction with school programs. They are provided through a system of "center programs" for children two through four years of age. Presently care is being provided for more than 30,000 children. In addition, the California Department of Education has adopted a proposal which provides for a statewide, voluntary system of education for four year olds. The goal of this program is to restructure primary education for all of California's public school children.

Aside from philosophical considerations, the cost of providing comprehensive developmental programs for pre-schoolers would seem to be prohibitive, and at the moment, given the inadequacies of school finance systems in this country, the costs would clearly be staggering. Instead of taking preliminary steps now to pave the way for the eventual establishment of early childhood programs, planning in this area should be long-range and include at least the following basic elements:

1. To establish cooperative working arrangements among state departments of education, institutions of higher education, and other agencies to formulate models for prekindergarten curriculum and parent education programs;
2. To institutionalize pre-service training and in-service retraining of teachers and aides for prekindergarten programs;
3. To formulate and disseminate to local school districts models for prekindergarten education curriculum;
4. To establish parent education and counseling programs in every school district offering early childhood education;
5. To provide in every school district by the end of the decade a voluntary prekindergarten program for children ages 3 and 4;
6. To screen and diagnose every pre-school child for learning disabilities.

Illinois, as noted earlier, has taken an important first step in the direction of institutionalizing early childhood programs by mandating such services for all handicapped children ages 3 and 4.

Participation in prekindergarten programs should be voluntary. The overriding aims of such programs should be to strengthen the family as the primary source for the development and education of young children and to help parents meet the special needs arising from their role. Early childhood programs can assist them in understanding the process of child growth and development. It is not enough that parents become merely the recipients of information; they must be involved in the planning, implementation, and evaluation of programs. Only in this way can educators hope that home and school will reinforce one another. Child development services must supplement, not supplant, the home environment.

What then should be the objectives of prekindergarten programs? The objective, to repeat an earlier point, should be something more than cutting welfare costs. Such programs can help rescue youngsters from the effects of affluence and isolation, as well as poverty and neglect. As the 1971 Forum on Developmental Child Care Services of the White House Conference on Children stated in its report to the President: "The members and delegates of this forum are shocked at the lack of national concern over the critical developmental needs of children. We urge the recognition of day care as a developmental service with tremendous potential for positively influencing and strengthening the lives of children and families, and we urge the eradication of day care as only a custodial, 'baby-sitting service'." The value of prekindergarten programs is to be found in their ability to enhance socialization and school readiness. They can help develop motivational systems and learning, language, and physical skills. And they also can help to heighten self-expression and aesthetic appreciation.

Socialization simply means learning to live within a large group of individuals of approximately the same age. This often is a much different process than living in a family group where the age differences tend to form a hierarchical system of authority. A prekindergarten program, on the other hand, can provide a child with an opportunity to learn to associate with others who have the same wants, needs and desires as he has. He learns that often he must vie for the attention of significant adults and that he is held personally accountable for his own actions. He also learns to anticipate the results of these actions before he produces them. And although recognition and respect must be given to the uniqueness of each child in such programs, a child begins to learn to respect the rights and privileges of others.

General school readiness involves, among other things, a child's learning how to become a cooperating member of the group. He learns the authority structure of the group and his position within this structure; how to be receptive to instruction; skills of manipulation, verbal skills, motor skills and attending (listening) skills; and various symbol systems of the group.

Because the value system of the group and those of the adult culture are new to the young child, he has an opportunity in a school setting to learn what it is that the group culture really values. He learns the value of cooperation as opposed to aggression, respect for the individual, and the necessity for a modicum of conformity.

The child needs opportunities to learn how to organize his knowledge. Of course, he has been learning since birth, but typically little effort has been made to assist him in organizing what he has learned, thus, his learning has been fragmented. If properly conceived, developmental programs can enable him to build concepts and generalizations which incorporate many specific learnings. He learns how to draw conclusions and how to evaluate what he experiences and learns.

Another learning skill often overlooked is the skill of working and learning within a group. Even advocates of individualized instruction are forced to admit that the child will not always have the benefit of a one-to-one relationship with an adult tutor and that the child must learn to work by himself or within a group for time periods within the day.

Children differ in their ability to speak and even to listen. For some children much training is needed to fill the gaps in these learnings. Other children need to learn the standard American dialect which is the accepted language of the educational community. Prekindergarten programs can facilitate the acquisition of basic language skills. There are many media of self expression, and the young child should become familiar with the variety of means open to him. These media may include: oral and written language; arts and crafts; music and rhythm; and the newer mechanical devices like the tape recorder and loud speaker. The child needs experiences in the variety of content of self-expression as well as experiences through which he will learn the effectiveness of the different forms of communication for him personally and for the type of message he expresses.

It is one thing to be involved in creating things through the arts but quite another to learn to become receptive to the creations of others. While appreciation of all forms of art is somewhat culturally bound, it is important to provide children with experiences through which they begin to develop their own personal standards of beauty. Early childhood programs should be a vehicle for such experiences.

Throughout the first five years of life, children experience rapid physical growth. During this period the young child develops skills involving large and small muscles. Children at this period need many opportunities to run, jump, climb, throw and catch; practice in movement and balance are also important for optimal physical development. So physical development activities should constitute an integral part of any early childhood program.

One final objective should be noted. Within prekindergarten programs or as an adjunct to them provisions should be made for early recognition, screening, diagnosis, intervention, and remediation of learning disorders and problems in pre-school children. It is crucial to a child's development that learning problems be identified early and for such cases to be referred to appropriate agencies for further diagnosis and treatment. It is clearly established that intervention at an early age can alleviate or eliminate future learning problems, particularly functional retardation.

While there is no agreement regarding the appropriateness of various approaches to prekindergarten education, there are compelling reasons for resolving the issue. If it is true that children learn through interaction and encounters with their environment and stabilize their perceptions of the world around them through observation, manipulation of objects, interacting and modeling, then it is obvious that children learn what they learn depending on what they are expected to. The significance of early childhood programs lies in their potential for providing the kind of experiences, materials, and opportunities for exploration and interaction among children which can optimize and facilitate each child's development.

The advantages of quality early childhood programs for all children are obvious. However, a word of caution is in order. An additional two years of schooling will not magically solve all the problems of growing up. And prekindergarten education is in no sense a panacea for all of the ailments of education. On the other hand, it is entirely possible that valuable lessons can be learned by programs which emphasize individuality, curriculum flexibility, a child-centered environment, and parent involvement—lessons which could help revitalize the entire system of public education.

Chapter V

Upgrading the Profession

Neither the present system of teacher certification nor teacher training institutions are doing an adequate job of preparing teachers for the jobs they are hired to do . . . or in specifying what skills teachers need to be successful.

Teacher Organizer

Traditionally, institutions which have prepared teachers have paid much attention to academic proficiency and teaching competence but very little to interpersonal relationships and intergroup conflict.

College President

No group has complained more bitterly about the lack of adequate preservice and ongoing inservice training than the teachers themselves.

Teacher

Professional Preparation and Growth

Since the success of the entire educational enterprise rests on the experience and intellectual capacities of those men and women who preside over our classrooms, the ways in which educators are educated and licensed is and should be a primary concern; this concern is not limited to teachers, but extends to counselors, school psychologists, curriculum supervisors, principals, and administrators. For those who share responsibility for the training and certification of these professionals, the task has been amply defined by the historian of education Lawrence Cremin, who with typical urgency has recommended that:

> [We] begin now the prodigious task of preparing men and women who understand not only the substance of what they are teaching but also the theories behind the particular strategies they employ to convey that substance. A society committed to the continuing intellectual, esthetic, and moral growth of all its members can ill afford less on the part of those who undertake to teach.[1]

Reform of the certification system must have priority, because no aspect of education generates greater unanimity of opinion than that teacher education needs a vast overhaul. To have been a teacher or to have discussed this subject with aspiring teachers or professionals in the field is to reveal the extent of the dissatisfaction. The issue, of course, is not whether teachers should receive special preparation for teaching, but the kind of preparation they should receive.

Undoubtedly, the quality of teacher preparation programs has been greatly influenced by the state certification process, a process which over the years has become increasingly stultified, highly mechanistic, and fundamentally clerical. Almost anyone can become a teacher, and, unfortunately, mediocrity is often the reward for a system which asks little more of future teachers than that they earn a bachelor's degree and complete about a semester's equivalence of professional education, including several hours of student teaching.

Mediocrity is a severe characterization. While this indictment is not made lightly, the pursuit of educational excellence is obviously not being served by current certification systems. Not only is the present system based almost solely on course completions and an outdated reverence for the self-contained classroom, but it makes few allowances for diversity or change, for inputs from students, teachers, or community representatives, and for continuing professional growth—and no allowances for alternative routes to certification.

Under these circumstances, it is hardly reasonable to hope that teacher training institutions will produce a product which the certification process neither compels nor encourages. A future teacher should possess some conception of the purpose and goals of education, how schools are and should be organized, how teachers should teach, and to what ends. Since any governmental or accrediting agency has historically been solely concerned with the establishment of minimal standards, it has been left to the teacher training institutions to go beyond these regulatory minimums. Unfortunately, the minimum, with few exceptions, has become the mode for teacher preparation programs. Clearly, the expectation that teachers can somehow be better prepared and more skilled than the present certification process requires is not only incongruous, but illusory.

The incongruity is most evident when one surveys or personally experiences the contents and procedures of some professional preparation programs. Few teachers would take issue with Charles Silberman's sweeping condemnation of those curricular offerings which so frequently:

> tend to be both intellectually barren and professionally useless. Some are so abstract as to have no contact with reality; what passes for theory is a mass of platitudes and generalities. Some courses focus entirely on the "how to" of teaching, presenting a grab-bag of rules of thumb, unrelated to one another or to any conception of teaching.[2]

All of this raises the question of responsibility. Who is to blame if a teacher possesses neither the requisite knowledge, appropriate skills, nor the attitudes to be a good teacher? Who is responsible for the teacher who is woefully incapable of performing skillfully and humanely in the classroom? Obviously, the responsibility must be equally borne by the state certification systems, teacher training institutions, and local school districts.

While there are exceptions to this generalization, certification has become a convenient crutch which spares some teacher educators from doing anything more than is legally required. It spares them the pain of having to justify, or even think about, their programs. It spares them from having to ask themselves why they are doing what they are doing or how it influences the kind of students they produce. So long as certification is based almost exclusively upon the completion of required courses rather than the tested ability of students to teach, these questions will remain unanswered.

When one considers that in Illinois over 34,000 professionals were licensed in 1971-72 alone, it is clear that certification has become a mindless process. It has nurtured institutional relationships between universities, local school districts, accrediting associations, and professional organizations which can justly be described as incestuous, for, in the case of colleges of education, certification has tended to preserve the status quo, rather than the search for continually improved programs of preparation. In fairness, it must be noted that teacher preparation programs and certification systems, despite their obvious infirmities, are improving. Colleges of education are doing a better job of preparing educational personnel than ever before, and clearly today's teachers are better prepared, more knowledgeable, and more sensitive than those who have gone before them.

This country's experiment in mass public education has not been a failure, but a success. It is success, however, which breeds restlessness, self-criticism, and renewed quests for higher levels of excellence. And it is in this spirit that many believe an incomparably better job of preparing educators can be done. The present system which often feeds on its own inadequacies deserves to be reformed. But reform, if it is to come, must be genuine and substantive; it must penetrate to the very heart of our discontent, for there is a "real danger," as John Dewey once warned, "in perpetuating the past under forms that claim to be new but are only disguises of the old."

Certification of educational personnel at every level must be governed by certain assumptions about the kind of professionals the schools want and need. A teacher, for example, should be certified on the assumption that he evidences the requisite knowledge, skills, and attitudes to teach.

He should be certified on the assumption that his own preparation has been individualized, permitting emphasis to be placed upon the reinforcement of desired attitudes and competencies as well as a diagnosis of his strengths and weaknesses.

He should be certified on the assumption that he has demonstrated an ability to teach and that his performance has been measured against clearly defined criteria.

He should be certified on the assumption that he is aware of and sensitive to the educational needs of minority, culturally deprived, and economically disadvantaged students.

These are the kind of assumptions which ought to be made about every teacher, and in the future it may be possible by significantly altering current concepts regarding professional education and certification. The training of professionals, for example, must now become the joint responsibility of colleges, local schools, students, professional educators, and state offices of education.

Based on these and other assumptions, a task force on certification in Illinois recommended a model, which if implemented, would very dramatically alter the manner in which educational personnel are trained and licensed.[3] The pre-service phase, as recommended, would require prospective teachers to attend a training institution which provides a program having the prior approval of the State Department of Education and the State Teacher Certification Board. In part, the approval of teacher-education programs would be contingent on an institution's showing that it is able to provide basic instruction and to evaluate the performance of its students on the basis of pre-established criteria—programs which would insure that its graduates acquire a broad education, special competency in a field, and the demonstrated ability to teach.

Colleges of education would be required under this proposal to provide their students with clinical experiences at the outset of their preparation. In fashioning a program for approval, colleges of education would be encouraged to experiment, to evaluate, and revise their program at every stage. They would be required to invite others to participate in this process, including college students, practicing teachers, administrators, community representatives, and, of course, the entire academic faculty, most notably those in liberal arts and sciences. The involvement of local school districts in this initial phase of teacher preparation would also be vitally important, for in addition to providing useful input for program planning, they could provide, as they have in the past, facilities for training, staff for supervision of clinical experiences, and assistance to university staff in evaluating prospective teachers. The public schools must serve not as a repository for student teachers, but as equal partners sharing their resources with the colleges. They must become a meaningful and integral part of the teacher education program. The public schools must serve not only the elementary and secondary student, but also the education profession.

To summarize, then, the pre-service phase would require three things of teacher training institutions: (1) to provide clinical experiences early in the undergraduate program; (2) to involve academicians as well as educationists in teacher education program planning; and (3) to base recommendations for licensure not only on course completions, but also on a prospective teacher's ability to perform competently in a defined educational role.

Under the second phase of this process, the in-service phase, the student who has successfully completed an approved professional education program would be issued what might be called *an initial certificate*. As recommended by the task force, an initial certificate would permit a graduate to teach, but such a certificate would only be valid for a limited and fixed number of years. Recognizing that teacher preparation should be a continuing process, the new teacher would be required to complete and school districts would be required to provide a program designed to insure his continuing professional growth and development. The initial certificate can also be thought of as an internship license which would allow the pre-service teacher an opportunity to perfect teaching skills before assuming full professional responsibility.

Just as the State Office of Education in consultation with the Certification Board would assist in the development, execution, and approval of *pre-service* educational programs, it would play a similar role relative to *in-service* educational programs. Local school districts would be encouraged to design a program which was sufficiently individual and flexible so as to satisfy the needs of its own educational personnel, pupils and community. And again the involvement of all publics having an interest in education, including teachers and teaching training institutions would be necessary.

In short, the local school or school district-centered program would be an avenue for assessing the initially certificated teacher and providing for his professional growth by reinforcing competencies and remediating deficiencies. A teacher's success in a renewal program of this nature would determine whether he would receive or be denied recertification, with such decisions being appealable to an impartial third party. A *continuing certificate*, valid for only a limited and fixed number of years, would be issued then to the holder of this *initial certificate* who had satisfactorily completed the in-service program.

Because the goal of in-service programs at the local level would be designed to achieve increasingly advanced and specific levels of educational competence, there would necessarily be a third phase to this process. Although continuing certificates would be renewable any number of times, the recertification of a teacher, regardless of his professional longevity, would be contingent on his periodically completing a renewal program and performance assessment. Clearly, the focus would not be how long a teacher has taught, but how a teacher might improve his teaching skills.

The task force also recommended that the State Certification Board choose a number of university centers to design alternate routes to certification and to assume the assessment and recommending responsibilities, as well. The rigidities of the present system are such that artists, scientists, mechanics, farmers, and public officials are artificially excluded from the teaching profession, and yet these are the very people who might help infuse the educational enterprise with rare and badly needed talent. For example, bilingual teachers are desperately needed in Illinois, a need the state could begin to meet if alternative routes of certification and compensatory training were opened up to those who have university degrees from abroad, but who are presently being relegated to assembly lines and other menial tasks due to narrowly drawn and inflexible standards.

On the whole, the recommendations of this task force are meritorious. Some of them are now in the process of being implemented. Others are being carefully assessed before moving ahead. For example, issues relating to professional tenure (which should not be cavalierly abandoned), certificate renewal, and competency-based criteria deserve further analysis. However, it would be a mistake to allow concepts like "competency/performance based teacher education" and "clinical and individualized experiences" to deter needed reforms in this area. At this time, the principal focus of concern should be the development or redevelopment of pre-service education programs for prospective teachers and administrative personnel. Emphasis should be placed on programs which assist pre-service teachers and administrators in gaining real experience and measurable success prior to licensing. The state education office is exploring with Illinois' teacher training institutions the need, as well as the methods, for establishing undergraduate competency-based teacher education programs.

There are certain characteristics which every teacher-preparation program should possess. Several come to mind. First, a teacher education program, as suggested earlier, should be the result of involvement not only of the entire university academic and professional education staff, including students when possible, but of public school teachers, administrators, and lay citizens. In addition, teacher preparation institutions should:

- formulate programs which provide sound curricular balance; broad experience in general studies including the humanities, the sciences and the social studies; a solid foundation of subject matter; and the professional experiences needed for a center in teaching.

- offer those educational experiences that lead to learning outcomes in the cognitive, affective, and psychomotor phases of personal and professional development, including a responsible commitment to the continuation of learning.

- select students for admission to teacher preparation programs and require continuous evaluation for retention in the program, giving consideration to good physical and mental health, good character, and interest in the learning process.

- provide systematic procedures for assessing the candidate's attitude and competency throughout the preparation period.

- provide experiences which will prepare the prospective teacher to be aware of and sensitive to the individual educational needs of all students.

- provide direct clinical experiences in classroom, laboratory and/or community services programs throughout the preparation period.

- recognize those abilities which the student may have already acquired and plan his program accordingly. A student demonstrating knowledge, skills and attitudes based upon previous experience in a given subject matter area may qualify for advance placement and/or credit by passing appropriate examinations as determined by the institution.

- provide their faculties with the opportunity to participate directly in public school programs so they may lend their expertise to the solution of public school problems and gain a continuing exposure to the different problems of public school instruction which may then be related directly to the teacher education sequence.

Education Courses—The Liberal Arts

It is easy to deprecate professional education courses but nothing suggested here should be interpreted as a signal to sweep them out of existence. Indeed, the history, philosophy, and methodology of education should occupy a central place in teacher education. While such courses by themselves do not insure a high level of craftsmanship, they can be enormously helpful in clarifying a prospective teacher's understanding of his own purposes and of the strategies and techniques available to him for achieving those purposes. This is not to suggest, of course, that such offerings should be immune from needed refinements and redefinition.

The growing emphasis, for example, on individualized instruction in our schools requires teachers to be able to transform learning theory into practice. A teacher cannot be expected to respond to each child's individual needs unless he perceives individual differences in personality and aptitude, and unless he realizes that individual learner needs are influenced by family, ethnic, religious, and socio-economic factors. So the academic components of teacher education must not be dismissed as unnecessary. The challenge is to transform those courses into a vital aspect of professional preparation.

With regard to curriculum, it is essential that the education of educators becomes a responsibility of the entire university. Teacher preparation is much too important a mission to be left solely to any one department, any one group, any one college. The melding of teacher education and liberal education is a movement which in Illinois began gaining momentum in the 1960s. By integrating content and methodology, a student is able to understand simultaneously a subject and how best to teach it to others. It makes no sense to exclude those persons from teacher preparation programs who are most knowledegable about those subjects which constitute the mainstay of the curriculum: English, history, foreign languages, mathematics, biology, chemistry, and physics. Those who possess expertise in these disciplines have in general enjoyed no significant policy-making function in teacher education and licensing. One would hope that a reform of certification would help facilitate an integrative approach to teacher education.

One of the underlying assumptions of the reforms outlined here is that earlier and more intensive clincial training of educational personnel is necessary. While it is generally agreed that practice teaching as a clinical experience is indispensable our current practices in this regard provide no basis for complacency. Anyone who has been a teacher or who has supervised student teachers knows that clinical training is much too brief, that feedback on performance is insufficient, that supervision is often perfunctory, and that the focus of both the trainee and his supervisor is often on the minutiae of classroom life.

Evaluation—Measuring Competencies

If clinical experiences are to be of maximum usefulness, desired outcomes of teacher preparation programs must be specified and their achievement measured. One of the most persistent criticisms leveled at the Illinois task force's proposal, calling for competency based instruction, is that the use of such criteria is complex and is unproven as an effective method for upgrading the quality of educational personnel. No one has ever suggested that the definition of performance outcomes would be easy.

On the other hand, it is inconceivable that in this day and age we lack the ingenuity and intelligence to determine whether a prospective teacher or practicing teacher is able to achieve his objectives, or relate to students, or evoke their interest, or diagnose their individual needs and problems, or evaluate their achievement.

The call for competency-based teacher education at the pre-service and in-service level is being echoed throughout the nation. Now that the hysteria is beginning to subside many of our teacher training institutions and state departments of education are moving forward toward the competency-based model. This movement is one of the most hopeful developments for teacher education in the past fifty years. However, the application of the competency-based model at the in-service level has not yet enjoyed the same acceptance or success as its application at the pre-service level. In fact, if the attempt to institute competency-based education created a storm among educators, attempts to impose an in-service competency-based program for evaluation and licensing have been met with a hurricane.

The problem of upgrading the professional skills of those presently in-service remains. Somehow a way must be found to instill in teachers a life-long love of learning. A way must be found to enable teachers to spend the time necessary to individualize programs for their students. A way must be found to deliver to all classroom teachers the advances that are occurring daily in the field of human learning. A way must also be found to convince teachers and administrators that they have a responsibility for their own evaluation which will be performed for the central purpose of improving the individual's teaching performance.

Educators cannot afford to abdicate the responsibility for upgrading their own profession. But then they face the possibility of legislatures, as happened in California, mandating a teacher evaluation program which is not only unreasonably stringent, but based on criteria which are educationally suspect. It should be noted that all but three of the sixteen principal teacher training institutions in Illinois are presently using some form of competency criteria, and that is a promising development.

While teacher evaluation is a good thing, it never should be punitive. Evaluation should be seen as an instrument for improving the instructional environment, as a diagnostic means of assessing performance so that weaknesses can be strengthened through in-service education. But to be meaningful, teachers themselves must assume a large part of the responsibility for developing the evaluative criteria and carrying out the actual evaluation process.

One of the legitimate fears of teachers is that professional evaluation will be undertaken in a vacuum. There are a multitude of variables which must be taken into account if judgments about professional performances are to be rendered in an objective and fair manner. The aspirations of parents for their children as expressed in broad goals and objectives of a school; the readiness of children to learn; working conditions, both material and interpersonal; and desired learner outcomes are all factors which must be taken into consideration if any system of teacher evaluation is to be effective. Teaching performance is only one factor which has a bearing on learner outcomes. Student skills, knowledges, values, and attitudes are the result of many influences, only one of which is the teacher. Any evaluative system which relies, for example, on the results of standardized achievement tests is not only destined to fail, but should be strenuously resisted.

An official of the National Education Association recently capsulized the differences between how teacher evaluation is frequently perceived and how it actually should operate.[4]

The Way It Usually Is	*The Way It Ought To Be*
• Evaluation is threatening to teachers.	• Evaluation should be something that teachers anticipate and want because it gives them insight into their own performance.
• They see it as something that is done to them by someone else.	• It should be something in which teachers have a part along with students, parents, and administrators.
• It is used mostly for determining teacher status relative to dismissal, tenure, and promotion, even though instructional improvement is often advertised as its major purpose.	• Evaluation should be used to diagnose teachers' performance so that they can strengthen their weaknesses through in-service education.

● Teachers often are unaware   ● Teachers should take part
  of the criteria used to judge   in developing or selecting
  them.   evaluation instruments so that
                                      they know the criteria against
                                      which they are judged.

The "ought to be" features of teacher evaluation, as set forth above, are sound. If they are incorporated into an evaluative system, teachers are likely to be more supportive of efforts to upgrade their profession.

The Role of Teachers

The responsibility for preparing and certifying educational personnel is one that properly should be shared by many educational interests. However, teachers ought to play a major role, if not *the* major role, in this process. On the other hand, the theory that educational policy ought to be controlled and dictated solely by teachers or any other element of the profession does not enjoy broad acceptance. The fact that the public schools are financed wholly out of public resources results in a relationship between educators and their profession which can never be as self-sufficient and self-determining as are professionals, for instance, within the legal and medical fields.

On the other hand, there is growing evidence that teachers are seeking the right to be held accountable for the future of their profession, and that is a positive development. Teachers must be more amply represented on state teacher certification boards. They must be permitted a voice in the fashioning of pre-service and in-service programs. They must be allowed to participate with local school districts in specifying evaluation procedures and performance criteria. And finally they should have responsibility for dealing with fellow professionals in the area of professional ethics and related matters. Impatience with teacher training is rather uniformly shared by teachers themselves. Experienced teachers have traditionally played a minor role in policy deliberations relating to their own profession. But as James Koerner has pointed out:

Teachers are usually critical of the status quo in teacher education. They manage most of the time to restrain their enthusiasms for certification standards and the teacher training programs they themselves went through. All attempts that I have ever seen . . . to find out what teachers think about teacher education—all attempts, that is, that guarantee teachers anonymity or protection from reprisal— bring in results that are as consistent as they are critical.[5]

Teachers are demanding, and they deserve, a much larger voice than they presently have in teacher education and certification. Their involvement is the best insurance that things will change for the better.

COLLECTIVE BARGAINING

Within the once complacent ranks of the teaching profession a growing dissatisfaction is evident. On the present scene teacher aggressiveness is manifesting itself in strikes, sanctions and other overt forms which would have been unbelievable just a few short years ago. The power of boards of education, once the citadel of educational authority, has been challenged—first by administrators who sought some power from the boards themselves, and during the past decade, by teachers, and more recently by students asking for greater participation. In each case conflict has been the result.

The conflicts that have and will occur are not new to our society, but they are relatively new in education. The challenge facing educators is a two-fold one: first to recognize that conflicts exist and second to discover methods and procedures to deal creatively with them. All disputes are not easily solved and all confrontations do not result in agreement. However, if confrontation is to exist, it is incumbent upon rational citizens to provide a framework in which order will prevail and a dialogue will be maintained.

Illinois is one of several states which does not have a legal and workable framework within which teachers and school boards can negotiate in good faith. Although teachers can organize and enter into a collective bargaining agreement, the final terms of such agreements are often an open question subject to judicial interpretation. No impasse machinery exists. No exclusive representation is permitted. There is no right to demand that school boards bargain, or that bargaining be in good faith. The law on collective bargaining in the public sector exists as a catch-as-catch-can proposition. As for work stoppages, they are viewed as unlawful, based on the premise that those who serve the public are presumed to have surrendered some private rights, including in this case the right to strike.

A school district, on the other hand, is not a free-wheeling, risk-taking entrepreneur. It does not enjoy the prerogative to react and act as does a business corporation. A school district is to a large extent subject to the state which may take and manage school facilities or abolish them altogether. These political and practical considerations have a bearing on the issue of collective bargaining.

Unfortunately, judicial fiat can never be a substitute for carefully thought out legislation, where conflicting views can be balanced in the public interest and the uniqueness of the public sector recognized.

Despite the state of the law in Illinois and similarly situated states, collective bargaining in education is a fact of life. The process is already mandated by statute in a majority of states, and in many states, like Illinois, all the large school systems, and many others, are actively engaged in the process. In fact, the vast majority of the school boards in Illinois have had some involvement in negotiations with organized teachers.

The process and practice of collective negotiations within the Illinois educational community is as varied as the state's geography, politics and demography. The state possesses among its 1,083 school districts, practices and resultant contracts that are as sophisticated, if not more so, than those held as models in the public sector. Also in considerable evidence are many school districts and teacher organizations where formal agreements between the two are simply viewed as inconceivable. When these realities are coupled with the fact that the Illinois Legislature has failed to provide statutory guidelines for conducting collective bargaining in the public sector one can easily see why public sector labor relations in Illinois can only be described as chaotic.

Because of the thrust of teacher organizations in gearing up for collective negotiations the chaos is particularly evident in the educational community. The absence of a statute has resulted, in many instances, in a crippling of educational services not only from work stoppages, but in a much more persuasive and dangerous weakening of the public's confidence in its elected school board as well as its employees.

In spite of a lack of legislated guidelines, collective bargaining activity in the public sector in general and in education in particular has been continuing at an increasing rate. This increased activity has been accompanied by multifarious responses by the various groups within the educational community. School boards in some instances have adopted the posture of simply not recognizing a group for bargaining purposes. In other situations school boards may have faced skilled teacher representatives who have taken advantage of the lack of bargaining acumen on the part of the board.

Teacher organizations in their zeal to obtain recognition and a subsequent contract often engage in practices that follow a "cook book" approach to bargaining. This practice involves following the parent organization's "sample agreement" to the letter without regard to the local situation.

The role of the superintendent and other school administrators is often unclear. This lack of clarity often results in needless suspicion among teachers and administrators, and is detrimental to the quality of education. It must be noted that as in the private sector, the majority of school districts and teacher organizations engaging in collective negotiations are able to reach agreement without a great deal of disruption to the educational community. However, the potential for difficulty is present in every school district in the state due to the absence of a legal framework.

Besides the lack of legislative guidelines other factors contribute to the negotiation problem.

1. Even though they are rapidly acquiring it, teacher organizations as well as boards of education have not had sufficient opportunity to develop the sophisticated expertise necessary for collective bargaining.
2. There exists in some quarters a "total victory" philosophy which if allowed to prevail will serve as an impediment to meaningful collective bargaining.
3. Inter-organizational rivalry often results in inordinate pressure for the teacher bargaining agent to "overachieve."
4. There are those on both sides who have not accepted the concept of collective bargaining.

5. The teachers' struggle for a greater share in the decision-making power of a school system.

In the private sector, and in those states which have had the fore-sight to enact legislation, mechanisms for the resolution of impasse exist. These mechanisms, while not providing guarantees against strikes and other disorders, do provide a framework which can lend a semblance of civility to the conflicts resulting from the collective bargaining process. Without a statute, boards of education and teachers upon reaching impasse, have resorted to a variety of methods in reaching an agreement. However, at present no consistent pattern and little statewide direction for the intervention of a third party neutral exists.

The absence of a collective bargaining law has made it incredibly difficult for the Illinois state office of education to intervene in controversies involving teachers and school boards. The authority of the state to prevent work stoppages and to balance, as judiciously as possible, the conflicting interests of all parties is at best implied. As a result, the agency's success has always been tempered by either the obvious limitations on its authority or by legal challenges to the exercise of that authority.

In Illinois, the state is charged with the constitutional responsibility of educating each individual to the limits of his capacity. In addition, the Superintendent of Public Instruction has the statutory responsibility to hear and determine controversies arising under the school laws of the state. Under these and other mandates, the policy of the state office in the area of collective bargaining in the educational community has been one of prudent involvement. Recognizing that conflicts between teachers and school boards exist and will continue, the basic task has not been to eliminate conflict, but to assist in every way possible towards managing it. In addition, the State Office of Education views as its most vital service the provision of a framework in which order prevails and a rational dialogue continues.

Initially, a department of teacher-school board relations was established within the state educational agency. This department was responsible for establishing the role of the state office in the arena of collective bargaining. The department formed an Advisory Committee on Collective Negotiations consisting of scholars in the field, a state education association representative and a representative from the state administrators association. This committee helped facilitate communication among the parties, and was very useful in assisting in the development of the role the agency was to play.

As events unfolded, it became more evident that the state office's role, as a third party neutral, could be enhanced in several ways. Consequently a program was developed involving various processes which had some positive effect on educational collective bargaining. Prior to becoming involved in any situation it is necessary to monitor as accurately as possible the climate at any existing moment. The state office, therefore, monitored school districts through as many individual and organizational contacts as could possibly be established. Most of these contacts, both formal and informal, proved quite valuable in determining situations where the state's involvement could be beneficial in reaching agreement.

The staff worked informally with both teachers through their organizations and with school boards and school administrators. During this informal stage assistance was provided so as to cause the parties to reach agreement without any intervention from the outside. Especially during this phase, financial or other factual data that could facilitate an agreement was provided. This informal state of involvement has been utilized in scores of districts. Normally, this was all that was necessary, and agreements were the direct result of the state office's involvement. In other cases further involvement has been necessary.

To assist in the resolution of more serious disputes a panel of mediators is carefully selected. These mediators are chosen for their expertise in the field of labor relations, education and in public sector dispute settlement. At the request of both parties or the encouragement of the state educational agency these mediators are made available to local school boards and teacher organizations. These mediators are also used as fact-finders when that process is appropriate.

In addition to these techniques and procedures, other forms of assistance are provided. During the summer months, the state office sponsors workshops involving all participants in the bargaining process: teachers, administrators, and school board members. These workshops attempt to focus on collective bargaining as a way in which agreements are reached, not as a partisan activity. The purpose is to not only raise the level of expertise for the participants, but to foster better communication among them.

When disputes become critical, it is occasionally necessary to summon both the teacher negotiators and the school board representatives from districts which are at or near impasse. By permitting both sides to present their point of view and to articulate their differences to the state superintendent, such meetings can have a positive impact on the resolution of conflicts. Most school districts settle their contracts without work stoppages. One school superintendent involved in such a meeting was quoted as saying: "This is a hell of a note. We drove 200 miles just to talk to each other. But, it helped!"

Not all confrontations, of course, are so easily resolved. In one city a bitter strike reached its tenth day. Because of the prolonged nature of the disruption of educational services, it was determined that direct intervention was imperative since the parties, even with the aid of a fact finder, were unable to reach a settlement. After repeated efforts to get the parties to reach agreement, all efforts proved unsuccessful. Therefore, a recommended settlement was drawn up by the state educational agency and presented to the teachers and the board of education. The teachers accepted the recommended settlement, but it was rejected by the board of education. At that point the Circuit Court was asked to order a solution. The court refused to grant the request, and the case was subsequently appealed to the Illinois Supreme Court. This was regrettable but unavoidable. It probably would not have occurred if legal guidelines for the conduct of collective bargaining in the public sector had existed. There are several conclusions one may draw from the Illinois experience.

It is possible to establish certain administrative guidelines to provide direction to the process of negotiations. It is also possible for a state superintendent to create a unit within the state educational agency that addresses itself to the negotiation process and informally assists both teachers and school boards in their quest for equitable agreements. State offices of education can also help upgrade the entire process by actively taking the lead in assisting the participants of the bargaining process in becoming students of collective bargaining. This can be accomplished through workshops, seminars and other educational experiences. For if the level of expertise on the part of the participants is raised, many problems due to a lack of experience on the part of negotiators can be reduced or eliminated altogether.

A state office of education can also select mediators who possess skill not only in private sector labor relations, but who also have expertise in settling public sector disputes and may have experience in educational confrontation. These mediators should then be made available to the parties. They could also be partially subsidized by the state office. A state office of education can also be of service in states where no law exists by promoting the passage of legislation that will facilitate cooperation on behalf of all those who are participants in making educational policy and decisions. While administrative guidelines and procedures can be of great assistance to the educational community as it enters the era of collective negotiation, they are at best stop-gap measures, stop-gap in the sense that they must do in place of the order that comes only with comprehensive legislation.

The dispute over the type and form that legislation should take is now raging in Illinois. To complicate matters, the state's two major teacher groups oppose each other. The Education Association wants a bill similar to the Hawaii and Pennsylvania statutes and the Federation has lined up behind a more liberal proposal. This type of inter-organizational disagreement has been a major obstacle to the passage of a public employee bargaining legislation in the past. These circumstances, among others, make it difficult to bring order to the present chaotic situation and pose a unique challenge for state educational leaders.

A collective bargaining bill should guarantee the right of teachers to bargain with their employers. It should define the participants of the bargaining unit and outline the role of each in the bargaining process. It should clearly define procedures for the resolution of impasse. Such procedures as fact-finding and mediation, if properly applied, should minimize the use of the strike. What is and what is not a fair labor practice should be clearly specified. And finally, a collective bargaining act should be administered by an independent and impartial agency to insure that all issues and perspectives are heard and weighed. The potential for conflict between teachers and school board has never been greater. In his inaugural remarks eighty years ago, Illinois Governor John Peter Altgeld made this observation:

> The reign of law has so broadened in this century as to cover almost every other controversy between man and man, and in the development of society some way must be found to subject the so-called "labor controversies" to law.[6]

Altgeld's advice is still relevant. It is time the reign of law was extended to labor controversies within the educational community. While such conflicts cannot be eliminated altogether, they can be uniformly managed.

Chapter VI

THE FINANCE CRISIS
*The Search for Equity, Efficiency, and
Effectiveness*

The history of this State's lack of responsibility to its children is a national disgrace. Race horses are treated with more respect and deference than are our children, and have infinitely less potential for contributing to the upgrading of our society.

Parent

We need nothing less than a totally new concept to pay for education. We might begin by discarding the personal property tax (it is doomed anyway) and by thinking about a general aid to education program.

Congressman

My taxes have increased 29 percent since 1967 and yet my net income per acre has only increased 15 percent. This is why we question a continued system of financing education as now exists.

Farmer

Our experience with the formation of a unit district during the past year leads us to believe that larger unit districts can lead to better educational programs at a more reasonable cost.

Teacher

The Finance Crisis: An Overview

Since educational offerings differ greatly among local communities, it is clear that the quality of a youngster's schooling is largely determined by the place of his birth and residence. These differences in opportunity are rooted more often than not in the system by which education is financed in this nation. The President's Commission on School Finance has summarized the problem.

> The decentralized control of American education, and the variations in both taxing ability and tax effort from state to state and from community to community result in dramatic disparities in the sums invested in the schooling of American youngsters. In 1969-70, per capita spending among the states ranged from $1,237 to $438; among local school districts within a single state, from $243 to $2,087. Financial disparities of such extreme degree inevitably affect school quality and, hence, equality of educational opportunity.[1]

The culprit, of course, is the property tax, or more precisely our heavy reliance on property taxes. Though only ten percent of the nation's income is derived from property, society continues to rely on that source to pay not only for a wide variety of educationally unrelated public services, but for fifty-six percent of the total cost of public schools as well. In Illinois, for example, it is estimated that this tax currently provides about fifty-five percent of the total cost of elementary and secondary education with the state contributing about thirty-nine percent and the federal government the remaining six percent. The school finance problems caused by the "local" property tax are much greater today than ever before because its use has been so greatly expanded. Property taxes extended in Illinois reached $2.7 billion during 1970—up 378 percent since 1949. During that same time per capita property taxes in Illinois increased from $65 to $243, an increase of 274 percent.

Since 1957, the first year that the property tax generated more than $1 billion in Illinois, this tax has grown even more rapidly due mainly to the accelerated expansion of property taxes for education. The proportion of total property tax revenues devoted to education has increased from 48.6 percent in 1957 to 59.9 percent in 1970; the property tax today is primarily a school tax.

While the property tax is not without its advantages, the school finance system is grossly unfair and inequitable. To an extent far beyond the recognition of most parents, the quality of their children's education depends upon the community in which they choose to live, a choice which is severely limited for many. A family that lives in a school district with little taxable property per pupil loses two ways: first, by paying high property tax rates for education directly or through higher rents, and second, by having less money spent on their children's education. On the other hand, a family that lives in a school district with substantial amounts of taxable property per pupil will benefit in two ways: first, by paying a lower tax rate for education, and second, by getting a more expensive education for their children.

The abilities of school districts to raise funds for education are reflected in the astounding variances in district wealth. In Illinois, for example, equalized assessed valuations per pupil for elementary districts ranged from $5,388 to $403,024; for secondary districts, $23,945 to $246,980; for unit districts, $3,544 to $101,908.

The magnitude of these inequities is frequently unbelievable. For example, families and businesses in Illinois' wealthiest elementary district are taxed at a rate for education that is less than one-fourth the rate paid by taxpayers in Illinois' poorest elementary district, while at the same time nearly two and one half times as much is spent for each student's education in the wealthier district. Among Illinois' high school districts, the ten wealthiest have more than four times the taxable property per pupil, a tax rate that is less than fifty percent as high, and fifty percent more expenditures per pupil than the ten poorest high school districts. The inequities among unit districts are similarly great.

Unfortunately, these are not isolated instances. Take Illinois' 588 elementary districts. Although the average taxable property per pupil for these districts is about $36,000, 159 districts are below $20,000, while ninety-seven are above $52,000. In other words, two out of every five elementary districts are more than forty percent above or below the average elementary district in ability to raise local money for their schools.

As a result, taxpayers living in the 159 relatively poor elementary districts must pay at least forty percent higher taxes in order to buy an average educational program, while the taxpayers of the ninety-seven wealthy elementary districts enjoy either an average educational program *plus* a forty percent or more tax break or an exceptional educational program with average tax rates. Once again, the pattern is similar for high school and unit districts.

To test further the existence of financial disparities among school districts, and "effort and ability" study of the Illinois' 1083 school districts was conducted by the state office of education. The purpose of the study was to determine the nature of the relationship between the wealth of a district, its tax rate, and the amount of money it spends on a child's education. One conclusion stands out: *as the wealth per pupil in a district increases, the tax rate goes down and the expenditures per pupil goes up.*

This condition exists not only within individual states, but also among the states. Two years ago New York ranked highest among the states on per pupil spending with $1,237 while Alabama ranked lowest with $438. In fact, by using almost any criteria for measuring educational expenditures—teacher salaries, pupil-teacher ratios, investment per pupil—it is evident that significant disparities exist among the states. This condition disguises the fact that poorer states, like poorer school districts, often tax themselves harder to finance education than do the more affluent states. For instance, Mississippi, which ranks fiftieth among the states in its ability to support education, devotes a larger percentage of its income to schools than does New York, which while taxing itself less than Mississippi still generates three times as much revenue.

There are other problems related to the property tax. First, it is extremely inelastic: that is, revenues do not expand as fast as the economy. A recent study indicates that during the 1960's the automatic growth of property taxes was only about half as rapid as Illinois' economy. Moreover, the property tax base is being eroded in some states as a result of either legislatively enacted or constitutionally mandated "homestead" exemptions, personal property tax exemptions and property tax freezes. By virtue of a recent U.S. Supreme Court decision, an amendment to the Illinois Constitution exempting taxpayers from personal property taxes, was upheld as constitutional. School district revenues will decline, therefore, by an amount estimated to be as much as $72 million a year, a loss which presumably will have to be made up from some other source. Add to this narrowing tax base the increasing difficulty of passing local tax referenda, and you have a problem of crisis proportions. Only six years ago more than sixty percent of such referenda were being approved; now not only do just thirty percent pass, but there are significantly fewer referenda. There is, of course, unhappiness about the schools; however, it is probably the absence of significant tax reform which really has taxpayers up in arms. An Illinois newspaper described the problem of tax friction this way:

> "Talk's cheap," so the saying goes. "It takes money to buy booze." It takes money to buy books and trained instructors. Americans spend billions on booze without a squawk; they spend billions on bombs and bullets with scarcely a whimper. But they tend to revolt when asked to spend billions for schools. They have very little control over the cost of booze or the cost of bombs. The local, public schools are about the only place where the consumer or voter can register a protest that will count.[2]

And that is precisely what voters have chosen to do.

What have the states done to alleviate these conditions? Most states have recognized the disparities in the tax-producing ability of school districts. As a consequence, most have adopted "foundation" laws which enable them to provide larger amounts of state-financial assistance to school districts with low tax bases than to those with high tax bases. The theory is that the state should provide all districts, regardless of their property wealth or degree of poverty, with funds necessary for an adequate educational program. In short, all districts are guaranteed by the state an equal starting point or foundation (in Illinois it is currently $520 per pupil in weighted average daily attendance) to which can be added revenues resulting from varying degrees of local tax effort.

Unfortunately, the foundation laws have failed their intended purpose of equalizing the resource disparities among local school districts. As presently constituted they have not narrowed the disparities in school financing between cities and suburbs or between

CHART NO. 1

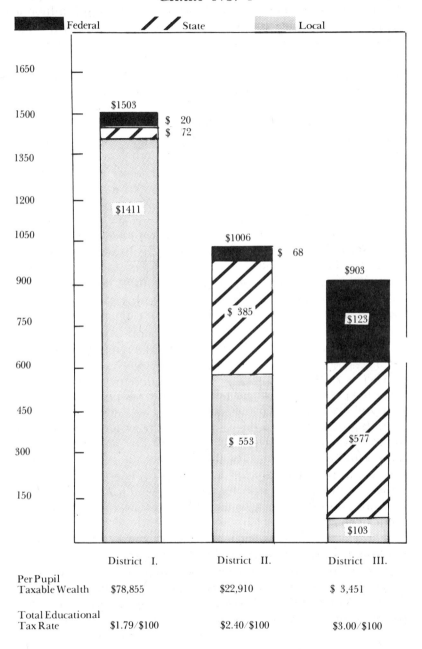

	District I.	District II.	District III.
Per Pupil Taxable Wealth	$78,855	$22,910	$ 3,451
Total Educational Tax Rate	$1.79/$100	$2.40/$100	$3.00/$100

affluent and poor communities. The "foundation" concept is sound. However, in the absence of a significantly larger financial input by the states, foundation aid cannot be expected to overcome the great disparities described above.

To illustrate the inadequacies of foundation laws, one need only look at three Illinois school districts of varying wealth. The richest district has $78,855 per pupil in taxable wealth. With a $1.79 per $100 tax rate, District I raises over $1,400 per pupil in local revenue. It receives an additional $72 per pupil from the state and another $20 per pupil from the federal government. Altogether, District I has $1,503 per pupil for educational purposes. District III, on the other hand, with twice the tax rate but only one-twenty sixth the wealth of District I can raise only $103 per pupil locally. Under the state aid formula District III receives eight times more in state resources and six times more in federal funds than District I. So has equalization been achieved? No! Despite the additional state and federal aid, District III has only two-thirds as much money available for its students as District I, $903 per pupil in District III compared with $1,503 per pupil in District I. As shown in Chart No. 1 on page 169, District II, which is in the median range of wealth for Illinois school districts, also falls far short of District I in revenue per pupil.

The limited effectiveness of present foundation laws is compounded by legislatively established school tax rates which limit districts with the least property wealth from setting high tax rates to equal the revenues of districts with high property wealth. It is doubtful, however, that a removal of tax ceilings would appreciably aid the quest for equalization. Most districts with low property wealth would not be inclined, and understandably, to bear the excessive tax burden required to raise revenues equal to those of districts with significantly higher property wealth. Some poor districts would have to raise their tax rates eighty times to yield the revenue available to some of the wealthiest school districts in Illinois.

Foundation laws generally have some equalizing effect. However, poor districts cannot hope to receive enough aid to enable them to spend at a level comparable to that of wealthier districts. And since every district is guaranteed a flat grant from the state, regardless of the district's wealth or its need for state assistance (in Illinois it is $57 per pupil), the inequalities are not diminished.

Frequently, inequalities are enlarged, too, when the school aid formula includes factors which are intended to attack specific problems, but because they are carelessly drawn serve only to make a bad situation worse. For example, a factor in the Illinois general aid formula is called the "density bonus." The "density bonus" provides the largest and most populous school districts with additional state funds, because large urban centers encounter higher differential costs than other areas with regard to providing public services unrelated to education. Unfortunately, several suburban districts which do not experience this municipal overburden receive the benfits of the bonus rather than districts having demonstrably higher differential costs related to education. The recipients in some cases have high assessed valuations per pupil or at least well above the state average. This failure to take into consideration the varying abilities of large school districts to meet their education costs has produced a windfall for some relatively affluent districts, at the expense of other districts which desperately need such assistance.

In addition to providing an "adequate" level of financial support for every student, most states also provide various forms of "categorical aid" to districts. Funds are earmarked to permit school districts to underwrite special programs for handicapped, gifted, and non-English-speaking children. Categorical assistance is frequently available for vocational education and pupil transportation. But because these funds are distributed without reference to the variances in wealth among districts, the unequal capabilities of districts to finance education are not alleviated but frequently reinforced. The granting of funds for programs of this nature do not contribute to equalization since poor districts cannot afford to supplement state funds with their own resources.

Therefore, despite various state financial programs for the schools, very significant disparities still exist. As the President's Commission on School Finance noted in 1972:

> The combined present local, state and federal mechanisms for financing education seem outdated, insufficient, or inadequate to overcome the great differences in taxing ability between state and communities within the nation.[3]

Having briefly surveyed the condition of educational finance, five general conclusions can be made.

1. Unacceptable financial disparities exist among school districts.
2. These disparities are produced by variations in district wealth and the priorities assigned by the citizens of each district to educational spending relative to other possible expenditures.
3. These fiscal disparities contribute, at least in part, to unequal educational opportunities.
4. State financing systems, including foundation laws, do not adequately reduce fiscal disparities.
5. These conditions will persist so long as the schools must rely heavily on local property taxes to finance education.

Court Decisions

When the father of John Serrano, a 7-year-old California student, learned five years ago that his local school district lacked the financial resources to provide his son with a decent education, he mortgaged his assets and scraped up money to move his family to another community. There Serrano found the education he wanted for his son.

John Serrano's father later concluded that he and similarly situated parents should not have to make personal sacrifices as he had and that good education should be available to all. The result was a lawsuit challenging the constitutionality of California's heavy reliance on property taxes as violative of the equal protection clause of the 14th Amendment. The California Supreme Court upheld the plaintiff's position, basing its decision on the principle that the level of spending for a child's education may not be a function of wealth other than the wealth of the state as a whole. The court further found that attempts at equalization and supplemental aid grants tempered but did not solve disparities resulting from vast variations in local real property assessed valuation throughout the state.[4]

In New Jersey, the State Supreme Court ordered the state to develop both a new school finance system and a new tax structure. A Minnesota case, *Van Dusartz* vs. *Hatfield* forced a thirty percent increase in that state's level of educational funding.[5] The system of financing schools in Texas was also successfully challenged in the *Rodriquez* case.[6] While one school district was raising a meager $21 per pupil from local property taxes, another with a lower tax rate was generating $307 per pupil.

To understand the potential implications of these lower court cases, one must understand what the courts said and did not say. They did not say that the property tax is unconstitutional or that a property tax levy for schools is necessarily unconstitutional. The decisions neither required equal spending for each pupil nor required the assumption by the state of complete and total funding for elementary and secondary education.

What the courts said in these cases can be generally summarized as follows:

1. The quality of a child's education may not be a function of the wealth of his parents, neighbors, or school district.
2. The quality of a child's education may not be a function of the willingness or unwillingness of the local electorate to vote funds for education.
3. There must be an equitable distribution of the educational tax burden.
4. The opportunity for an education is a right which must be made available to all on equal terms.
5. The accidents of geography and the arbitrary lines of local school districts can afford no ground for financial and the concomitant educational inequities among the school children of a state.

These are the principles which are echoing throughout the country and have provided the foundation for the recent school finance reform movement. The pervasiveness of the problem is to be found in the fact that there are currently over fifty *Serrano*-type suits before courts in thirty-one states.

Stimulated by the *Serrano* decision and those that have followed, Illinois has examined this issue at close range. In November of 1971, the Superintendent's Advisory Committee on School Finance was established. A short time later Governor Richard Ogilvie established a Commission on Schools which, among other things, studied the question of school finance. The reports of both of these groups contain many recommendations for change in the present system and call for a substantial increase in the state's share of school funding. Together they outline the kind of school finance system which policymakers should seek over the long run, as well as indicating some of the paths which lead in that direction. The rate at which reform proceeds will be greatly influenced by the availability of increased state and federal resources.

Reform will also be influenced by the U.S. Supreme Court's decision in the *Rodriquez* case. On March 21, 1973, the Supreme Court reversed the earlier lower court *Rodriquez* decision by a five to four vote. This historic decision was based on two overriding principles. First, the court declared that education is not a fundamental right guaranteed by the federal constitution. It denied that Texas law had either created a class of citizens based on wealth or that such a classification, if it existed, was suspect as are classifications based on race and other standards tending to deny a constitutional right. Second, the court said that it was reluctant to become entangled in state tax and educational issues. Speaking for the majority, Justice Powell said:

> It has simply never been within the constitutional prerogative of this court to nullify statewide measures for financing public services merely because the burdens or benefits thereof fall unevenly, depending upon the political subdivisions in which citizens live.[7]

At the same time the Supreme Court declared that "the need is apparent for reform." It did not deny that present methods of financing education produce hardships or inequities. Relief from those conditions, however, was not to be found under the equal protection clause.

> The need is apparent for reform in tax systems which may well have relied too long and too heavily on the local property tax. And certainly, innovative new thinking as to public education, its methods and its funding, is necessary to assure both a higher level of quality and greater uniformity of opportunity.[8]

The effect of this decision, of course, has been to place the burden of reform completely on the shoulders of the states. The court insists that school finance is a political question and that "ultimate solutions must come from the lawmakers and from the democratic pressures of those who elect them." Whether sweeping reform comes or not remains to be seen. Clearly, had it been court-induced, reform would have come more quickly.

If the *Rodriquez* reversal has taken some of the impetus out of the reform movement, what can the states reasonably be expected to do in the near future?

One would hope that state legislatures would approve programs which not only substantially increase state funding, but distribute those resources so as to achieve greater equalization than present formulas provide and so as to recognize the differential needs of underprivileged children and the higher cost of effectively educating them. In addition, state aid programs should be formulated so as to complement efforts presently underway to provide greater property tax equity. The categorical programs, discussed above, should be incorporated into state aid formulas so that the programs are retained while assistance is provided in an equalized manner, thus permitting poor districts, as well as rich, to offer effective specialized educational programs.

Ultimately, however, the efforts of the states in this area must lead them to one of two possible conditions neither of which, unfortunately, was specified by the U.S. Supreme Court. Those possibilities are that (1) each district in the state must have access to the same resources per weighted pupil as any other district that is making a comparable effort, or (2) that the state will have nearly total responsibility for financing education, with local discretion being reserved for enrichment programs exclusively and expenditures per weighted pupil being nearly equal through the state. At present many states are striving to achieve the first, while recognizing that it may ultimately be necessary for them to satisfy the second.

Remedies

It seems clear that the remedy in the equal protection cases will involve state initiative and undoubtedly a substantial increase in educational funding by the states. Among the alternatives most frequently discussed are full state funding, or a revised joint state-local funding program by which all districts would have equal access to property tax resources.

Full funding would involve a distribution of funds on the basis of equal grants per pupil. Variations in spending to accommodate differential costs and special education needs would be allowed. Under this approach, a state might choose to fund education with no provision for local taxes, or it might provide a basic flat grant per pupil while permitting local school districts to supplement state revenue up to twenty percent with revenue obtained from a local tax levy.

Full state funding, in short, would require the state to assume explicit responsibility for the collection of revenues and for the distribution of these revenues to school districts according to a state-defined system of goals and priorities. Such a system would be able to address itself to the equity problems described above, and would seem to be in accord with the recommendation of the President's Commission on School Finance, namely, that the states should assume nearly the full cost of elementary and secondary education.

> The Commission recommends that state governments assume responsibility for financing substantially all of the non-federal outlays for public elementary and secondary education, with supplements permitted up to a level not to exceed 10 percent of the state allocation. The Commission further recommends that state budgetary and allocation criteria include differentials based on educational need such as the increased costs of educating the handicapped and disadvantaged, and on variations in educational costs within various parts of a state.[9]

Not only does the Commission support full-state funding, but it has also recommended a program of federal incentives to stimulate the states to move toward full funding over a reasonable period of time.

With respect to joint state-local funding methods, two different approaches might be used to satisfy the court decisions. On the one hand, many of the existing state aid formulas could be modified to guarantee that every district received a foundation equal to the per-pupil spending level of the wealthiest district. On the other hand, equalizing formulas such as *power equalizing, percentage equalizing,* and *resource equalizing* would require that equal local tax rates result in equal per weighted pupil expenditures.

Where a district's assessed valuation at a given tax rate does not produce the prescribed revenues, the state would pay for the difference. In cases where a given tax rate generates more revenue than is needed for the allowable level of spending, local districts would be allowed some leeway and discretion to spend excess dollars.

The arguments for and against these various approaches are multitudinous. The proponents of full state funding claim that their approach will equalize educational opportunity, provide needed tax equity, reduce inter-district competition, promote far more efficient school district organization, and allow local schools to determine more easily priorities and the efficient use of resources. The opponents of full state funding insist that such an approach will produce a "levelling down" for certain high-expenditure districts. They claim there will be a regression toward mediocrity, a dilution of local control, a diminution of diversity, and a loss of flexibility.

While no particular route of escape is endorsed in this book, it is clear that alternative methods of escape do exist and are under serious consideration in many quarters. It would be a mistake, of course, to permit subjective attitudes relative to the Supreme Court's decision in *Rodriquez* to stampede policymakers prematurely in one or another direction. On the other hand, its decision should not become a basis for inaction by the states. One would hope that the widespread publicity which has attended the revelations regarding school finance disparities would hasten reform.

Change in the system of financing education is inevitable. It would have come more quickly if it had been decreed by the courts. In any event, reform, whether court decreed or legislatively prescribed, must satisfy and be evaluated in terms of certain criteria.

1. *Equity in taxation*—the system should work to eliminate wide disparities in tax burden between taxpayers in similar circumstances. Equal tax effort should produce equal revenue.
2. *Adequacy*—the system should distribute sufficient funds to provide a reasonable level of education for all children.
3. *Affordability*—the system should require funding within the financial capabilities of the state and its taxpayers.
4. *Equalization of access to educational opportunity*—the

system should improve the access of each student to a quality education.

5. *Efficiency*—the system should help promote educational practices which provide the most favorable ratio between costs and the benefits to be derived. The system should not foster or preserve inefficient practices and organizations.

6. *Decentralization of decision-making*—the system should provide for a reasonable balance of decision-making power among the state, the educational profession, elected school officials, the local community, and the student and his family.

7. *Constitutionality*—the system must be consistent with both state and U.S. constitutions.[10]

The fact that few state systems for financing education can begin to meet these standards is not only a cause for concern but the most persuasive argument for reform. The states ought to resist pressure for quick and easy solutions to what are clearly complicated economic, social, and educational problems. Some of the options available to the schools have been suggested. Each deserves serious and careful consideration.

There are people who argue that the movement for educational finance reform while perhaps defensible on grounds of equity will make little difference from an educational point of view. Christopher Jencks proposes, for example, that "unequal expenditures do not . . . account for the fact that some children learn to read more competently than others, nor for the fact that some adults are more economically successful than others." It may be true, of course, that reform of school finance will not make life "better in the hereafter," but even Jencks agrees that "it can be justified on the grounds that it makes life better right now."

> Some schools are dull, depressing, even terrifying places, while others are lively, comfortable, and reassuring. If we think of school life as an end in itself rather than a means to some other end, such differences are enormously important. Eliminating these differences would not do much to make adults more equal, but it would do a great deal to make the quality of children's (and teachers') lives more equal. Since children are in school for a fifth of their lives, this would be a significant accomplishment.[11]

The case for reform can be made on legal, educational and moral grounds. One can reasonably argue that until steps have been taken to equalize the quality of children's lives in the schools, it is premature to make definitive judgments about the impact of equal educational opportunities on the achievement of students or their performance as adults in the larger society. Because educational evaluation and available tools for insuring accountability are primitive at best, the burden of proving that equal educational expenditures have little or no effect on the quality of education rests with the critics. The inconclusiveness of much of the current research in this area is due in large measure to the inadequacy of evaluative instruments as well as this society's failure to give equal educational opportunity, in its broadest sense, a chance to succeed.

How the schools are financed has a direct and unmistakable relationship to the existence or non-existence of equal educational opportunities. As the Fleischmann Commission noted:

> One of the functions of an educational system is to act as a sorting device. Classification of people on grounds of ability and aptitude occurs all the time, and schools often act as a transmitter of the process. But if primary schooling of some children is of vastly greater quality than that of other children, the sorting process is ineffective and dangerous. Local tastes for basic educational services should not distort the function of the sorting mechanism and possibly undermine students' potentials and achievements.[12]

Clearly, such distortions are occurring and will continue to occur until the various states reform their systems for generating and allocating educational resources.

AID TO NONPUBLIC SCHOOLS

One of the factors complicating the already complicated school finance picture is the pressure being exerted on the states to provide financial assistance to the nation's hard-pressed nonpublic schools. State legislatures find themselves torn between two principles. First, all children should share equitably in the resources available for education. Second, no public programs should be undertaken that violate the constitutional prohibition against any governmental establishment of religion or the guarantee of free exercise of religion. Whether these two principles can be reconciled has not yet been definitively determined. The ultimate arbiter in these matters will be the U.S. Supreme Court.

What really is at issue here is not only the future of nonpublic education in this country but the future of the public schools as well. The so-called nonpublic school problem is, in the final analysis, really a public school problem. Current expenditure for nonpublic schools is estimated at over $4 billion a year. Permit these schools to close down, and public school costs will increase substantially. Permit these schools which presently enroll 5.6 million of the nation's 51.6 million elementary and secondary students to close down, and the public schools will experience not only an unacceptable level of overcrowding in existing public facilities, but greater demands for capital construction. Permit these schools to close down and both freedom of choice and diversity will be sacrificed, two concepts traditionally cherished in this country.

To understand the gravity of this issue, one must first examine the conditions which underlie the present crisis and second the alternative methods for dealing with it.

The situation in Illinois is typical of the conditions to be found in every state. The nonpublic schools have lost about 117,000 students in the last four years. Although Illinois' Catholic schools had ninety percent of the total nonpublic enrollment in 1966-67, they have experienced ninety-eight percent of the enrollment decline in recent years. As a matter of fact, all the other nonpublic schools of the state actually gained 311 students during this period, and nine of the twelve types of schools, denominational and otherwise, had increased enrollments. Some of these increases were quite sizable. For example, Jewish schools increased their enrollment by nearly twenty percent; the Greek Orthodox schools by about fifteen percent; and the Episcopalian schools by nearly thirty-five percent.

One reason why Catholic school enrollments have been declining is that the birth rate for Catholics, as well as others, has been declining. In the city of Chicago, for example, Catholic baptisms fell from 60,200 in 1960 to 45,000 by 1969 with nearly three-fourths of the decline occurring in the last five years. Although the number of Catholics living in Chicago declined during this period, it is hardly possible that this reduction was as great as the twenty-five percent decline in baptisms. As a consequence of the accelerating decline in baptisms, even a greater decline in first grade enrollments can be expected during the next five years than has already been experienced. Recent reductions in Catholic first grade classes have been greater than at any other grade level.

A second important factor causing the decline in Catholic school enrollments has been the out-migration of potential Catholic school students from central cities where these schools tend to be concentrated to suburban areas where there are fewer Catholic schools. Although the suburbs totally have a larger population than the cities, they have only twenty-five percent of the Catholic elementary schools and nineteen percent of the Catholic high schools, while the cities have thirty-three percent and forty-nine percent respectively. During the last decade, an estimated 550,000 white people moved out of the city of Chicago to the suburbs, while many black people moved into the city. The effect has been to increase the proportion of students in the public schools of Chicago and to reduce the Catholic school enrollment in the city. Between the school year 1968-69 and 1972, the Catholic elementary school enrollment in Chicago alone declined by nearly 20,000 or 13.8 percent.

The Elementary and Secondary Nonpublic Schools Study Commission of Illinois has noted that the relative attractiveness of public and nonpublic schools changes dramatically as one moves from the city, where public schools are bitterly criticized, to the suburbs, where public schools are in high repute.[13] In reaching this conclusion, the Commission relied upon the questionnaire which was answered by nonpublic school principals. The Commission found that only 18.8 percent of suburban nonpublic school principals thought parents viewed these schools as "much superior" academically to public schools, while forty-one percent thought so in general urban areas and fifty-seven percent thought so in urban poverty areas. One conclusion was unavoidable: "In the suburbs, where public schools usually are characterized by more adequate funding, fewer students with severe difficulties, more mutual understanding vis-a-vis their communities, and less racial strife, nonpublic schools do not represent such a vital option for parents." Limited state aid to nonpublic schools is not likely to stop the migration of Catholics from city to suburb and, therefore, is not likely to significantly affect this cause of nonpublic school enrollment loss.

The most popular explanation for the decline in Catholic school enrollment has been the increased tuitions that have taken place. Average tuition fees for the first six grades rose from $67 to $138 per year between 1966-67 and 1970-71. During this period, Catholic school enrollments decreased by 15.5 percent. It appears that Catholic parents are not as willing to absorb tuition increases as they have been in the past or as parents who are presently supporting other denominational schools. To the extent that state aid will reduce the rate of tuition increase in Catholic schools, it has some potential for reducing the rate at which students leave the Catholic schools. However, Pennsylvania's experience with parochiaid does not offer much encouragement in this regard. Although the state provided $5,000,000 in 1968-69, $17,500,000 in 1969-70, and an estimated $20,000,000 in 1970-71, the nonpublic school enrollment of the state has declined by over ten percent in less than two years. In addition, it is reported that the two major Catholic systems (Pittsburgh and Philadelphia) are both under great financial pressure, although they received over $5 million and $8 million in state aid respectively. This situation has worsened in the wake of the Supreme Court's ruling in 1971 that the Pennsylvania law was unconstitutional.

Another important factor which has contributed to the Catholic school enrollment decline has been the rapid reduction in the availability of religious teachers. The number of full-time religious teachers in the five dioceses of Illinois, excluding one, declined by nearly 1,000 from the 1967-68 school year to a level of only 6,778 only two years later. This represents a thirteen percent decline in two years and means that only about forty-eight percent of all Catholic school teachers now belong to religious orders.

The decline in the availability of religious teachers has two major effects on the enrollment picture of the Catholic schools: (1) it substantially increases the operating cost of the school because of the enormous differential between the stipend paid the religious teacher and the salary that must be paid to the lay teacher; and (2) the influence that the reduction in sisters has upon the religious image of the school. If parochiaid is to become a permanent fixture, it is clear that a substantial amount of it will undoubtedly be absorbed in replacing religious teachers with higher paid lay teachers. However, no amount of state aid will greatly influence the decline in the number of religious teachers available to the Catholicschools.

Finally, there is a good deal of evidence that indicates that attitudinal changes on the part of Catholic parents are also responsible for the observed decline in Catholic school enrollments. As noted earlier, statistics indicate that the proportion of baptized children attending local Catholic schools has declined substantially during the last five years. The proportion of families which belong to a parish and send their children to the parish school has also declined perceptibly during the last five years. In June of 1970, the Gallup Poll indicated that seventy-five percent of the adults surveyed thought "religion as a whole" was losing its influence in American life. Comparable percentages for 1965 and for 1957 were forty-five percent and fourteen percent. Other surveys indicate that church attendance is at an all-time low. Once again, the future looks no brighter than the past and the enactment of limited aid to nonpublic schools is not likely to have much influence.

These findings reveal that the parochial school problem is not simply a financial one, and, as a consequence, a strictly financial solution is not really a solution. The Catholic school of the future will not be the same as in the past, no matter how much state aid is forthcoming. Indirect state aid may defray some of the cost increases that are coming and may reduce the rate of tuition increases, but it will surely not stop, or even significantly retard, the rate of Catholic school enrollment loss. Nonpublic schools will continue to lose students, because modest amounts of state aid will not significantly influence the birth rates of Catholic families, the migration of Catholic families from cities to suburbs, the decline in religious vocations, or the increasingly secular attitudes of Catholic parents.

What then can and should be done? There are four alternatives that have been suggested by those of varying viewpoints for dealing with this crisis.

The first alternative is to do nothing and let those nonpublic schools which cannot sustain themselves close their doors. Those who would choose this option are primarily concerned about the constitutionality of the other alternatives and the effects the assistance would have on the public school system itself. These are legitimate concerns, but, unfortunately, the dilemma which faces the nonpublic schools and the dilemma which would face the public schools if the nonpublic schools were to close are considerations of equal importance. Consequently, this alternative has been rejected by most observers as not being in the best interest of all the people, nor of all the children, whether they be in nonpublic or public schools.

A second suggested approach would ease the "phase out" of the nonpublic schools by providing a modest amount of financial or non-financial aid. Included in this category are proposals which would:

1. Provide auxiliary services, such as textbooks and student services including medical, psychological, and counseling assistance;
2. Allow limited shared-time arrangements using public school facilities;
3. Permit the purchase of secular educational services using limited amounts of state money;
4. Establish a voucher program which also involves the same modest amounts;
5. Authorize income tax exemptions (both state and federal) for all educational expenditures;
6. Allow "Bingo" games to be conducted by church-related organizations so long as the proceeds are used for educational purposes; and,
7. Provide impaction aid to public school systems affected by nonpublic school closings.

Each of these proposals have differing constitutional prospects, as well as various advantages and disadvantages. However, all suffer individually or collectively from the fact that they do nothing to insure the continuation of educational pluralism in this country. An additional problem with most of these approaches is that they hold out the hope of future increases in the aid level and, consequently, retard effective planning for realistic educational endeavors. The primary effect of each of these proposals is to temporarily offset the rapidly rising cost of nonpublic education and, thereby, permit some time for planning the phase out. If Pennsylvania's experience is indicative, that breathing space will be very short, if not non-existent.

The third alternative is to stop the decline in nonpublic school enrollment through *substantial* amounts of financial assistance from the state. It has been estimated that a subsidy of $250 a year for each nonpublic school pupil over a five-year period would be required in order to stop the decline in nonpublic school enrollment. The present annual cost of such a program would be approximately $110 million. Several serious problems are created by such a plan, the foremost of which would undoubtedly be the development of innumerable, new, private schools whose educational programs might seriously detract from, rather than enhance, the achievement of our national goals. A related problem would be the probable loss by the public school system of its better students and its most interested parents. As a result of this alternative's lack of feasibility, plus these disadvantages, this alternative does not enjoy widespread support.

The fourth and last alternative is to alter the existing arrangements between the public and nonpublic schools of an area so as to preserve the nonpublic schools and also improve the overall quality of education afforded to all students, both public and nonpublic.

Aid to nonpublic schools, of course, is not unprecedented. The Elementary and Secondary Education Act of 1965 extends benefits to students in nonpublic schools on the theory that the various types of aid it offers go to qualifying children, not to their schools. Research grants, scholarships, construction grants and loans have been available to religiously affiliated colleges and universities for years, and curiously enough, with little public controversy. "Supporters of nonpublic schools," the President's Commission on School Finance notes, "wonder why the constitutional line should be drawn at twelfth grade."[14]

Several states have adopted laws which are designed to reimburse teachers from nonpublic schools for a portion of their salaries for instruction in secular subjects. Others have adopted or are considering tuition-grant plans which would enable a youngster to obtain his education at approved nonpublic schools. Still others have or are proposing to increase present programs of public aid to nonpublic schools. And a number of states and the federal government are considering a variety of tax-credit proposals. Almost all of these efforts are in various stages of litigation due to unresolved church-state entanglement issues.

In 1972 the Illinois General Assembly enacted a series of parochiaid bills. The "Nonpublic State Parental Grant Plan to Low Income Families Act" provides for reimbursement to parents of children as partial payment for the educational expenses incurred. This per child grant is to be equal to the actual per pupil amount contributed by the state to the public school district within which the particular nonpublic school child resides. As the act's title suggests, these grants are to be limited to parents whose family income is less than $3,000 per year due to payments under the state's aid to families with dependent children program. The Chicago District Court found this act unconstitutional, a decision which was appealed to the Illinois Supreme Court.

A second bill, the "Nonpublic State Parental Grant Act", called for the furnishing of textbooks and auxiliary services to nonpublic school children by public school districts. The public school district is then reimbursed at the end of the school year for monies spent in providing these services. Under this act districts which provide free textbooks to their students are obligated to provide free texts to nonpublic students, while those which rent books must rent them at the same rate to nonpublic schools. However, if a district sells textbooks to public students, it is not obligated to provide free textbooks to nonpublic school children.

The auxiliary services covered by this legislation refer to health, guidance, counseling, psychological, and remedial and therapeutic programs. As with textbooks, these services are to be provided to nonpublic students on the same basis as they are provided in a public school. For example, if a public school district has one hundred students requiring remedial instruction and provides four remedial teachers, then the district must furnish one remedial teacher for every twenty-five students needing such service in nonpublic schools. Or, if a public school has one nurse for every 5,000 students, then provision must be made on the same basis for nurses in nonpublic schools. On the other hand, public school districts are not required under this act to provide any auxiliary services to nonpublic students which are not provided their own students. This act was declared to be constitutional by the Chicago District Court. However, this decision, too, was appealed to the Illinois Supreme Court.

In October of 1973, the Illinois Supreme Court struck down as unconstitutional the $20.5 million appropriation to provide textbooks and other services to students in non-public schools and the

$4.5 million grant to reimburse low-income parents who send their children to such schools. The court tended to side-step the issue of separation of church and state, having concluded that the principal provision of the law "does not treat all students alike." This, the court said, is because books and services for public school children are provided by local taxpayers, while those for non-public school children would under this provision be paid for by the state. The smaller grant to low-income families was found violative of the Constitution because, in the court's view, it was an effort to provide desired financial support for non-public, sectarian institutions.

The U.S. Supreme Court's actions with regard to nonpublic school aid provide no basis for optimism. Pennsylvania and Rhode Island laws have been found to be unconstitutional under the religion clauses of the First Amendment, because in the court's view they fostered excessive entanglement between government and religion. The court concluded that entanglement arose because of six conditions:

1. The religious purpose and operation of church-related elementary and secondary schools;
2. The enhancement of the process of religious indoctrination resulting from the impressionable age of pupils, particularly in elementary schools;
3. The necessity of state surveillance to insure that the teachers, who were subject to control by religious organizations, observed the restrictions as to purely secular instruction;
4. The state's examination of the parochial schools' financial records to determine which expenditures were religious and which were secular;
5. The probable intensification of political divisiveness along religious lines resulting from the annual appropriations required under the statutes, benefiting relatively few religious groups;
6. The self-perpetuating and self-expanding propensities of the statutory programs.[15]

It is too early to tell whether a statute can be drawn to satisfy these and other constitutional concerns. As Justice Douglas has pointed out, "sophisticated attempts to avoid the Constitution are

just as invalid as simple-minded ones." In any event, it is obvious
that in the absence of a major legal breakthrough the nonpublic
school problem will increasingly become a public school problem.
Any effort to reform school finance, therefore, must take into consideration the future of nonpublic education in this country. And
its future, at least at this point in history, is very much in doubt.

MANAGEMENT OF EDUCATIONAL RESOURCES

At a time when the schools are demanding greater resources, it
is incumbent upon them to use existing revenues more efficiently
and effectively. The issue of economies in education prompted the
President's Commission on School Finance to suggest recently
that if American schools are to succeed in gaining public confidence,

> it is imperative that administrators assess their management
> practices and adopt techniques that maximize the effective-
> ness of educational resources. Education administrators have
> given serious attention to this problem and have produced
> both cost savings and improved management techniques.
> Too often, however, successful experiences in one location
> remain unknown elsewhere. There exists a need to identify
> and disseminate these results as well as new techniques for
> increasing the utilization of people, facilities, and other
> resources.[16]

Public education is a mammoth enterprise. The annual expenditure necessary to support this undertaking is now in excess
of $60 billion annually, five percent of the nation's GNP. Over
fifty million pupils are enrolled in the schools, an increase of
almost twenty percent in the past decade. The Illinois system
alone involves 175,000 full-time individuals, three billion dollars
a year, and over two million students. Therefore, the potential
for waste and inefficiency within public education is always
present. In late 1972 a task force on business management practices
estimated that $240 million or ten percent of all money spent for
education in Illinois was being wasted at all levels of the statewide

educational system on account of inadequate management procedures.

It is time we placed the schools on a sound management basis. It is time educators looked to the private sector for management procedures and techniques that can be adapted to a public agency, always with an eye toward better utilization of scarce resources. There is a growing interest in adopting industrial and commercial management techniques, particularly long-range planning. Some schools are experimenting with Planning, Programming and Budgeting (PPBS) concepts, developing management information systems, and moving toward program budgeting to demonstrate not only how educational dollars were spent, but how much gain in achievement they produced. Some school districts extricated themselves from the building business by transferring all capital construction matters to private architectural consulting firms. Others have realized economies by turning over other support services—textbook warehousing and distribution, cafeterias, and building maintenance—to commercial firms.

The fact that educational funds are often functionally and directionally fragmented at all levels is a concern of educators and lay citizens alike. Unfortunately, given the local character of schools, most state departments of education have little enforcement responsibility for either insuring cost effectiveness within the schools or requiring the adoption of sound business policies and methods. The task, however, is to devise ways of running the schools like any other self-respecting, large-scale enterprise. The task is to equip educators at all levels, like executives in the private sector, to maximize productivity while minimizing costs.

Those educators who are at last beginning to operate through management objectives, program planning and budgeting, management information systems, system analysis, and performance evaluation, suggest that improvements are possible. The widespread use of such techniques will hopefully equip educators to answer the common complaint that we pour both our children and money into the schools, and are never given an accounting of what happens to either. The failure of two-thirds of local educational tax referenda in recent years is only one indication that people feel generally overwhelmed.

However, the challenge is not an easy one. The educational system of Illinois, unlike a large corporation, is segmented into

1083 school districts. Each is vested with prerogatives associated with local government. And because these districts serve a variety of cultural, social, educational, and economic needs, there are few prescriptions which can be uniformly applied to everyone. So while much must be done to improve the management of educational resources at all levels, it must be understood that there are conditions peculiar to education which will make needed improvements in this area difficult.

First, of course, state departments of education should be themselves models of fiscal efficiency, for it is unreasonable to expect the vast systems they oversee to succeed if they have failed. Thus one of the objectives of every state department must be to point the way to better management of educational resources.

In Illinois the state education office is putting management principles to work internally and externally. *Action Goals for the Seventies*, a statement of educational goals and priorities, discussed in Chapter II, has provided program managers within the state office a blueprint from which to design program planning statements and objectives. As a result of this process, agency-wide priorities have emerged and a system of management by objectives has been established. Those objectives accorded high priority have received primary consideration in the allocation of resources. In a few cases, where program objectives demonstrated no relationship to the educational mission of the state, they were either curtailed or eliminated altogether. Similarly, local program planning and the statewide assessment program, both of which were described in Chapter II, will eventually have a significant impact on the use of financial resources.

The goal must be to secure greater productivity, that is, to provide more and better services to the educational community within the framework of reduced budgets. A business-like management approach has permitted the state education agency to reduce the operating budget of the state office three consecutive years, an achievement which is attributable in large measure to internal management improvements.

Management improvements efforts cannot be confined to state education departments. So in Illinois, the state is currently engaged in the development of a new financial accounting manual for local school districts. This new manual will allow local districts to maintain their accounting records on a program basis. This program was implemented in a number of pilot districts which then instituted these new accounting procedures for the 1973-74 fiscal year. Successful completion of the development and conversion phase of the project is anticipated during the remainder of fiscal year 1973 and the successful implementation during fiscal year 1974. Eventually this program will be expanded to involve scores of additional districts.

In addition, grants, totalling $500,000, have been awarded to school districts and cooperatives in fulfillment of the expectations of the Educational Effectiveness and Fiscal Efficiency Act of 1972. This program is designed to foster better and wider use of data systems techniques in educational administration by tapping computer-age technology. The availability of new data will hopefully lead to improved decision-making with regard to educational programs.

The state office is now utilizing computer technology to accelerate payments of grants and reimbursements to local school districts. One aspect of the school finance problem has been the unavailability of cash to meet local obligations. Recognizing this as a problem within the state's means to correct, grant and reimbursement payment procedures have been automated to help alleviate local cash shortages. These are just a few of the activities which a state can undertake to insure more efficient and effective use of school funds.

As noted earlier, a group of Illinois businessmen reported in 1972 that millions of dollars could be saved through the adoption of new management techniques by the schools. Because of their general applicability to other states, some of the task force's recommendations are set forth as are the estimated annual savings for Illinois to be derived from each.

- Consolidate districts with an average daily attendance of 1,000 students or less ($6.4 million).
- Accelerate the reduction of Superintendents of Educational Service Regions to 12 (presently 102) by the end of 1973 ($4.1 million).
- Establish a data process network under the Department of Finance to serve all districts in the state ($5.1 million).
- Adopt a pay-as-you-go method for funding employer contributions to the teacher retirement plans ($33.7 million).
- Initiate a four-part program to improve the collective buying

power of Illinois schools, including cooperative buying and
warehousing ($12.6 million).
- Establish large cooperative bus fleets and centralized maintenance shops owned by participating districts ($3.05 million).
- Utilize public health facilities for school health programs
($4.6 million).[17]

If these recommendations are implemented, Illinois schools stand
to save as much as $70 million a year. However, it is not that easy.
Neither the state department nor the state's school districts presently have the legal authority to engage in any of the above activities. In fact, more than seventy percent of the task force's sug-
gestions, and many are worthwhile, would require legislative
action. Without such action, school districts are powerless to move.
So if the schools are to make significant progress in this arena, the
cooperation of all branches of government is required.

In 1972, the office of the State Superintendent of Education
drafted and introduced into the General Assembly a financial planning bill. This legislation would have required district superintendents to submit reports indicating budgeted expenditures and
revenues for the current fiscal year and anticipated expenditures
and revenues for the coming year. The objective was to provide
the General Assembly with more and better information with which
to make their general educational aid decisions. The bill passed
the General Assembly, but was later vetoed by the Governor, although his own task force on school management practices later
recommended such a procedure as being consonant with sound
management practices. The point is that there are a multitude of
ways in which the schools can better use available resources; they
cannot be expected, however, to do the job alone. State statutes, in
many instances, must be overhauled, and the expertise of the private
sector must be forcibly brought to bear on the management process.

State departments of education should explore the possibility of
creating a pool of management talent from the business community
to assist local schools in resolving management and financial
problems. Although most state departments of education provide
technical assistance to school districts, resources available to them
for this purpose are very limited. The schools, like any other
resource-using activity, can achieve something resembling optimal
economic efficiency, but the sustained involvement and counsel of
the private sector is needed.

School District Organization

The achievement of educational efficiency is difficult, because of the vastness and diversity of the nation's school system. It is riddled with built-in constraints which inhibit higher levels of efficiency. And, of course, it should come as no surprise to anyone that there are many individuals within the educational establishment who view the activities already described with undisguised horror and hostility. The resistance to reform, which is formidable in some quarters, is exemplified by the issue of school district organization.

Fifty years ago there were more than 100,000 local school districts in the United States. As a result of consolidation, there are fewer than 17,000 school districts today, a large percentage of which are found in Illinois. The problem of school district organization is not one which is confined to Illinois, but to understand the implications of school district disorganization in terms of achieving economies and equal educational opportunities, the situation in Illinois is worth examining.

Since 1945 the total number of school districts in Illinois has been reduced from approximately 12,000 to 1,091 in the 1972-73 school year. Of these present districts, 509 are elementary districts, 146 are secondary districts, and 436 are unit districts. Whether the present organization of Illinois school districts is consistent with the State Constitution's requirement that the state provide "an efficient system of high quality public educational institutions and services" is an issue which is being reviewed by the state courts.

Two hundred forty-nine (249) school districts presently enroll less than 300 students. At least seventy-eight elementary school districts have fewer than one teacher per grade. The assessed valuation per pupil in Illinois school districts ranges from $3,451 to $355,386. These and other circumstances have prompted the state to re-evaluate its system of school district organization which permits the continued existence of districts incapable of providing high quality education.

A survey of school districts has been completed to determine the relationship of district organization and related state financial policies to the ability of districts to provide an efficient system of high quality education. The survey results clearly demonstrate that in many instances programs provided students are inadequate to meet their needs; comprehensive services are not available; expenditures of resources among districts are unequal; and resources at the local level are inefficiently used. In many cases, these conditions are directly attributable to faulty district organization.[18]

The enormity of the problem is clear. The data reveal that of the many factors affecting the quality of local educational opportunity, district size is perhaps the most critical. Districts of minimal size are generally inadequate to the task of providing the increasingly broad range of educational programs and services demanded of today's school. This situation appears to be largely true regardless of the wealth, organizational type, or geographic location of such districts.

On the other hand, a large enrollment, in and of itself, does not seem to guarantee that a district is able to provide a wide range of learning opportunities to its students, or that large districts, as a class, necessarily provide their pupils with a better education than small districts. However, there appears to be a high degree of correlation between the size of districts and significant trends in programs, practices, and policy.

The evidence suggests that small districts are generally unable to derive maximum benefit from their investment in education. Excessively small teacher-pupil ratios, limited facilities, and disproportionate administrative costs cause operating costs per pupil in small districts to run higher than those of larger districts. The result is that small districts often provide only limited programs at a disproportionately higher cost.

Moreoever, because of the sizable difference in the wealth of districts, pronounced disparities presently exist in the ability of local districts to provide the level of personnel, facilities, and services necessary for a quality school program. To the degree that the present patchwork pattern of fragmented districts tends to isolate pockets of both poverty and privilege, it appears that many small districts tend to perpetuate this fiscal injustice. Clearly, such fiscal inequities should be remedied.

This new information requires that the assumptions upon which district organization has rested for over a quarter of a century be examined and reformulated. In terms of quality education and economic efficiency, school district reorganization is defensible. Savings derived from reduced operating and administrative budgets alone would involve millions of dollars. But these facts alone will not guarantee that the issue will be dealt with forthrightly now or in the foreseeable future. Considerable pressure will inevitably be brought to bear on state legislatures to preserve the status quo.

What may be needed and is presently under consideration in Illinois is a legislative plan for effective and orderly reorganization of existing school districts through the retention of certain districts and the combination of other districts in order to enhance educational opportunity for the children of the state. The goals of this reorganization plan are: (1) to enable each school district to provide a range of high quality programs adequate to meet the needs of every student; (2) to make it possible for every student to provide a comprehensive range of educational support services; (3) to insure that every child is assured an equal opportunity for quality education; (4) to provide for a more equal expenditure of educational resources among school districts; and (5) to achieve the most efficient use of educational resources at the local level. The plan would concentrate on the reorganization of districts which do not meet minimum enrollment and taxable wealth standards. The primary burden of the reorganization process would be assumed by committees in each educational service region, with provisions for extensive local input, and final approval of all reorganization proposals reserved for the state office of education and local voter approval.

In the absence of sweeping financial reform, school district reorganization alone can help equalize educational opportunities, reduce some of the enormous financial disparities among districts, and effect economies in the day-to-day operations of the schools.

The Year-Round School

One of the more obvious and promising possibilities for improving school management practices revolves around the use of existing school facilities. While the utilization of schools twelve months a year would undoubtedly increase operating expenses at least initially, policy makers are only beginning to understand this concept's potential for reducing capital expenditures, which in recent years have skyrocketed. And this is particularly the case in highly urbanized areas where land and construction costs have resulted in disproportionate capital expenditures by school districts.

The construction and rehabilitation of school facilities represent a major strain on school district resources. In Illinois, an average of $173 million was expended annually between 1966 and 1970 for land acquisition, new buildings and improvements. The anticipated demand between 1973-78 is estimated to be $200 million to $250 million annually.[19] This basic pattern in capital expenditures is found across the country. Obviously, this drain on dollars available for education must be stemmed. One step in the process should involve experimentation with the year-round school and frank assessment of its success.[20]

The nine-month school and three-month vacation calendar is a remnant of an agricultural society. As President Nixon has said, the nine-month school year "may have been justified when most youngsters helped in the fields, but it is doubtful whether many communities can any longer afford to let expensive facilities sit idle for one-quarter of the year." In an effort to deal with current problems, provide meaningful education, and meet the demands of taxpayers to reduce costs or, at least, hold the line on spending, educators and others must look for workable alternatives. As obvious and apparent as it may be, schools can no longer afford to be empty for long or short periods of time.

Today, most of our public elementary and secondary schools are organized around a 180 school-day calendar. Many of these schools are closed during the summer months with little or no use made of their resources. Whether this is a great waste of valuable equipment, professional skills, and learning time is a question which must be answered. Countless numbers of teachers seek temporary employment in unrelated occupations during the summer because they cannot practice their profession. Scores of students plagued with the inability to find summer jobs have inherited many hours of boredom.

Interest in year-round schools is increasing. A growing number of school districts around the country are operating year-round programs, and many others are considering the adoption of a year-round calendar in the near future. Also impressive is the number of state education agencies and state legislatures that are studying the possibility of assisting local districts in implementing year-round programs.

The full year school calendar is not a new idea. In the early part of this century, many schools were providing recreational programs during the summer months. Later, these "vacation schools", as they were called, began to assume a more academic orientation. Probably the best known and largest of these attempts to implement a year-round calendar was a program which began in Newark, New Jersey, in 1912 and continued until the depression forced the adoption of a more limited school program in 1931. At that time this was only one of very few programs, but today year-round schools are not so few in number.

What is the year-round school? How does it work? And, why does it appeal to so many?

There are many names associated with the concept: year-round school, extended school year, expanded calendar, but they all have the same basic aim. That aim is to make maximum use of all facilities and expand the choices offered to both students and teachers.

Basically, there are three organizational plans that seem to be most popular: the modified summer school plan, the multiple trails plan, and the staggered quarter plan.

As the name implies, the modified summer plan is the regular 180-day school year, plus summer school. However, rather than providing only remedial courses, make-up and enrichment courses are offered during the summer. The major aim of this program is to enable the accelerated student to finish his program in three years. The cost of operating this program is usually higher than other year-round programs, but a total commitment to year-round schools is not necessary.

The multiple trails plan necessitates the complete reorganization of secondary schools, and emphasizes individualized instruction and economic gains. The school day is rescheduled into time modules of varying lengths. Some modules are fifteen minutes and others are thirty minutes or longer. Classes do not meet as often. The school year is about 210 days with vacations in July or August. The traditional Easter and Christmas vacations are maintained. Continuous progress for each student is the ultimate aim of this program. Instead of the traditional grade lines, a pupil is able to move along a subject trail at his own rate. Also, the traditional curriculum is reorganized into broad resource units which can be completed in four, five or six weeks.

Probably the most popular of all year-round school programs is the staggered quarter plan. It provides a forty-eight week school year divided into four terms of twelve weeks. Students are divided into four equal sized groups and attend three of the four quarters. At any time, then, three-fourths of the students are attending class and one-fourth are on vacation. Generally the students can choose the quarters they wish to attend and the teachers have the option of working three or four quarters with additional compensation if they work four. Under the basic plan, there would be twelve work weeks each quarter or a total of forty-eight work weeks, and thirty days' vacation each year. This plan is usually favored by districts that desire to reduce the need for new buildings and furnishings. Adjusting to a new vacation pattern appears to be one of the major obstacles of this plan. Also, some problems arise in scheduling extracurricular activities and in dividing students into groups under voluntary staggered quarter plans.

A variation of the basic staggered quarter plan is the 45-15 plan. Generally used in elementary schools, this program involves forty-five days of class and fifteen days of vacation. Holidays and the traditional Christmas and Easter vacation account for the balance of time out of school.

The only school district in Illinois operating a year-round school program, the Valley View Elementary District No. 96 in Lockport, employs this type of plan. Valley View's 45-15 plan is, in effect, the basic quarter plan. Students do not have the option of choosing their vacation quarter.[21]

Because of the overwhelming support from the community, the teachers, students, and the officials at Valley View say the program is a definite success. The apparent reason for this success has been a result of thorough planning and community involvement. Valley View began the year-round program to avoid constructing additional school facilities. This involved informing the public of the problems and seeking support for this plan over less desirable alternatives. Over an eight year period the district had been hit by fifteen different tax increases, and it had reached the limit of its bonding power for building. The alternatives facing Valley View were clear: house over 60 students in some classrooms, hold double sessions, or keep the schools open all year. The district chose the latter alternative. Greater building utilization, bus utilization, lower summer juvenile crime rates, and less school vandalism have been the most obvious benefits. The district has discovered, too, that fewer desks, textbooks, library books, audio-visual aids and other items have had to be purchased, even though the district's student population is increasing.

So the year-round school program has appeal for taxpayers and businessmen who feel that it makes more sense to have facilities in use throughout the year. Many communities are no longer willing to pass building bond issues without first looking at the year-round alternative. It is rather easy to predict that the cry for financial accountability will continue to be a strong determinant in whether or not a school district changes its school calendar.

In addition, the benefits to students and teachers are many. More flexible enrollment practices, new types of courses, individualized instructional programs, and other instructional changes usually accompany year-round programs. In addition, since vacations would be shorter and more frequent, the amount and rate of learning can or should be increased, while the forgetting rate, usually resulting from a long summer vacation, should be reduced. Teaching and learning should be more pleasurable. Teachers would benefit since the program would provide twelve-month positions for those who wanted them. Also teacher sabbatical leaves could be taken at times most beneficial to the school's administration. Instead of losing one full year of teaching time, the teacher could work the summer term thereby saving the district twenty-five percent of the usual cost of sabbaticals. The board of education is much more responsive when costs for a leave are reduced.

Of course, there is criticism of the year-round school concept. Ironically, opponents of the concepts often use the same financial argument that proponents use, but, of course, in a completely opposite approach. Many feel that the year-round school is more costly. This is true in terms of instructional materials and salaries, but savings in building costs and a lower per pupil cost for instruction are still realized. Most educators would agree that operational costs remain about the same, but that building costs are reduced appreciably.

Another argument frequently offered against the year-round school is that the existing school system is in need of reform, and, therefore, should not be extended. Some feel that cosmetic changes, like lengthening the school year, will not insure the making of important changes. Some predict problems with an increased number of people in the job market and increasing numbers finishing high school and college a year or two earlier. Of course, there is the disruption of traditional vacation schedules. This also applies to teachers who, some say, need a three-month vacation each year to renew themselves.

These different viewpoints are reflected in the opinions of teachers, administrators, students, and businessmen. Businessmen generally favor the plan for economic reasons, although some who operate seasonal businesses are not always in agreement. Administrators favor the plan for economic reasons and add that there are many more opportunities for curricular revision. Teachers and students are more divided. Many teachers cite the advantages of twelve-month employment and the increased flexibility in programs. Others are afraid that the year-round school may cause more problems and solve few. The major opposition from students involves the elimination of the three-month vacation. Most students, though, usually agree that the option to attend class all year should be available for those who wish to attend.

Two bills passed by the Illinois legislature permit the operation of a year-round school and provide funds for operation, thus making it easier than in most states, should a district choose to adopt a year-round school plan. In 1969, a bill changing the method of computing state aid payments, to be based upon the average daily attendance for the best six months of the fiscal year, was passed. In 1970, the legislature passed a law that permits districts to operate schools on a full year basis with the approval of the state education office. This bill requires that students be in attendance for a minimum of 180 school days and that teachers not be required to teach more than 185 days.

Another piece of legislation, called the "Full Year School Incentive Bill," is designed to encourage interested school districts to study the feasibility of the twelve-month school and authorizes the state to aid in the preliminary transition costs if a district decides to adopt a full-year plan. A number of school districts are now involved in this program, and it is hoped that their experience will provide a basis for meaningful research into the successes and failures of the twelve-month school.

It is evident from the programs now in operation that not all plans will solve all needs within a district. The year-round school is not a panacea for all educational ills. No matter how much research is done on year-round schooling, each individual district will have to decide for itself which type of basic plan will best suit its needs. But in view of the alternatives available to school districts, the twelve-month school must be considered one of the most promising.

EDUCATIONAL VOUCHERS

Conservatives, liberals, and radicals have all complained at one time or another that the political mechanisms which supposedly make public schools accountable to their clients work clumsily and ineffectively. Parents who think their children are getting inferior schooling can, it is true, take their grievances to the local school board or state legislature. If legislators and school boards are unresponsive to the complaints of enough citizens, they may eventually be unseated, but it takes an enormous investment of time, energy, and money to mount an effective campaign to change local public schools. Dissatisfied though they may be, few parents have the political skill or commitment to solve their problems this way. As a result, effective control over the character of the public schools is largely vested in legislators, school boards, and educators, not parents.[22]

Since parents cannot rely solely on the political process to influence educational affairs, mechanisms must be set into motion which enable them, in the words of the Center for the Study of Public Policy, "to take *individual* action in behalf of their own children." Increasing the control of parents over the education of their children requires reform, like the local participatory planning discussed in Chapter II. However, there is a growing school of thought in this country that such reforms, though well-intended, will only superficially enhance the control of parents. Educators, the critics charge, simply will not allow real and substantive reforms to take root.

The only way to humanize the curriculum, improve the performance of teachers, insure equal educational opportunity, and provide genuine accountability is to break down the monopolistic character of public education. This is the message coming from those who believe that only the forces of competition and the marketplace can truly transform elementary and secondary education. Many people who view the present educational system as hopelessly beyond redemption believe that "education vouchers" are the key to a more promising future. Under this system, the government or some other public authority issues vouchers to parents. Parents take their children and, of course, their vouchers to the schools of their choice. The schools then return the vouchers to the government which in turn sends the schools checks equal to the value of the vouchers. The end result of this process is that educational funds go only to schools in which parents choose to enroll their children. Those schools which cannot attract applicants either improve or simply go out of business.

There are numerous and diverse voucher systems on the drawing boards. The differences among the various schemes advanced thus far involve sharp differences of opinion about the extent to which the educational marketplace should be regulated. All of the proposals, however, promise to develop and make available to all parents alternatives to education. The use of vouchers, according to the Center for the Study of Public Policy, "would make it possible for parents to translate their concern for their children's education into action. If they did not like the education their child was getting in one school (or if the child did not like it), he could go to another. By fostering both active parental interest and educational variety, a voucher system should improve all participating schools, both public and private."[23]

The debate over vouchers finds the educational establishment in general very substantially on the side of opposition. The American Association of School Administrators, the American Federation of Teachers, the National Education Association, and at least a score of other national education organizations have gone on record for varying reasons against vouchers. And because of a fear that an unregulated voucher system could intensify racial and socioeconomic isolation in the schools, some civil rights organizations, including the N.A.A.C.P., have expressed strong reservations.

The proponents claim, on the other hand, that such a plan would free the public schools from the burden of trying to be all things to all pupils, make teachers and administrators more accountable for the learning of their students, give parents and children of all socio-economic groups real educational alternatives, and provide more equal educational opportunities for disadvantaged children. These claims have prompted L. Jackson Newell to observe that "any reform proposal that promises to ameliorate so many of the central problems of education deserves very careful attention.[24]

However, many believe that the schools, as we know them today, can be made to do an incomparably better job of equalizing educational opportunities and providing new alternatives, and they can do so without reverting to a voucher system. Unfortunately, those who blindly oppose vouchers often do little or nothing to transform the existing system with the result that public impatience grows and sweeping reforms, as represented by education vouchers, gain wider public acceptance. Unless the educational community deals forthrightly with some of the hard issues discussed in this book, a point could be reached in the not too distant future when the public will demand a radical departure from traditional methods. If the schools and their personnel fail to become more client oriented, the current, limited enthusiasm for vouchers could grow substantially in the years ahead.

Since it is quite possible that the voucher system will eventually take root it would be foolish to have a closed mind on the subject. (Much of the turmoil in public education today is the direct consequence of past close mindedness). Because there has been so little experimentation with vouchers it is impossible to generalize about either their workability of their advantages. Even the proponents of vouchers admit that the system does not ensure that every child will get the education he needs, even though it may make such a result more likely. However, this judgment is based on a theoretical model, not empirical evidence.

Therefore, it is clearly impossible to say with certainty at this point that competition would be technologically inefficient in the field of education; or that consumers (parents in this case) are incompetent to distinguish between good and bad educational products; or that competition among schools would encourage consumers, particularly those with financial means, to maximize their private advantages in ways that are not in the public interest. These are among the principal arguments lodged against a voucher system, and, of course, in the absence of countervailing evidence, they are very persuasive. Educators must steadfastly oppose any program which intensifies economic and racial segregation, or produces public support of sectarian instruction, or encourages "hucksterism" in education. Such eventualities are quite possible from both a theoretical and practical standpoint under an unregulated voucher system.

The major experiment involving education vouchers is being funded currently under a continuing Office of Economic Opportunity grant to the Alum Rock Union Elementary School District in San Jose, California. The objectives of this experiment are (1) to improve the education of children generally, but in particular disadvantaged children; and (2) to give all parents in the school district more control over the kind of education their children get. In order to accomplish these objectives the O.E.O. model is a "regulated" one. Recognizing that disadvantaged children are likely to suffer no less in a competitive than a monopolistic market, the Alum Rock plan is structured so as to prevent student isolation based on race, income, or ability. And because of the differential costs involved in educating disadvantaged youngsters, the Alum Rock plan provides substantially more money to schools enrolling disadvantaged children than to schools enrolling only advantaged children.

The Rand Corporation is under contract to evaluate the Alum Rock project, and that analysis, which is expected to be completed in 1975 or 1976, will hopefully allow policymakers to make some rational judgments about the efficacy of vouchers. Of particular interest will be the answers to questions regarding the benefits, if any, derived from *parent choice*. Those questions have been outlined by James Mecklenburger:

- What social and political tensions or benefits emerge when parents usurp this "professional" prerogative?
- Does the educational market place function as some might predict, i.e., do new programs and options develop? Are the customers satisfied? Does the cost of education change?
- Do students learn more, or differently, or worse, than under conventional school patterns?[25]

Until educators have the answers to these questions, they will have to play the wait-and-see game. Until the evidence is in, definitive judgments regarding the efficacy of vouchers should be postponed.

Meanwhile the schools ought to be doing now whatever is necessary to equalize educational opportunities, to nurture a healthy diversity in the school, and to open up alternatives for parents and students. Failure to deal with these vexing problems can only hasten the search for more radical solutions. While no voucher system may be flawless in theory or in practice, such a system may prove in the years ahead to be more perfect and more promising than the present system. In the final analysis, the performance of the schools will determine the course of educational reform.

Chapter VII

STUDENT ADVOCACY
The Issue of Student Rights

The best way to teach dignity and democracy is to make our schools experiences of these important commodities. Education is never a neutral thing—it is either used for the domination or the liberation of people, their domestication or their humanization. And we all know how much our society desperately needs liberated and humanized people.

Community Leader

There is so much debate about whether or not students have rights that many observers have concluded that the issue is part of a much larger question. The question regards the position of young people generally in society. Senator Walter F. Mondale has correctly asserted that "our national myth is that we love children." In many ways, that myth influences what we do and don't do in the schools.

Young people are not allowed to shape the policies which affect their lives. They have little control over their own fate. They can't vote. Society expects them to adjust their behavior to environments created by adults and for adults, environments which too often are designed to meet the narrow needs of adults rather than the unique needs of children.

In fact, despite the myth, ours is not a child-centered society. The unwillingness to feed hungry children, for example, is a devastating statement about the regard this nation—the richest on earth—has for its most valuable resource. The penchant for running kids into court and placing them in detention facilities for indiscretions that never constitute adult offenses is simply unjust. Saddling the juvenile courts with the duty of rehabilitating children who run away, smoke, drink, or refuse to attend school is a measure of society's failure. Day care centers are warehouses for the most part. And, of course, the law gives parents almost every opportunity to reclaim battered children.

Since our society is not child centered, it is not surprising that the schools and what happens inside them reflect in various ways our attitude about young people. This attitude is seen every day in the formulation of policy. Those who steadfastly resist educational reform frequently lose sight of the child. Self-interest, especially among school people, too often outweighs any consideration of what is in the best interest of children. Looking back on the interminable, often acrimonious, discussions the state educational agency has had with school people about desegregation, reform of certification, individualization and other matters, one thing stands out: the infrequency of expressed concerns about the impact particular programs or activities will have on students.

Is desegregation good for students or is it bad for them? Do students need and deserve better teachers or not? Unfortunately, these more fundamental issues are obscured by adult concerns with convenience, local control, and professional prerogatives.

Young people need advocates. They need voices that represent their interests in an adult-dominated environment. There is more than a grain of truth in the observation that in this country societies for the prevention of cruelty to animals have far more members and money than societies for the prevention of cruelty to children. Although no single agency in a community can presume to speak for all children, one of those agencies should be the school. Schools can speak for children by creating an atmosphere in which young people enhance their understanding of the world around them, their capacity for growth, their powers, their regard for freedom, and their worth.

But since our society is not child-centered and since the schools are an extension of society, many schools are hopelessly incapable of igniting and sustaining the joy and exhilaration derived from learning. "Sit Down!" and "Be quiet!" are not only the most favored classroom catchwords, but they tell us a great deal about what is happening in the schools and about our attitudes toward children. In his book, *The Underachieving School*, John Holt explains what the schools often do to youngsters.

> There is much fine talk in schools about Teaching Democratic Values. What the children really learn is Practical Slavery. How to suck up the boss. How to keep out of trouble, and get other people in. "Teacher, Bill is. . . ."
> Set into spirited competition against other children, he learns that every man is the natural enemy of every other man. Life, as the strategists say, is a zero-sum game: what one wins, another must lose, for every winner there must be a loser.
> He learns, not only to be hostile, but to be indifferent. . . .
> He comes to school curious about other people, particularly other children. The most interesting thing in the classroom —often the only interesting thing in it—is the other children. But he has to act as if these other children, all about him, only a few feet away, were not really there. He cannot interact with them, talk with them, often even look at them.

> Splendid training for a world in which, when you're not studying the other person to figure out how to do him in, you pay no attention to him.[1]

These are the conditions which exist in many schools. And they are allowed to persist knowing full well that formal education, for better or worse, helps shape children's personal values, their outlook on life, their opinion of others, and their view of the world. The fact is that although we love our children, we really don't like or trust them very much! This ambivalence helps explain why popular expectations regarding the kind of students turned out by our schools often have little relationship to the final product. The debate over student rights dramatizes this stress between what society wants its young people to be and what they often become.

Society likes to believe, for instance, that all students acquire over the years an appreciation for and positive attitudes toward persons and cultures different from their own. Society likes to think that young people learn that every individual possesses dignity and worth, learn that every person has the right to achieve the best that is in him, and learn that equality of opportunity is, or ought to be, a national preoccupation.

Society likes to believe that our schools and classrooms are laboratories for democracy, places where students acquire habits and attitudes associated with responsible citizenship, places where they not only learn to believe in free society, but how to operate effectively within it, and as a result they become worthy of a free society.

Society hopes, too, that as a consequence of their educational experience students understand constitutional forms and have become thoroughly imbued with a healthy regard for their rights and responsibilities in a democratic society.

But are these really reasonable expectations?

Is it possible, for example, to acquire a sensitivity for civil liberties if high schools are not communities where such principles are exemplified?

Is it possible for students to learn how to strike a balance between the principle of order and the principle of liberty if they are forbidden to exercise initiative or responsibility within their own schools, if regimentation and authoritarian discipline are unbridled?

Is it possible for students to engage intelligently in the free contest of ideas if arbitrary limitations are imposed on what they are allowed to hear, to read, and to say? Is such a clash of ideas possible, if expressions of opinion and points-of-view are limited to what is currently fashionable and orthodox in a given community?

Is it reasonable to expect young people to grow to the political and social maturity required in a democracy if they are denied opportunities to practice, as is practicable, some of the rights of citizens?

These questions have implications not only for the quality of public education, but implications for the quality of American life itself. Many people were alarmed by the delayed public indignation to the revelations surrounding the "Watergate caper." The clandestine designs of those who sought to disrupt and undermine our political processes in 1972 by means of spying, sabotage, and other criminal acts, should have evoked immediate and unmitigated outrage. Perhaps, as Father Theodore Hesburgh has suggested, "we have been so engulfed for so long with so much evil on such a massive scale that our nerve ends are numb." And, as a result, says Father Hesburgh, "we tune out." Tuning out is easy. It is safe to predict that severe and direct penalties await a society which in time of moral crisis tunes out, turns its back on citizens who suffer invasion of privacy by government or anonymous organizations. To tune out is to permit an erosion of all of our freedoms.

The reactions of Americans to the revelations surrounding the break-in of Democratic Party Headquarters tells us something about what is happening and not happening in the schools. Regrettably, and perhaps unintentionally, public education in this country has produced generations of Americans who are either totally alienated by politics and insensitive to constitutional guarantees or who have so little faith in the democratic process that they revert easily to the techniques of disruption and sometimes to violence. That is the price society pays for sheltering students from the real world, for discouraging them from becoming politically involved, for punishing free expression and reasonable dissent, and for permitting students no opportunity for institutional governance and meaningful decision-making.

At public hearings, students have repeatedly told representatives of the state office of education that one of their overriding concerns is decision-making, having a choice in the making and enforcement of rules within their schools. They talk about dissent—being able to criticize and to protest when circumstances warrant. They are asking for due process, a system by which a person accused of something might have a fair chance to defend himself.

These are fundamental virtues in a democratic society, but traditionally there has been no room for them in the schools. How is it possible then for high school graduates to become responsible and alert members of the larger body politic? The truth of the matter is that too many never do, and would not know how if they tried. While civics courses at best superficially and platitudinously portray the virtues and workings of democracy, young people are forbidden to inspect those virtues and workings at close range. Paradoxically, the schools have assiduously guarded against any exercise by students of their democratic prerogatives within or around the schools. Even student government, typically lacking any power and relegated to the most meaningless tasks, is woefully incapable of firing the democratic spirit of young people.

These conditions should concern all citizens, because they help breed cynicism among many well intended and purposeful young people. And that cynicism is frequently carried over into later life. The end product is an adult citizenry whose view of government and whose relationships to other institutions in our society are characterized by skepticism, incredulity, and abandonment. One observer has noted, and he is right, that it is idle to talk about civil liberties to adults who were systematically taught in adolescence that they have none. It is sheer hypocrisy to call or to even hope that such people could be freedom-loving.

So we are confronted with this question: how is it possible, given its incredible successes, that public education has conspicuously failed on this front? "In the United States", de Tocqueville noted in the 1840's, "politics are the end and aim of education." This relationship of politics and education helps explain the predicament in which the schools find themselves today. Historically, in this country, the political goals of public education have transcended in significance the goals associated with scholarship and intellectual development.

When Governor Coles recommended in 1824 that Illinois establish a system of free public schools, he reminded the state legislature that:

> Intelligence and virtue are the main pillars in the temple of liberty. A government founded on the sovereignty of the people and resting on and controlled by them cannot be respectable or even long endure unless they are enlightened. To preserve and hand down . . . that liberty, we must make provisions for the moral and intellectual improvement of those who are to follow us. . . .[2]

What all this meant, as a practical matter, was that the public schools were to civilize people and to tame their anarchistic instincts, and to do so by imposing discipline and respect for authority and by infusing the curriculum with moral instruction and patriotic exercises. And because political aims always overrode intellectual aims, the schools did what they could to eliminate any semblance of highly individualistic conduct on the part of students.

The best guarantee that young people will become useful and law abiding citizens, according to the above viewpoint, was by their being steadfastly obedient to the rules and regulations prescribed by the schools. Unfortunately, this notion conveniently avoided any debate as to whether or not such rules and regulations were reasonable or likely to contribute positively to the educational and personal development of young people.

The expense of public education was always justified, and, to a large extent, continues to be justified in terms of a rather parochial perception of citizenship training. When at the turn of the century, the Georgia Supreme Court declared that public education would be "more of a curse than a blessing", if it "fails to instill in the youthful mind and heart obedience to authority", it sounded a theme which even today is an influential, if not a predominant, view of the student and his proper place in the classroom.[3]

Traditionally, the courts, local school boards, school administrators, and parents have uniformly viewed a free public school education as a privilege which could be granted or withheld at the discretion of the state. Because it was a privilege, almost any standard of conduct could be demanded of students—even if constitutionally protected freedoms were routinely violated. Today, however, public education is being increasingly regarded a right rather than a privilege, a right which must be protected from arbitrary interference. Flowing from this new posture are new demands that students be permitted to speak freely and assemble peacefully, be protected from invasion of privacy and be guaranteed due process of law.

The subject of student rights is a concern because clearly students and administrators are not certain about what rights and responsibilities they have in relation to one another. The absence of guidelines pertaining to such matters at both the local and state levels has only increased the likelihood of future conflicts and confrontations. As a consequence, guidelines are needed to clarify questions relating to freedom of expression, freedom of the student press, freedom of association, participation in school governance, individuality in student appearance, and procedural standards for disciplinary cases.

The conceptual framework of these guidelines deserves some attention, as do those principles and understandings which constitute their foundation.

First, it is clear that students as persons have constitutionally protected rights. The Supreme Court of the United States has stated that "neither the Fourteenth Amendment nor the Bill of Rights is for adults alone."

Second, if students are permitted to exercise these rights within clearly understood limitations, schools can contribute substantially to the development of those skills and attitudes commensurate with good citizenship. On this point, the Supreme Court observed almost thirty years ago that:

> Educating the young for citizenship is reason for scrupulous protection of constitutional freedoms of the individual, if we are not to strangle the free mind at its source and teach youth to discount important principles of our government as mere platitudes.[4]

Third, young people have a right to a public education, and, as students, peculiar rights accrue to them. Every student, for example, has the right to a safe environment within his schools. Likewise, every student must be guaranteed equal access to a quality education, regardless of his race, sex, ethnic background, language, wealth, or marital status. Some people believe that student opinions on matters relating to curriculum development and teacher evaluation should be systematically solicited and considered.

Fourth, every right has a corresponding responsibility whether we are talking about students as citizens or as consumers of education. Guidelines should define those responsibilities, because only through the scrupulous maintenance of this balance will the rights and responsibilities of everyone—students, teachers, administrators, and parents—be preserved.

To be sure, no protected right should ever be construed as license to engage in disorder, or to disrupt classwork, or to interfere with disciplinary processes, or to invade the rights of other students and school personnel, or to express contempt and derision for others because of race, color, or religion.

In short, substantial interference with the educational process is not constitutionally defensible and, therefore, should not be tolerated. If in the exercise of their rights, students are not civil, fair-minded, and solicitous of others, they run the risk of bringing the educational system to a grinding halt. But then that possibility has always existed. There is no reason to believe, as some excitedly predict, that allowances for student freedom will inevitably encourage higher levels of permissiveness or that the educational process will come crashing down around society's head. Such speculation does not take into account either the intelligence and good judgment of most students or the generally high regard with which young people are perceived by others.

Although there is a need for statewide guidelines, local school districts should assume the primary responsibility for guaranteeing the rights of students, teachers, parents, and administrators. Because different communities have special needs and unique problems, every school district should constitute a representative group to formulate a local statement of student rights and responsibilities and to develop practical methods for monitoring grievances relating to the exercise of citizen rights in a school.

Due process must be the principal responsibility of local schools. Formal disciplinary hearings, particularly those involving serious penalties, should probably take place before the school board or a hearing officer appointed by it. The student accused of wrong-doing deserves a fair and impartial hearing. He deserves to be informed of the charges against him, represented by an advisor or an advocate of his choice, given an opportunity to present his own case, and allowed to confront his accusers, and to cross-examine adverse witnesses. These are the most obvious elements of due process. Built into this process should be a procedure for appealing judgments rendered by local school districts, and of particular concern should be those cases involving the expulsion of students.

Given the broad conceptual framework of the guidelines, what specific and desirable outcomes should be sought?

Students should be able to participate meaningfully in the planning and execution of a school's academic program and other activities.

Students should have well-defined and easily accessible avenues of communication with their school boards and administrative personnel.

Students should be free from unreasonable or demeaning abuses, including, of course, excessive corporal punishment.

Students should be free to express sincere and honest opinions and points-of-view in a responsible manner, even if they are unpopular.

Students should be able to dress as they wish or wear their hair in any style, unless there is danger of substantially interrupting the teaching process.

Student files should be considered confidential and closed to persons outside the school system unless this right of confidentiality is waived by the student and/or his parents.

The student press should not be subjected to prior restraint, censorship, or financial threats, and student editors and staff members should not be subject to administrative harrassment or the arbitrary exercise of authority.

A student should not be expelled from school unless it is determined beyond a reasonable doubt that he has engaged in conduct of such a serious nature that removal is necessary to protect other students or preserve their right to get an education. Caution in such cases is warranted, for as the courts have said, terminating a student's education ". . . is . . . to apply the terrible organized force of the state, just as surely as it is applied by the police, the courts, the prison warden, or the militia."

Rights, of course, are not absolute and unabridgeable. Rights do not represent an invitation to disrupt the educational process or to interfere with the education of fellow students. Often forgotten is the fact that parents, taxpayers, administrators, and teachers also have rights and responsibilities with regard to public education. If conflicts are to be avoided, all parties, including students, will neeed to be sensitive to the impact which an assertion of their rights will have on the rights of others. This requires a fair degree of sophistication and reasonableness on everyone's part. A large part of the democratic experience involves balancing assertions of rights by contending individuals and groups. While this process inevitably requires some accommodation and compromise, there should never be a necessity in society to completely abridge any-one's rights.

It must be noted that the law, including judicial decisions, is not entirely clear or unanimous as to what rights students actually have. Because of this legal gray area, it would be inadvisable to require the schools to make allowances for student rights beyond what the law or the courts have decreed. State guidelines, if they are to be effective, should make such distinctions. Administrators and boards of education should be informed of what the law requires with respect to student rights and perhaps encouraged to extend those rights, so far as practicable, beyond present legal requirements.

Democracy has a place in our schools. If it is imperfectly practiced there, and all too often it is, one cannot reasonably expect it to function more perfectly in the larger community. While school administrators bear the major responsibility for insuring the proper operation of our schools, students must also share in that responsibility. The notion that we live under a government of laws, not men, can be given new substance and meaning if those who are concerned and directly involved in public education clearly understand and respectfully observe one another's rights and responsibilities as well as the rules and regulations under which the schools must function.

With clear and precise guidelines on paper, administrators, who often are placed in untenable positions, will be equipped to come to terms with the Constitution, student ferment, and community resistance. It is not an easy task. It is obvious, however, that the great majority of administrators being men and women of good will would welcome an agreement of this matter among students, school boards and themselves. It would permit administrators to move on to some of the larger and more fundamental concerns of education.

Thomas Jefferson believed that there was only one safe depository of the ultimate powers of society and that was the people themselves. If the people did not use power wisely, the remedy was not to take it from them, but to teach them how to use it wisely. And that is what is being advocated here—teaching people how to use their power wisely. Those lessons, most people would agree, are better learned in the schools than in the streets.

The establishment of a student affairs unit within the state education office, its interest in seeing students serve on local school boards in an ex-officio capacity, and its concern with students rights are an outgrowth of the agency's belief that students can make a good and lasting contribution. After all, it is the young people of this country who in this last decade have brought to the fore a heightened perception of reality. It is young people—starting with the civil rights struggle in the South and with its demand for an end to an unjust war—who have compelled others to see the difference between the way things are and how they might be. It is young people who in response to John Kennedy's call have sought to give "enlightenment, vision, illumination" rather than "the sneer of the cynic or the despair of the faint-hearted."

Furthermore, it is the young who appreciate more fully than others that freedom is never an accomplished fact, that freedom is not a fixed and unalterable condition, but a process which is best defended by enlarging it and by exercising it. Viewed from this perspective, it is important that educators address themselves to the question of student rights.

Chapter VIII

THE CHALLENGE OF CHANGE

We have had . . . some success in reducing the size of the curricular smorgasbord for the brighter students and possibly in reducing the more frivolous ways in which many average and below average students used to spend their time in school; but we are a long way from either forcing or persuading the establishment to give all students a sound basic education.[1]

James D. Koerner

Our psychologists and politicians alike are puzzled by the seemingly irrational resistance to change exhibited by certain individuals and groups. The corporation head who wants to reorganize a department, the educator who wants to introduce a new teaching method, the mayor who wants to achieve peaceful integration of the races in his city—all, at one time or another, face this blind resistance. Yet we know little about its sources. By the same token, why do some men hunger, even rage for change, doing all in their power to create it, while others flee from it? I . . . found no ready answers to such questions. . . .[2]

Alvin Toffler

To anyone who has been involved in American public education in the last decade nothing can be more obvious than the need for fundamental changes within the educational system. Yet equally clear is the immense difficulty in bringing about such change, and therein lies the dilemma and frustration of public education today. Serious questions are raised by this situation. Why is change difficult? What are those forces supporting and opposing educational change? What really is wrong with the educational system today? What should be discarded and what should be retained? Other questions reach into the very heart of the American experience itself: What really is the American commitment to education?

These are not questions that lend themselves to quick and easy answers. They are difficult, because they touch so many aspects of the nation's experience, both past and present. The educational system reaches out into the social, economic and political fabric of the nation. To dissect the educational system today is to look at more than teachers, books, curriculum, and buildings. It requires that we examine history, taxation, powershifts, vested interests, national priorities, partisan politics, and the national value system. In many ways educational analysis is self-analysis, for society's hopes and fears, its aspirations and angers are explicitly and implicitly revealed in what it does for and expects from the schools. A time may have been reached in our national history when the average citizen, helpless as he feels about his ability to direct any decisions that affect his life, looks to the schools as the remaining avenue of action. It is there where he can strike out against rising taxes; it is there where he can seek to control values and a moral system which seem to be disintegrating elsewhere; and it is there where he can check any alien public or political philosophy which is counter to what he embraces.

Thus, educational change takes on a more difficult dimension, for change in this realm challenges what is perceived by Americans to be one of the last vestiges of what they control, what they can influence. It is in many ways a last stand against the increasing bigness and anonymity of government and society. And whether the arena is athletics, politics, or education, last stands are emotional and sometimes violent experiences. The phrase "last stand" is used guardedly, for it does not imply that the educational era of local control and leadership has ended. Rather, we may be on the threshold of an era where local control will be considerably increased, but in forms which are strikingly different than we have known.

Some of the challenges facing public education and suggested possible approaches for dealing with them have been described. There is, of course, no unanimity of opinion about any of these matters. Everyone agrees that educational planning is a good thing and ought to be undertaken at every level of the educational system. And in principle at least, no one opposes equal educational opportunity, a more humane and individualized curriculum, better prepared teachers, and a more substantial and equitable financial endowment for the schools. However, when one tries to deal with these principles in a concrete way, one quickly discovers that reaching an agreement on almost any subject is next to impossible.

Every step forward requires a delicate balancing of conflicting opinions. This places an incredible strain on any state department of education which desires to provide leadership. While a state department must be aware of and often responsive to these disparate interests, its perspective must always be statewide in scope and conditioned by a perception of what is in the best interest of all citizens. To bow consistently to the wishes of one or another group is to jeopardize the support of the larger community, and without broad public support significant change in education is impossible. In many ways, it is a miracle that anything ever improves. Fashioning a consensus on any one issue is a herculean task, and when it is completed no one is ever completely satisfied.

Richard Hofstadter once noted that "the history of American educational reformers often seems to be the history of men fighting against an uncongenial environment."[3] Personal experience has revealed just how uncongenial and unyielding that environment can be at times. Educators are frequently asked why this or that is not happening in the schools. Unfortunately, there is little appreciation by an impatient public of the stresses and strains that accompany every forward movement in education. There is little appreciation for the emotionalism generated by last stands. This is not to suggest that change is not possible, because as Irving Kristol, has correctly observed, schools "are changing all the time—

but at their own tempo, in their own evolutionary way, with a massive and exasperating inertia."[4]

The best way to understand some of the dynamics which are at work in education is to allow the critics to speak for themselves. Every week the state office receives hundreds of letters, telegrams, and petitions from citizens, many of whom are educators, and while the vast majority are generally supportive of various programs and activities of the state office, many are not. A sampling of these communications with respect to *Action Goals for the Seventies,* program planning at the school district level, desegregation, and reform of teacher certification reveal the anger, antagonism and suspicion which reform efforts invariably generate.

Action Goals for the Seventies

The process of defining goals and priorities for Illinois education was viewed by some participants as a move by the state office to take control away from local school districts. One administrator put it this way:

> Too many of the proposals initiate action at the state office level rather than at the local level. Many of the proposals appear to be a power-grab by the state office and a direct contradiction of the demands by communities for control of their schools.

Another administrator added:

> The overall concept of local autonomy is being threatened here. We are moving toward too much regulation at the state level and a loss of local determination of education.

One participant viewed the planning process as an exercise in futility:

> When my sister was in kindergarten, she came home complaining that the teacher was wasting the student's time by asking them what they wanted to do during the day's "planning time" when the teacher had all the plans made already. This has been nothing more than a clever "planning time" for adults.

Some people felt the state was moving too fast:

> The administration needs to prove itself in practical man-
> agement to build confidence before mounting the white
> charger.

Local Educational Planning

Opposition to statewide educational planning has been modest
in comparison with the consternation generated by the state's
insistance that school districts formulate local program plans. This
requirement, as detailed in Chapter II, calls upon school districts
to assess local needs, to identify objectives, to specify activities for
the accomplishment of those objectives, to devise evaluation procedures, and to involve the community in the planning process.
Again, a dominant concern is local control. A group of district
superintendents noted in a letter:

> The document (*Illinois Program for Evaluation, Super-
> vision and Recognition of Schools*) still contains the phi-
> losophy of eroding the powers of local Boards of Education.
>   The document seems to consolidate more powers in the
> office of the Superintendent of Public Instruction which can
> create a total state school system. This is in conflict with the
> philosophy of the Legislature which has wisely delegated
> to the local communities the operation of the schools.

The idea that the larger community—parents, students, teachers,
and other citizens—should be given an opportunity to participate
in the planning process has been sharply criticized by some professionals.

> I would like to object to making mandatory the involvement
> of a Citizen's Committee in this area. In some school dis-
> tricts this will work and work well, and in others it will not.
> The Board of Education of each district is made up of seven
> members representing citizens' views.
>
> It would seem to me that in some districts there are so many
> committees and involvements with one or two administra-
> tors to serve with them that it begins to become somewhat

of a task to pro-rate time. This time could be much better given working in the school setting to formulate and implement desired improvements. Also, it seems that authority is being taken away from the Board of Education.

Others claimed that the new standards exceeded the authority vested in the state office and represented an usurpation of legislative prerogatives.

It is indicated that pursuant to carrying out this authority that "every school shall involve their respective local communities in the development of school policy."

Whatever the merit of the pronouncement it seems clear that the Superintendent of Public Instruction does not have the authority to mandate certain kinds of behavior for school boards to follow in meeting their responsibilities. . . .

It does seem that the legislature . . . has given thought to the question of public participation in policy making for schools and the State Superintendent of Public Instruction cannot redirect this process through a set of guidelines for recognition of schools . . . Boards of Education are chosen by popular election and the proceedings of these boards take place in open meetings.

And, of course, the idea that students might have something to contribute with regard to the formulation of school policy struck a sensitive nerve.

"Every student shall have the right to meaningful participation in the planning and execution of a school's academic programs and other activities." This section is sufficiently vague to cause a great deal of difficulty in interpretation of terms such as "every student" and "meaningful participation" and if used as written would leave the school wide open to criticism. . . . by every contentious or disenchanted student. This is another high-sounding section that can cause great difficulty at the local level and yet the state office stands out in some heroic proportion.

In early 1973, a series of workshops were held throughout Illinois for district superintendents, local school board presidents and teacher representatives to discuss the "ins and outs" of program planning. These workshops were jointly sponsored by the administrator's association, the school board association, and the Superintendent's office. One aspect of each program involved the submission of written questions and comments to which members of the staff would try to respond. Many criticisms were well-intentioned and constructive. Others, however, eloquently explained the predicament in which public education finds itself today.

- To save time now, and later when we are evaluated by our own goals, would it not be to (our) advantage to set these goals low?
- What happens if a board refuses to use community involvement? What happens if a board refuses to submit a plan?
- Is it not true that while these new standards may well not have been purposely written to put small schools out of existence, they can very easily cause this to occur, even though the residents of those districts might be well satisfied with their children's educational opportunities?
- What will happen to the planning discussed today if Dr. Bakalis is not appointed to succeed himself?
- There will likely be many additional higher expectations from citizens because of their participation in the planning process. Are there any plans by the state office to publicize successes by the Illinois public schools to help place this clamor in perspective?
- Can you tell us how Dr. Bakalis can be impeached?
- Is it the state office's long range intention to make teacher certification, licensure, and tenure decisions on the basis of student achievement of stated behavioral objectives?
- Can you categorically deny that Dr. Bakalis will eventually recommend the use of the objectives set up by a school as a basis for, or in addition to, or in place of our present tenure law?
- The state office has a legitimate concern with requiring districts to meet minimum standards. It does not have a legitimate concern with requiring local districts to account to the state office for how it plans to meet those standards. Local boards should account to the electorate for such plans.

- When we start involving the public, may we, like the state office, pick a time when most of the irate publics cannot attend the meetings, invite only our friends or people that agree with our initial plans, be certain the majority present agree with our point of view and then tell the public and the state office that the public was included in our planning?
- What would be the action taken by the state office if a school district said, "The hell with it! It's our school and we will not allow the 'Big White Fathers' at Springfield to 'take over' and dictate to our community?"
- From when are the teachers supposed to steal the time required to write the guidelines, fashion evaluations, and make publicity speeches to the local community? Is this time supposed to be stolen from the students we are teaching or our own children? We notice that nothing concerning monetary remuneration has been mentioned.
- You talk about asking what the people want, but if you've had any marketing experience you know that most people don't really know what they want. Ask the average person what he'd be more apt to buy, then manufacture it; you'll most likely have a flop. Most people don't truly know what they want; they usually react more on an emotional or subconscious level; so can such things as surveys or interviews really be considered valid?
- Did you know that the American flag is on the wrong side of the podium?
- Who was responsible for this farce this afternoon?

Some superintendents who opposed these new standards seized upon the fact that Illinois will have a new state board of education in 1975 and petitioned the General Assembly to pass a resolution recommending that the state office not promulgate the new standards. The following are excerpts from the resolution:

Such sweeping and costly regulations would if presently mandated have the Public School Districts of the State of Illinois in many instances cause administrative burdens and economic hardship . . .;

The General Assembly of Illinois will create by appropriate legislation a State Board of Education which will be assigned the governance of Public Education in the State of Illinois, *in conformity with maximum practicable local autonomy*;

If the proposed . . . Illinois Program for Evaluation, Supervision and Recognition of Schools, or any other guidelines that are filed with the Secretary of State were to be adopted as a binding scheme of regulations applicable to all local school districts of the State of Illinois, the role of the State Board of Education would be unduly constricted and narrowed.

Inherent in this strategy was the view that if local program planning, as proposed by the state office, could be delayed a year or two a new administration and a new state board of education comprised of lay citizens would be easily persuaded, or at least more easily persuaded than the present administration, to abandon the new standards altogether. The resolution eventually died in the House Education Committee.

Desegregation

As pointed out in Chapter III, sentiment on issues relating to equal educational opportunity while varied is always pronounced and laden with emotionalism. It is not surprising that those who write the state office in support of the concept of quality integrated education are greatly outnumbered by those who oppose any movement in this direction. Frequently, the authority of the state office to deal with this problem is questioned.

I feel you have disregarded our Constitutions as well as the courts and laws of these United States. I am prone to think that you are a character of mind to tender S.D.S. or Y.S.A. chapters for all schools in this state. When and if I should see a petition for your resignation, I assure you my name will be on it.

Invariably concern is expressed for the use of student transportation.

In no way will you force busing of white children living on the north-west side of Chicago. We maintain parental supremacy supercedes your political aspirations. Our fight will not end on November 7th. Never underestimate the intelligence of John Q. America. In suggesting or intimidating school boards throughout this state to meet racial quotas you, sir, as an elected public official are violating state law and should be jailed. Must we revert to cowboy law to preserve our inalienable rights.

Another citizen reminded the agency that:

Even the President is opposed to the forced busing of students to achieve racial balance in our schools. But who the devil is the President to be telling you what to do. Right!

Some citizens make it clear that they are prepared to go to jail before permitting their children to be bussed.

According to your edict you are making our Republic a radical dictatorship. Well, I wish to inform you that you will not tell me where I shall or shall not educate my child. Are your children bussed long distances from their neighborhood or perhaps they attend exclusive schools? *WHY ARE YOU TRYING TO DESTROY OUR PUBLIC SCHOOL SYSTEM?*

Underlying many of these protests is a fear of violence and disruption in the schools.

Please stop a moment and think through clearly what you are doing, and ask yourself if you will be able to live with yourself if your plan works out all wrong and causes civil strife or possible war, or an all black state of Illinois.

One letter from a student predicted dire consequences.

I used to go to a . . . school where they had bussed in blacks. These children did not like me no more than I liked going to school with them. All they did was cause a lot of trouble. I don't believe that busing us to their school and them to ours makes any sense. If for some reason you do bus them in and us out I tell you one thing: a lot of kids will not finish their education. They will quit school because of it.

After admitting that every child should have equal access to quality education, a teacher wrote that "integration is leading to inferior education for all children." She reflected on her own experience.

I am teaching in a school experiencing integration for the first time. How inferior our education is this year, and parents are furious. Most of my time is spent on discipline. Only two of the black children are making progress and are not discipline problems. The others are constantly disturbing, stealing, hitting, pushing. I am running far behind last year's progress. Isn't that something. These black people they want better education for their children. Their presence alone makes it inferior education. What they are getting at this former all white middle class school is not better than what they were getting at the ghetto school, because we are spending more time just trying to keep order.

And, of course, the agency is occasionally reminded that integration is neither natural nor divinely sanctioned.

Have you even given the word "segregation" *per se* any research? Thru all recorded history, segregation has been the law of nature. Every living creature from man to insects stays with its own kind. "Birds of a feather stay together." Deuteronomy 22, verses 9 and 10, say it very plainly: "Thou shalt not sow thy vineyard with divers seeds, lest the fruit which thou hast sown, shall be defiled." Verse II: Thou shalt not plow with an ox and ass together."

Teacher Preparation and Evaluation

A task force to the state office recommended sweeping reforms for the training and certification of educational personnel. Although these proposals, described in Chapter V, have not been fully endorsed by the state office, reactions to these preliminary findings came swiftly and furiously. One teacher summed up his feelings with this observation:

It is my humble opinion that the recommendation of the state office's task force would be a return to the dark ages.

Another teacher provided this critique:

I take a jaundiced view of your program of recertification for teachers. Your proposal is not specific enough. Your proposal excludes teachers' associations. Your proposal circumvents tenure. Your proposal has not involved teachers in its development.

The proposals were immediately interpreted as a means of abandoning teacher tenure.

As it now stands, teacher tenure does allow for dismissal by due process. In doing away with tenure, we are reverting back to the time in which teachers were under pressure to belong to the "right" church, to speak up on personal or political convictions only if they agreed with the school board's, and so on. In what other profession are such unfair pressures exerted?

One writer suggested that there were other dark and sinister forces at work.

It would be too easy for a district to get rid of its expensive teachers. Even if they are good teachers, it is a temptation to get two teachers for one.

Many teachers suggested that the only fair and reasonable way to upgrade the teaching profession was to give teachers considerable, if not complete, control over their own profession.

After reading the *Report of the Task Force on Certification,* I must honestly admit I was in a state of minor shock. This plan would deny teachers the right to be held accountable for their own profession.

This Task Force has no recognition of the changing relationships between the organized body of hard working teachers and the local and state agencies responsible for administering educational programs of the State of Illinois.

My associates and I realize the fact that the public needs teacher accountability, but the teachers become the scapegoats for institutional failure. The growing frustration resulting from this process of unfair victimization compels stronger and stronger opposition to any plan which promises more of the same.

One writer characterized the proposals as a "disaster which we cannot allow to happen." However, he made a counterproposal.

The legislature should pass a professional practices act mandating that teachers control who comes into their profession, that teachers provide a system of evaluation and growth, and that teachers determine who is unfit to belong in the profession. This step would finally equate us with the plumber and morticians.

A teachers' representative strongly advised that the recommendations of the task force "be discarded before they produce any further discredit to the Superintendent's Office." The objective of re-certification, he continued, was "to make 'whipping posts' of teachers for the failures of politicians who have done nothing to meet real problems that teachers face day to day in their classrooms." Therefore, he recommended that teachers oppose:

1. the evaluation of teachers for certification purposes by persons who are not qualified teachers;
2. any proposal that threatens to destroy the teaching certificates of qualified teachers for any reasons except moral turpitude or cruelty to children;
3. any involvement of local boards of education in the certification process, except as may be provided by agreements with teacher-training institutions and teacher organizations for student teaching or internship programs.

The purpose in allowing the above critics to speak for themselves is to demonstrate that the educational enterprise is not and never has been a hothouse of affability. The purpose is not to demonstrate that the educational establishment is hopelessly conservative. What these criticisms show is that educational reform does not take place in a vacuum, but within a human framework, and what happens or does not happen is heavily conditioned by a complex network of human relationships. So in formulating educational policy, conflict is unavoidable, and it must be admitted that such conflict is often very healthy. What is not widely understood, however, is that serious and interminable disagreements can create logjams that make real progress impossible. Educators can try to avoid controversy by doing nothing, as they frequently have in the past, but obviously in an age when people are demanding educational leadership that is an unacceptable alternative.

The fundamental problem is that state educational leadership has neither common understanding nor acceptance. There are other positive forces, briefly alluded to in the opening chapter, which call for this leadership function to be expanded and institutionalized. And these forces, like criticisms set forth above, must be taken into account and perhaps accorded even greater importance in the formulation of educational policy. Hansen and Jesser have summarized those factors as follows:

1. The increasing number of people who have begun to understand that the mere establishment of standards and detailed regulations (that often are unrealistic in the light of emerging needs) for aspects such as the curriculum or certification is almost meaningless and may tend to discourage needed improvements in education;
2. The increasing demands that the provisions for education be modified continuously to meet the needs of a rapidly changing society;
3. The rapidly growing recognition that changes in education can and should be planned on the basis of careful statewide studies of existing and emerging problems, inadequacies, and inequities—rather than made on a piecemeal basis primarily as a response to the efforts of special interest or pressure groups, or to a "crisis situation" that may have constituted an unrecognized obstacle to progress for many years;
4. The development of new federal programs and the provision of additional federal funds designed to help state agencies and local school systems to plan for effecting needed changes and to evaluate progress; and
5. A strong demand by increasing numbers of lay citizens and

educators for better ways of measuring performances and progress in improving education in each state and the recognition that this will be possible only when the state education agency is headed by an unusually competent leader and staffed by highly qualified personnel.[5]

Given these forces and counterforces, it is infinitely easier to dispatch men to the dark side of the moon than it is to reconcile firmly held and disparate attitudes about what the schools should be doing. One is a technological problem, the other essentially a human problem. People simply cannot be manipulated like computers. Because people are people, it is a mistake to think that they can be molded to embrace any idea which is fashionable at the moment. But this fact does not alleviate the need for educational leadership, for a basic issue must still be addressed, and that issue is whether society will control and manage the forces of change or whether those forces will manipulate and mismanage society.

The emergence of state educational leadership will not resolve this issue alone nor will it markedly reduce the resistance to educational change. However, leadership can help rationalize that resistance, especially if the public and the profession are forewarned that the schools must begin to train youngsters to cope with the equivalent of a millenia of change within the compressed span of a single lifetime. An individual educated in 1873 was essentially prepared to deal with the world of 1900. The current ambivalence about change, however, raises serious doubts about our willingness and capacity to prepare youngsters in 1973 for a meaningful existence in the year 2000.

Resistance to educational change can also be rationalized if citizens are informed of what is happening in their schools. With modern methods of communication readily at our command, there is no reason why people should not understand the purposes of their schools, what is happening in those schools, why certain programs and methods are being used, and what the anticipated and practical outcomes of public education are. Perhaps more than any other single factor, this breakdown in communication between those who run the schools and those who are served by them is preventing continuous renewal of the education system. Why should the public be sympathetic to sweeping reforms in education when it understands neither the systems nor the proposals intended to change it?

Educators cannot permit themselves to be overwhelmed by the prospects of change. There is an impulse to strike out at it, to flee from it. Difficult as it may be to face, however, the fact remains that change is a constant and unalterable condition from which there is no escape. Whether one talks about individualized instruction, schools without walls, or finance reform, each innovation in education has been an effort of sorts to keep pace with the changes relentlessly thrust upon the schools by shifting circumstances. Of course, almost without exception such reforms are resisted, and sometimes with conspicuous success.

More than reform is required. First, the public must be brought into the confidence of educators. It must be constantly and candidly apprised of those existing and anticipated conditions which threaten to incapacitate the educational process. Second, educators and non-educators together must take stock of the future and decide how best to deal with its distant and unpredictable exigencies. It will not do any longer to think and act as if the future were but an extension of the present without diminishing further the future significance of our schools. Any resemblance between the schools of today and the schools of 2001 should be purely coincidental.

Despite all the rhetoric about education preparing children for life in the future, the primary focus of students, parents, and most educators has been either the past or the present. Many people, including many educators actually yearn for the good old days when attending school meant regimentation, no individualization, rigid systems of seating, grouping, grading, and disciplined and authoritarian teachers. The best insurance for the future, they steadfastly believe, is to teach children to live for the present. What is not commonly understood is that in preparing children to survive in today's world we are talking about a mode of existence that will be dead before they are.

The bias in education for the past has largely given way now to a bias in favor of the present. It is time educators once again shifted our time-bias forward and looked the future straight in the eye. This is an age when man's accumulated knowledge doubles every ten years, a phenomenon which renders much of what we learned yesterday or today obsolete tomorrow. Kenneth Boulding, an eminent economist, has observed that "the world of today . . . is as different from the world in which I was born as that world was from Julius Caesar's. Almost as much has happened since I was born as happened before."

The challenge facing education today is the intellectual development of men and women who have the future in their bones—"who can," as Alvin Toffler recommends, "make critical judgments, who can weave their way through novel environments, who are quick to spot new relationships in the rapidly changing reality."[6] The task, in short, is to increase the speed and economy with which an individual can adapt to continual change, and that will require change, perhaps radical change, within the educational system itself.

In reaching for new standards of excellence in education, the only impediment is a fear of change. The future is not a menace, if its inevitability is accepted. And the forces of change can be effectively harnessed, if what is done is based on a sound assessment of future needs and is not totally lacking in logic, cohesion, and direction. The challenge of change is a constant condition; it is not, however, an excuse for inertia. As Justice Holmes once observed: "I find the great thing in this world is not so much where we stand, as in what direction we are moving." We ought to be moving toward educational excellence. That road is too infrequently travelled. For many people it is too hard, too rigorous, too demanding, too disciplined. But it is the one way that can make a difference.

Americans demand much of themselves and their institutions. If there is a crisis in education, it is because our reach almost always exceeds our grasp, and that is nothing to be ashamed of. If there is a crisis in education, it is due to our persistent, intense, sometimes touching faith in the efficacy of popular education, and we need not be ashamed of that either. The crisis is really only a reminder that our work is not completed, that our work is never completed, that we must seek out and rectify our educational weaknesses and build on our strengths and successes.

Notes

Foreword

1. *Newsweek*, December 6, 1971, p. 81
2. Burnell Heinecke, "Progress in State Education," *Chicago Sun Times*, January 3, 1974.
3. John F. Kennedy and Allan Nevins, ed., *The Strategy of Peace*, Popular Library, 1961, p. xix.

Chapter I

1. Dr. James Bryant Conant, *Shaping Educational Policy*, McGraw-Hill, 1964, pp. 37-38.
2. Roald F. Campbell and Gerald E. Stroufe, "The Emerging Role of State Departments of Education," *Strengthening State Departments of Education*, University of Chicago, 1967, p. 91.
3. J. Myron Atkin, "Schools Serve as Society's Battleground," *Champaign-Urbana Courier*, January 1, 1973.
4. James D. Koerner, *Who Controls American Education?*, Beacon Press, 1969, pp. 94-95.
5. Michael J. Bakalis, *Action Goals for the Seventies: An Agenda for Illinois Education*, Office of the Superintendent of Public Instruction, May, 1972.
6. Dr. James Bryant Conant, *Shaping Educational Policy*, McGraw-Hill, 1964, pp. 37-38.
7. Warren L. Anderson, "School Board—To Be or Not To Be," *Pathfinder Report, Illinois School Board Journal*, September, 1971, p. 26.
8. Terry Ferrer, "Conant Revisited," *Saturday Review*, March 18, 1967, p. 73.
9. Kenneth H. Hansen, "The State Education Agency at Work," *Six Crucial Issues in Education*, National Association of State Boards of Education, 1972, p. 43.

Chapter II

1. Michael J. Bakalis, *The Illinois Program for Evaluation, Supervision, and Recognition of Schools,* Circular Series A, No. 160, State of Illinois, Office of the Superintendent of Public Instruction, 1973.

2. Michael J. Bakalis, *Guidelines for Local District Educational Planning,* State of Illinois, Office of the Superintendent of Public Instruction, January, 1973.

3. "Bakalis Request is Realistic," *Champaign-Urbana Courier,* November 26, 1972.

4. Glaue, Gerald, "Get On With The Planning," *The Illinois School Board Journal,* June, 1973.

5. "The $50 Billion Question—How Can Schools be Tested?," *The Argus,* January 31, 1973.

Chapter III

1. *Brown v. Board of Education of Topeka,* 347 U.S. 483 (1954).

2. "Armstrong Act," *Illinois Revised Statutes* 1971, Chapter 122, S. 22-19.

3. *HEW-News,* June 18, 1971, pp. 1-11.

4. *Report of the National Advisory Commission on Civil Disorders,* Bantam, 1968.

5. Michael J. Bakalis, *Rules Establishing Requirements and Procedures for the Elimination and Prevention of Racial Segregation in Schools,* State of Illinois, Office of the Superintendent of Public Instruction, November, 1971.

6. *Swann v. Charlotte-Mecklenburg Board of Education,* 402 U.S. 1 (1971); and *Ronald Bradley et al v. William G. Milliken et al,* 438 F. 2d 945 (1971)

7. Weinberg, Meyer, *Desegregation Research: An Appraisal,* 2nd Edition, Phi Delta Kappa, May, 1970; *School Desegregation in Ten Communities,* United States Commission on Civil Rights, June, 1973; Nancy St. John, "Desegregation and Minority Group Performance," *Review of Educational Research,* Volume No. 1, 1970.

8. Christopher Jencks, "Do Our Schools Really Hold the Key to Equality," *The Chicago Daily Tribune,* December 18, 1972.

9. Christopher Jencks, "Will Equal Opportunity Make Us Equal?," *The Chicago Daily Tribune,* December 17, 1972.

10. Christopher Jencks, "Adding Up Our School Days, Getting . . . What?," *New York Times,* December 12, 1972.

11. *Ibid.*

12. Harold Howe II, "Start with the Schools," *Saturday Review,* March, 1973, p. 20.

13. Studs Terkel, *Division Street: America,* Avon Books, 1968, p. 386.

14. Rafaela Elizondo de Weffer, H. Ned Seelye, and K. Balasubramian, *Preliminary Report on the Achievement of Children in Bilingual Programs,* State of Illinois, Bilingual Education Section, Office of the Superintendent of Public Instruction, December, 1972.

15. Michael J. Bakalis, *Rules and Regulations to Govern Administration and Operation of Special Education,* State of Illinois, Office of the Superintendent of Public Instruction, 1973.

16. Charles Silberman, *Crisis in the Classroom, The Remaking of American Education,* Random House, 1970, p. 186.

17. *The Costs to the Nation of Inadequate Education,* Select Committee on Equal Educational Opportunity, United States Senate, February, 1972.

18. Walter F. Mondale, "Educational Neglect Costs Nation Billions; Finding Contained in New Mondale Report" (press statement), Select Committee on Equal Educational Opportunity, May 13, 1972.

Chapter IV

1. Ernest Ludlow Bogart and Charles Manfred Thompson, *The Centennial History of Illinois; The Industrial State, 1870-1893,* Illinois Centennial Commission, 1920, p. 36.

2. Charles E. Silberman, *Crisis in the Classroom, The Remaking of American Education,* Random House, 1970, pp. 172-173.

3. Jerome Bruner, *The Process of Education,* Harvard University Press, 1965, p. 52.

4. For fuller discussion of Illinois Network for School Development see: Michael J. Bakalis, "The Illinois Network for School Development," *Phi Delta Kappan,* March, 1973, pp. 475-476.

5. John Holt, *How Children Fail,* Dell, July, 1972, pp. 209-210.

6. Nathan Glazer and Daniel P. Moynihan, *Beyond the Melting Pot,* The M.I.T. Press, 1970, p. 289.

7. George Overholt and Don Martin, "The Vendetta in the Schools: An Exercise in Ethnocentrism," *Phi Delta Kappan,* February, 1973, p. 410.

8. *Ibid.*

9. John Dellenback, "Report on Proprietary Vocational Schools," *Congressional Record,* August 12, 1970.

10. John Holt, *How Children Fail,* Dell, July, 1972, pp. 207-208.

Chapter V

1. Charles E. Silberman, *Crisis in the Classroom,* Random House, 1970, p. 374.

2. *Ibid.,* pp. 439-440.

3. Michael J. Bakalis, *The Report of the Task Force on Certification,* State of Illinois, Office of the Superintendent of Public Instruction, May, 1972.

4. Bernard H. McKenna, "Teacher Evaluation—Some Implications," *Today's Education—NEA Journal,* February, 1973, p. 55.

5. James D. Koerner, *Who Controls American Education?,* Beacon Press, 1969, p. 181.

6. Henry M. Christman, ed., *The Mind and Spirit of John Peter Altgeld,* University of Illinois Press, 1965, p. 58.

Chapter VI

1. *The President's Commission on School Finance, Progress Report,* March 22, 1971, p. ii.

2. Norma Skamenca, "Schools are Target of Taxpayers Revolt." *Edwardsville Intelligencer,* February 14, 1973.

3. *The President's Commission on School Finance, Progress Report,* March 22, 1971, p. 33.

4. *Seranno v. Priest,* 5 Cal. 3d 584 (1971).

5. *Van Dusartz v. Hatfield,* 334 F Supp. 870, (D. Minn. (1971).

6. *Rodriquez v. San Antonio Independent School District,* 337 F. Supp. 280 (W. D. Tex. 1971).

7. "Supreme Court OKs Property Tax for Schools," *Chicago Sun Times,* March 22, 1973.

8. *Ibid.*

9. *Schools, People, and Money: The Need for Educational Reform,* The President's Commission on School Finance, 1972, pp. 36-37.

10. *A New Design: Financing for Effective Education in Illinois,* The Governor's Commission on Schools, Task Force on School Finance, 1972, pp. 66-67.

11. Christopher Jencks, *Inequality: A Reassessment of the Effect of Family and Schooling in America,* Basic Books, 1972.

12. *Report of the New York State Commission on Quality, Costs, and Financing of Elementary and Secondary Education,* 1972, p. 46.

13. *Findings and Recommendations of the Elementary and Secondary Nonpublic Schools Study Commission,* State of Illinois, April, 1971.

14. *President's Commission on School Finance, Progress Report,* March 22, 1971, p. 23.

15. *Lemon v. Kurtzman,* 403 U.S. 602 (1971) 91 S. Ct. 2105; and *William P. Robinson, Jr. Commissioner of Education of the State of Rhode Island et al v. Joan Di Censo et al.,* 403 U.S. 602 (1971) 91 S. Ct. 2105.

16. *The President's Commission on School Finance, Progress Report,* March 22, 1971, p. iii.

17. *Survey and Recommendations, Report of the Business Management Task Force,* Governor's Commission on Schools, November, 1972.

18. *Opportunities for Excellence, Findings, Conclusions, and Recommendations of a Survey of Illinois School District Organization,* The Governor's Commission on Schools, Committee on School Organization, April, 1973.

19. *A New Design: Financing for Effective Education in Illinois,* The Governor's Commission on Schools, Task Force on School Finance, 1972, p. 100.

20. Kenneth L. Hermansen, James R. Gove, *The Year Round School at Work,* ETS Publications, 1974.

21. Kenneth L. Hermansen, James R. Gove, *The Year Round School—The 45-15 Plan,* Linnet Books/The Shoe String Press, Inc., 1971.

22. *Education Vouchers, A Report on Financing Elementary Education by Grants to Parents,* Center for the Study of Public Policy, December, 1970, p. 1.

23. *Ibid.*, p. 2.

24. L. Jackson Newell, "Education Vouchers: Plague or Panacea?," *Planning & Changing—A Journal for School Administrators*, October, 1971, p. 118.

25. James A. Mecklenburger, editor, *Education Vouchers: From Theory to Alum Rock*, ETC Publications, 1972, pp. 387-392.

Chapter VII

1. John Holt, *The Underachieving School*, Dell Publishing Co., 1969, pp. 19-20.

2. *Illinois Blue Book*, Illinois Secretary of State, 1925-26, p. 418.

3. *Flory v. Smith*, 134 S.E. 360 (1926).

4. *West Virginia State Board of Education v. Barnette*, 319 U.S. 624 (1943).

Chapter VIII

1. James D. Koerner, *Who Controls American Education?*, Beacon Press, 1969, p. 164.

2. Alvin Toffler, *Future Shock*, Bantam, 1971, p. 3.

3. Richard Hofstadter, *Anti-Intellectualism in American Life*, Alfred A. Knopf, 1970, p. 301.

4. Irving Kristol, "Lag Found in Tempo of Reform," *The New York Times*, January 8, 1973, p. 62.

5. Kenneth Hansen and Edgar Morphet, "State Organization for Education," *Emerging State Responsibilities for Education*, Denver, Improving State Leadership in Education, 1970, pp. 43-44.

6. Alvin Toffler, *Future Shock*, Bantam, 1971, pp. 402-403.

Index

DATE DUE

JUL 30			
MAR 1 6 2001			
GAYLORD			PRINTED IN U.S.A